Ray W. Pierson
POST OFFICE BOX 158
PAYSON, ILLINOIS 62360
PHONE (217) 222-5478

P9-CSE-191

Protestant Preaching in Lent

Harold J. Ockenga

PROTESTANT PREACHING
in Lent

1957

WM. B. EERDMANS PUBLISHING CO.
GRAND RAPIDS, MICHIGAN

PROTESTANT PREACHING IN LENT
by Harold J. Ockenga

Set up and printed, January 1957

LIBRARY OF CONGRESS CATALOG CARD NUMBER: 57-6672

PRINTED IN THE UNITED STATES OF AMERICA

To

HAROLD JOHN, JR.
*Who already has heard
the call to preach
this great Gospel*

CONTENTS

CHARACTER CONFLICTS AT CALVARY

INTRODUCTION

Dr. Ockenga believes that "in preaching resides the power of evangelical Christianity." He rejoices in the current trend of the Protestant pulpit towards a larger observance of Lent and of Holy Week. During the past twenty-five years he has devoted each Lenten season to sermons about Christ, and the days of every successive Holy Week to messages about His Death. Out of these Lenten and Holy Week sermons he has drawn the materials for a book that seems to me unique.

The volume consists of seven series, each including from four to eight sermons. In successive years such messages would suit the purposes of the Sundays in Lent, or else the evenings of Holy Week. Not every pastor has the opportunity and the courage to hold weekday meetings during Lent, year after year. Whatever the local situation, every parish minister ought to consider the need of such messages during Lent and throughout Holy Week. The stress ought to fall, as it does here, on Christ as the Son of God, and increasingly on truths relating to His Death as our Redeemer. In other churches at times, the man in the pulpit seems to feel chiefly concerned about "the human nature of Jesus."

These sermons from Park Street Church in Boston do not appear in full. They assume the form of extensive discussions, more largely developed than in the most complete outlines, and all in the form of consecutive sentences. Three of the series have to do mainly with the earthly ministry of our Lord prior to Calvary: "The Dinner Parties of Jesus"; "Questions Asked of Jesus. The Last Week"; "Jesus, Pray for Us." All of these discussions, the author hopes, will "stimulate further creative activity on the part of the local preacher."

The opening series, "The Dinner Parties of Jesus," has a tone color all its own. It consists of expository sermons about "life situations" in the Gospel records. While equally biblical, more than a few of the later messages consist in topical discussions of Bible doctrines, as they stand out in royal texts. Four of the series have to do with "the day of the Cross": "Glorying in the

7

Cross"; "The Suffering Messiah"; "At the Cross of Christ"; "Character Conflicts at Calvary." Thus with seven series the volume begins and ends strongly, presenting truth full of human interest and divine power.

Whatever the form, these messages contain little save biblical materials. The style throughout is simple and clear, thoughtful and informative, rather than beautiful and inspiring. At the old Park Street Church through the years, Dr. Ockenga has attracted and held throngs of eager hearers, many of them men. He has taken for granted that on the Lord's Day and during the week in Lent both men and women want to bring their brains to church and keep them busy there; that they relish manly sermons which show the meaning and the glory of old evangelical truths about the Christ of the Cross. In order to attract the man in the street, Dr. Ockenga seems never to stoop to intermittent entertainment.

In a different sort of pulpit a minister may feel obliged to do much the same sort of preaching in other ways. In a rural parish, or in a village with only one church, the pastor may choose to present less truth in only one sermon. If he ministers to men and women of average ability, or even less, with their growing boys and girls, he may decide to serve less meat and more milk. Even so, any pastor anywhere should seriously consider following the practical philosophy that undergirds this book. So should every young man in a divinity school seriously consider the wisdom of adopting such a philosophy of life. As the minister of a church without fixed forms of worship, Dr. Ockenga says, in effect, two things that lie at the heart of gospel preaching for today:

1. During Lent preach regularly about the Lord Jesus as day by day He draws nearer to Calvary.

2. During Holy Week, in sermon after sermon, bring every hearer face to face with the Christ of the Cross as the world's only Redeemer and King. In every such message claim the promise that rings out from one of Dr. Ockenga's texts: "I, if I be lifted up from the earth, will draw all men unto me" (John 12:32)

ANDREW W. BLACKWOOD

PREFACE

Lent is a time when Christians are predisposed toward considering the great events in the life of Jesus Christ which constitute the gospel. Protestants have not taken advantage of this seasonal opportunity for preaching the central facts of the Christian faith. A new trend may be detected in Protestantism toward observance of Lent by the employment of preaching.

In preaching resides the power of evangelical Christianity. By proclamation of the Word of God come enlightenment, knowledge and conviction. Then why not utilize every opportunity to preach, especially when the minds of men are conditioned to receive the message of the gospel? Lent is a time when men expect to hear about the life, death and resurrection of our Lord Jesus.

Twenty-five years ago I resolved to redeem this seasonal opportunity and to observe Holy Week by daily preaching of a series of sermons designed to present the primary truths of the gospel, namely that "Christ died for our sins, according to the scriptures, and that he was buried, and that he rose again the third day according to the scriptures" (I Cor. 15:3, 4). Since that time I have regularly participated in Lenten preaching in addition to Holy Week, recognizing the value of such observances. Lent may well be redeemed by Protestantism and directed to the most spiritual season of the Christian year.

Once a pastor has determined to observe Lent, the problem of union services will arise. Always there are those who wish to merge and pool the resources for the support of such services. This is an encroachment upon the opportunity, privilege and initiative of the preacher. This also militates against the full support of the mission by his congregation. The sense of responsibility lessens when the effort is broadened to be cooperative. Let a pastor prayerfully and studiously plan his messages and a congregation dedicate itself to a community witness through these services. I have steadfastly resisted all such urgent invitations to cooperative effort and have built at Park Street Church over a twenty-year period a far greater attendance and interest

9

than exists in the union services held by a dozen cooperating churches. The season is a delight to me as a preacher, a blessing to the congregation, a witness to hundreds of visitors, and a means of evangelism whereby some make a first commitment to Christ.

The suggestions for Lenten preaching given in this book are in groups subsumed under weekly topics. Thus they may be a pattern to be followed during Holy Week alone, or also during Passion Week, or during the whole of Lent. They are given merely as suggestions to stimulate further creative activity on the part of the preacher.

THE DINNER PARTIES OF JESUS

THE DINNER PARTIES OF JESUS

INTRODUCTION

In the following dinner parties of Jesus, we are only giving four of many possible such sermons. A more full series of suggestions, and on each one of which I have preached a message, is as follows:

1. A Sinner Entertains or Levi's Dinner (Luke 5:29)
2. A Dinner a Prostitute Attended (Luke 7:36)
3. A Dinner Which Satisfied (Luke 9:10-27)
4. A Dinner Which Divided a Family (Luke 10:38ff)
5. A Dinner Where a Hypocrite Was Rebuked (Luke 11:37ff)
6. A Dinner Filled With Table Talk (Luke 14:1ff)
7. A Dinner Which Cost a Rich Man Half His Wealth (Luke 19:1-10)
8. A Dinner With Most Precious Fellowship (Luke 22:14-27)
9. A Dinner With Thanksgiving (Matt. 26:6-13)
10. A Resurrection Dinner (Luke 24:30ff)
11. A Dinner Where the Cross Was Remembered (Luke 24:36-48)
12. A Dinner Where Love Reigned (John 21:15ff)

These dinners attended by Jesus, graced by His actions of love, rebuke and instruction, and filled with His teaching form a rich repository of preaching material. The attitudes and reactions of the human beings involved offer a springboard for the analysis of the human character of our present day. We strongly suggest the use of this series some time in the Lenten season.

1

A DINNER WITNESS TO SOCIAL OUTCASTS

Wednesday — First Day

Text: Luke 5:32. "I came not to call the righteous, but sinners to repentance."
Scripture: Luke 5:27-35

The home of Levi the publican was Capernaum. We would not know that Levi the publican was Matthew the disciple unless Matthew himself had revealed this unto us. Mark and Luke refer to the conversion of Levi but Matthew tells us that the name of this publican was Matthew and thus identifies himself with Levi. Capernaum was the adopted home of Jesus after He had been rejected at Nazareth. This was His center for His Galilean ministry and here He performed many of His miracles. The call of Matthew came immediately after one of Jesus' most controversial miracles, namely, the healing of the paralytic (Luke 5:17-26).

The Pharisees and doctors of the law had come out of the towns of Galilee and Judea and from Jerusalem itself to evaluate His work. There was nothing wrong in this, for we are not to follow every new religious teacher or religious movement. We are to try the spirits to see whether they be of God or not. Nevertheless, the Pharisees were hostile to the Lord Jesus. When the Lord in this healing of the paralytic equated His healing with His forgiveness of sins, the doctors of the law and the Pharisees reasoned that this was blasphemy, for only God has the authority to forgive sin. They, of course, erred in their judgment, for they did not recognize the identification of Jesus of Nazareth with the Messiah, or the Son of God. They were sound, however, in their conclusion that only God has the right to forgive sin.

The effect of Jesus' words on the man who had been suffering from palsy was immediate. He was healed so that he could take up his bed and walk, and he departed to his own house glorify-

13

ing God. The effect upon the people who saw the miracle was instantaneous. They were amazed, filled with fear and they glorified God for such power being given to a man.

Then it was that Jesus threw down the gauntlet to the religious leaders of His age, making the claim to equality with God by saying, "Whether is easier, to say, Thy sins be forgiven thee; or to say, Rise up and walk? But that ye may know that the Son of man hath power upon earth to forgive sins. . . ." Here was one of Jesus' direct claims to deity, to the exercise of the prerogative of deity, namely, the right to forgive sin, and this was substantiated by credentials of the Messiah in miracle-working power.

It was immediately following this that the Lord called Matthew. Here we see a fallen man converted, a great feast of testimony, and the Great Physician working.

I. THE FALLEN MAN CONVERTED

In the conversion of Matthew we have one of the great transformations of character recorded for us in the Scriptures. Matthew was a great sinner, a social outcast, a self-condemned man, and he was totally and completely transformed by the power of the Lord Jesus Christ. Such conversions have taken place throughout the history of the Christian Church whenever the Lord Jesus has been presented in His true person, position and power. We should be expecting such conversions to occur now.

Let us look at this conversion as it related to the place of the meeting of Matthew with Jesus, the person or status of Matthew, and the power of Jesus to change Matthew.

A. THE PLACE OF MEETING WITH JESUS

The Lord had just returned to Capernaum from a tour of Galilee and a brief visit to Jerusalem (John 5:1-18), had resided in Peter's home where He had healed all the sick whom they brought to Him and where undoubtedly the paralytic had been healed. Now He had gone out of that home into the streets of the city which led Him to the confluence of the caravan road to the east and the edge of the Sea of Galilee.

Capernaum may still be recognized by the ruins of the grand synagogue, the extensive market place and by its described location. Capernaum was important because it was located on the Via Maris from Damascus to Achor on which all the caravans from the east passed and from which customs were exacted. It was the chief Jewish city in this area and was quite populous. It was beautifully situated where it could overlook the lovely lake of Galilee and it was a happy location for much of the Lord's ministry.

The customs house located at the confluence of the road; the lake and the city, no doubt, were on the east of Capernaum. It would be marked by a stone building, by gate barricades and by a group of officials of whom, no doubt, Matthew was the authority. Past here came traveler bands, soldier troops, commercial caravans with bearded sheiks, and priests in flowing robes. It was Matthew's business to collect the taxes at this station. He served under Herod Antipas, the king, who in turn paid revenues to the Romans. He and his class were hated and despised and ostracized by their fellow-countrymen as traitors, extortioners and outcasts. His people had no social intercourse with him.

B. The person of the publican Matthew

Mark and Luke name this publican Levi, but there is no Levi in the apostolic list; yet this call was certainly an apostolic call and Matthew 9:9 leaves little doubt that the new name which Jesus conferred upon Levi was Mattathias, or "the gift of God," just as He gave Peter to Simon. Thus we know that at least one of the apostles was of the low class of publicans, a traitor to his own people, who sold out to Rome and to his own greed. He assisted in continuing the galling yoke of foreign exploitation which robbed the people of their income and saddled upon them the support of the foreign power with its soldiers, its brutality and its exploitation. These publicans generally lived up to their reputation, indulging in all manner of sin and having for friends other social outcasts and harlots and living for this world only in which they had their reward.

C. The power to change a sinner

1. The life of Levi in Capernaum

Levi was irreligious, worldly, unprincipled, indulgent and frivolous. Perhaps he was also generous, hearty and unselfish but it is certain that he was impervious to his social standing or to any thought of the future. His philosophy and that of the publicans was "Live for today for you are a long time dead," make as much money as you can, increase your desires and satisfy them, whether through liquor, lust, laughter, or levity.

Such a pattern of life is seen in every community and age. Yet Matthew must have had misgivings with such a life. He must have had more serious moments of questioning, of hungering after abiding satisfaction, of longing for the commendation of his conscience and of society. There is a moral spark in every man which will not permit him to go on in such a life without giving him warning. Either he must silence that inner voice or he must be disturbed by it.

Matthew's condition as a publican may have expressed his maladjustment with the society of his day, his revolt against Pharisaism and the false restrictions and shibboleths of the religion of his day. We may be sure that there had been injected into Matthew's life before this meeting with Jesus some knowledge of the teachings of Jesus. He could not have been ignorant of his works and words performed and given in Capernaum, for business must have stopped when Jesus was teaching and healing by the lake. In this Nazarene he sensed power, authority, integrity, purity and sincerity. He was shaken by Him, he was convicted of sin, dissatisfied with life and had a desire for something better. He must have remained at his customs position with resistance, conflict and defense against his own convictions.

2. The look of Jesus

Then it was that Jesus met him in front of the customs. Luke says he "fixed his eyes attentively on him." The penetrating power of that look was all that Matthew needed to see himself as he was and as he ought to be. It was the same look that the Lord gave to Peter in Caiaphas hall and to Zaccheus as he was in the sycamore tree. New possibilities opened before Matthew and the past was swallowed up in the wondrous bliss of the present.

Then he heard the words, "Follow me." It was an apostolic call like that given to the first four disciples. In a moment's time he counted the cost, he made his decision which he never reconsidered, he left his work, the despicable source of his wealth, he made a clean breach with his past, he consecrated himself to Jesus and he "rose up, and followed Him." Let us never deprecate the will of man and the possibilities thereof. What Matthew did, others can do; in fact, you can do.

II. A GREAT FEAST OF TESTIMONY

A. THE CELEBRATION

Matthew was a fallen man among fallen men and he determined that the transformation of his character would not go unwitnessed by his fellows in sin. All of us have a group with whom we are intimate. Any action or transformation in our lives will have its effect upon them.

Thus Levi made a great feast ". . . and there was a great company of publicans and of others which sat down with them." The place was Levi's own house, a great structure used to accommodate such a company. Probably it was in a fine area of Capernaum and luxuriously appointed with the wealth which he had obtained in his ill-advised way. At the feast were sinners, winebibbers, harlots, gluttonous and convivial. These were the socially ostracized and the totally indifferent to the mores of society. Many times in this home they had made the rafters ring with their ribald levity and had kept the neighbors and the community awake. Now it was Matthew's intention to introduce them to Jesus, to bear his own testimony, and to let Jesus speak to them.

No man should break with his sinful companions and his past without giving a testimony. His testimony will raise a new barrier between himself and them. He must make a clean breach from them. One can imagine how Matthew told them of his inner misgivings, of his final decision, of his new intention and then of Jesus' own teaching to them.

B. THE CRITICISM FROM THE PHARISEES

It was in the midst of the feast, while these publicans were having a new and a strange relationship to one of such an impeccable character as Christ, that the Pharisees, observing, began their criticism which no doubt was expressed to the disciples of Jesus rather than to Jesus Himself. They said, "Why do you eat and drink with publicans and sinners?" Jesus' association with outcasts implied to them that He had violated the Levitical law. Eating was a sign of intimacy and for Jesus to eat with these sinners placed Him on their level in the eyes of the

Pharisees who observed a strict separation from all social out-casts. Those who would minister and serve among such people may have their greatest protection in the possession of a character like unto that of Jesus.

III. THE GREAT PHYSICIAN AT WORK

The answer Christ made was, "They that are whole need not a physician but they that are sick. I am not come to call the righteous, but sinners to repentance."

A. THE MISSION OF CHRIST

Christ came to call sinners to repentance, to forgiveness, to life eternal. Both the publicans and the Pharisees understood Him rightly and therefore the interest and sympathy of the publicans grew and the hostility and the antagonism of the Pharisees grew. His teaching cut across every teaching of tradi-tional theology, religion and morality as it was known in Judaism. It was for this reason that He gave the parable of the new wine in old bottles and of the new cloth in the old garment. The old forms and organizations were not able to take care of the new spirit and new life. The old covenant was legal, of works and of justification by obedience; the new covenant is by faith, or evangelical obedience. This distinction is expounded in Romans and Galatians. There can be no patching up of the old system. The old must be discarded for the new and the new life must create its own form.

B. THE MEANING OF CHRIST'S STATEMENT

There was an apparent implication here that the Pharisees considered themselves to be well and to need no physician but that the publicans considered themselves ill and did need a physician. Unless men know themselves to be sick, they find a physician useless. Judaism was self-righteous. Its morality was one of works, of self-help, of being blameless according to the law of God. Jesus opposed this by proclaiming salvation to sin-ners as sinners and not that they should become righteous first. The Pharisees said, "God's ear is open to the righteous" but Jesus said, "God's ear is open to the unrighteous."

C. THE MULTITUDES WHO RESPONDED

The sinners, the irreligious and the irrespectable hung upon Jesus' words, accepted Him as their friend, rallied around Him and followed Him. They understood the basic principles of His teaching. They knew that that was the day of repentance and thus they rejoiced in His coming and His ministry. They knew the meaning of His statement, "I will have mercy, and not sacrifice" for they were the sinners to receive that mercy. If Matthew, if Mary Magdalene, if Zaccheus could be saved, so can we. If there is a stirring in the human breast which makes us dissatisfied with our sin, it is a sign that God's Spirit is striving with us and that there is hope for us sinners.

2

A DINNER ATTENDED BY A PROSTITUTE

THURSDAY — SECOND DAY

TEXT: Luke 7:47. "Her sins, which are many, are forgiven; for she loved much: but to whom little is forgiven, the same loveth little."

SCRIPTURE: Luke 7:36-50

We often find Jesus at meals, and these meals reveal a great deal about the Lord. This is in contrast with John the Baptist, for he came neither eating bread nor drinking wine, whereas the Lord Jesus came eating and drinking (Luke 7:33,34). John was unacceptable to the Pharisees for the one reason, and Jesus was unacceptable for the other reason. On this occasion we find Him in the home of a Pharisee who desired Him to eat with him. It was probably a wealthy, well appointed, favorably situated home. As such, it would have a view of that incomparable lake, Galilee. It would have the livability of the eastern structures which were marked by walled gardens, fountains, colonnaded patios, an atrium and small balconies at the windows from which it was possible to get the beautiful vista over the lake of Galilee. It was customary, according to the laws of hospitality, to offer water to wash one's feet of the dust of the road, and oil to anoint one's head, face and hair, and to give a kiss of welcome for a table companion. In this case, all these amenities were omitted. The host was attentive, but critical. He thought of Jesus as "this man." He accepted Him as a teacher, but not as a prophet or anything more than a prophet. Hence, he did not accord Him the common civilities and amenities in the supercilious attitude which he displayed toward Jesus. It is apparent that Jesus felt this quite keenly.

I. THE INCIDENT

A. Her courage to face this self-righteous Pharisee

1. *The condition of the woman*

It was while Jesus and the Pharisee were in this attitude of mind that a woman, who was a sinner, appeared upon the scene. We are to understand that she was a prostitute, or a harlot, or in modern terminology, a call girl. In our day, women of this type are not marked by geographical areas as Theodore White in *Thunder Out of China* says they were in Chungking, or by a badge as Nathaniel Hawthorne in *The Scarlet Letter* says they were in early New England, or by long hair as they were in Jesus' day. They now appear in the AA hotels, in fine neighborhoods, in university sororities and in good society. Some movie celebrities are nothing but women of the streets, namely, sinners.

2. *Her coming to this house*

The Pharisee and his guests reclined on couches with their heads toward the table, their weight on their left elbows, their feet outward as they conversed and received the delicacies prepared for them. Then it was that this woman came up the steps from the courtyard, through the antechamber into the atrium where the dinner was being held. How did she get in? Apparently she knew the house, as she was known by the Pharisee. Edersheim (Vol. I, p. 564) thinks the Pharisee knew her too well.

3. *Her conversion*

Somewhere this woman had heard Jesus' teaching, possibly His invitation for all those who labor to come to Him. She had believed His word and now she had come to appropriate His peace and rest. Others would gladly have weighted her down to hell, but Jesus held out hope for her.

I wonder where she heard Him? Was it the Sermon on the Mount? Or the sermon on the plain? Or His sermon by the lake? I wonder how she looked at Simon, the Pharisee, and his friends as she entered? No one evidently spoke to her. I wonder why Jesus said nothing but in silence let her proceed as all eyes were upon her? It is interesting that this woman is totally unidentified. There is no ground for identifying her with Mary Magda-

lene or with Mary of Bethany. There is a fine delicacy in the
Gospels in such matters. She may have become someone well
known in gospel history.

B. HER CONTRITION

Having come, she "stood weeping, and began to wash His
feet with her tears." Is this hyperbole? Never. A truly broken
heart, whether by sorrow, disappointment, gratitude or love will
weep copiously, sometimes uncontrollably. Her past life
weighed upon her; perhaps poverty, weakness, temptation, in-
fidelity may have led her into the life of sin. Hers was a guilty
conscience, a sense of shame, the reproach of society, ostracism
from accepted places and possibly a condition of sickness. But in
the light of Jesus' person, teaching and presence, she saw these
moral aberrations with a hatred of evil, self-abhorrence, conviction, sorrow, repentance and a desire to change. This is called
"sorrow toward God" or "true contrition."

C. HER CONSECRATION

She "began to wash His feet with tears, and did wipe them
with the hairs of her head, and kissed His feet, and anointed
them with the ointment." His feet which were not cleansed by
water now were washed with tears and wiped with her hair.
What a washing of the dust of the way this was. She kissed His
feet and worshipped (Psa. 2:14). To have had her guilt lifted
and life changed made her love and worship Him. She anointed
His feet with ointment. This was not ordinary ointment, but
myrrh, a perfumed unguent of great value — possibly it was the
price of her own security and possibly the price of her sin. By
these acts, she confessed openly that she had come to Jesus as
He had invited.

II. THE INDICTMENT

Here we have two indictments — one of Jesus by the Pharisee
and the other of the Pharisee by Jesus.

A. OF JESUS BY THE PHARISEE

The Pharisee "spake within himself, saying, This man, if he
were a prophet, would have known who and what manner of
woman this is."

1. *Things we say within ourselves*

The Pharisee thought that no one heard him or knew what he was thinking. However, our thoughts have effects upon us. If one would take great triumphant texts of Scripture such as Philippians 4:13, II Corinthians 2:14, Romans 8:36 and bear them in mind, they will have a great effect upon life. Our thoughts even have effect upon others. We emanate attitudes. If our thoughts are negative and critical, they will have an influence upon ourselves and also upon others. We do not think alone. Therefore, it is wise for us to keep our thoughts pure.

2. *The thoughts he had*

This Pharisee's thoughts about Jesus were in error. He considered Him not even a prophet. How much the Pharisee missed which the woman had gained. His thoughts about the woman were incomplete. He thought she was a sinner. She had been a sinner, but now she was changed. This he did not understand. He only knew her past. His thoughts about himself were in error. He considered that he knew that he was righteous, that he could sit in judgment on others. He was a perfect illustration of the parable Jesus gave of the publican and the Pharisee going to worship in the temple. How little this Pharisee knew of himself.

3. *That God knows these thoughts should shock us*

Jesus said that lust in the heart is adultery, hate in the heart is murder, wrong criticism is lying, envy is stealing. And God knows all these things. God desires truth in the inward parts. What condemnation may be ours!

B. Of the Pharisee by Jesus

1. *The personal address*

Jesus said, "Simon, I have somewhat to say unto thee." And Simon replied, "Master, say on." This should have warned Simon, but his self-confidence deceived him. He had no idea that Jesus was answering his thoughts nor did he know the trap into which he was falling, namely, that he would be brought to condemn himself by Jesus' use of the Socratic method.

2. *The parable or illustration*

A syllogism is involved here. Its major premise is that love is measured by benefits received. That is a very materialistic premise but one which the Pharisee would understand. The minor premise was that the man forgiven five hundred pence received the greater benefit. The conclusion was that therefore this man would love the most. Simon assented all the way through. The similarity was that this woman had been forgiven much. Simon thought he had little to be forgiven. Therefore, the woman was most grateful and loving. The sense here is not that Simon was forgiven, but the thrust was to open his eyes to his own condemnation.

III. THE PRINCIPLE APPLIED

Of the woman, Jesus says, "much sin," "much forgiveness," "many tears," and "much love." Of Simon there is the implication that there is no sense of sin, no sorrow, no forgiveness and no love. What if the principle were applied to you? Is your heart cold and unresponsive to Jesus? If so, what does it reveal about your spiritual state? For one who is greatly forgiven, no act of service, worship or sacrifice is too great to express his love.

A. HER ACTION WAS THE RESULT OF HER LOVE

The inference that love is the condition of salvation is not warranted here. This of course is the argument advanced by those who preach salvation by works. The impulsion to action, worship, sacrifice and service is love (II Cor. 5:14). The infusion of love by the Holy Spirit into a justified soul leads him to love God, Jesus, the brethren, the Word and the things of God.

B. HER LOVE WAS THE RESULT OF HER FORGIVENESS

The testimony to your forgiveness and salvation is the love you bear Jesus Christ. After all, love is the test of Christianity. John the Beloved puts it by asking, "Do you love Jesus?" Love should triumph in a regenerated, converted life. Away then with all Pharisaical bitterness, and criticism and judgment.

C. HER FORGIVENESS WAS THE RESULT OF HER FAITH

Faith is the instrument of justification and salvation (Rom. 1:16,17; 3:25; 5:1). Faith works by love which is the fruit of faith (James 2:14; Gal. 5:8). Faith in Christ's person and work was not shared by those at the meal. They had no realization of forgiveness.

CONCLUSION

This woman's tears, faith and love testified to a forgiveness already received. God grant that we may weep over our sins, believe for our forgiveness, and love Christ sacrificially.

3

A DINNER WHICH COST A RICH MAN
HALF HIS WEALTH

Friday — Third Day

Text: Luke 19:5,8. "I must abide at thy house . . . Behold, the half of my goods I give to the poor."
Scripture: Luke 19:1-10

Common things like eating, drinking and sleeping take a place of prominence in the New Testament. The occasions of the Lord's dinner parties were used for self-revelation and impartation of truth.

A. Jericho

The meaning of Jericho is "perfumed." Situated by the flowing waters of the Jordan, its own water supply largely supplied by the brook Cherith, graced by acacia trees, smoke trees, oleander, coconut palm, date palm, balsam, banana, fig, olive, pomegranate and all kinds of citrus trees as well as flowers, the city is a veritable garden. It has its rich and its poor sections. The waters of the brook Cherith are brought into Jericho by an aqueduct from the hills. The climate is warm in contrast to the biting sharp winds of Jerusalem.

B. The house

This rich man had a house of brick or stone covered with stucco, all on one floor such as a modern ranch house, although it was Roman in form. The atrium contained a pool. From it led porticoes over which there was no roof, so that the water reflected the stars and the balmy fragrance during the cool night entered the banqueting hall. The rooms clustered around the pool and the garden. Outside a high wall surrounded the property into which were built the rooms with a tile roof. At hand was the Arabian master of the slaves, the steward who controlled the treasure room of silver, jewels, linen, money and valuables, and the wife and children of the family who were the center of the wealthy man's interest and love. This man's name was Zakki which meant innocent. Possibly he was just and had won his wealth by shrewdness, quickness and ruthlessness, but harmonious with honesty.

C. THE FEAST

The house had been prepared for friends who had been invited to a party, for even a publican had his friends. Common people going by the wall would spit at it. Honest publicans only collected the taxes and a reasonable percentage in addition. Dishonest ones feathered their own nests. All of them were ostracized from society. Thus it would be a social strata of his own kind which would be invited to this party, probably from neighboring towns, for all were glad to spend time in Jericho, the watering spa of Israel. For them, choice viands, wines, entertainment, music and dancing girls were prepared. Everything they liked would be there for Zakki was a very rich man.

I. HIS PURPOSE

A. THE KNOWLEDGE OF EVENTS

Sometime before this, Matthew the publican had been converted and it was noised around among all publicans. Jesus' teachings, miracles like the healing of blind Bartimaeus and His claims could not be hidden. Already He had raised the daughter of Jairus, the son of the widow, and Lazarus from the dead. Already authoritative plots to put Him to death expressed the antipathy of the rulers. All of this the intelligence officers of Zakki had reported to him.

B. THE KNOTTY PROBLEMS

Apparently Zakki believed the law and the promise and looked for the Messiah. He must have wondered whether Jesus could be this Messiah or just a plain teacher. He had long ago broken with the Pharisaical laws, interpretations and the bondage of them. This had led him into the activity of a publican. He wondered how Jesus would interpret the law — with mercy and judgment, or as the Pharisees did. At least he was interested in the strange things which Jesus said about the

Pharisees and the publicans. Zakki had a conviction that Israel ought to be able to get along with Rome and not to revolt against her. He believed these spiritual matters should be divorced from the political.

C. THE NEED TO MEET, TO HEAR, AND TO TALK WITH JESUS

About this time, one of Zakki's men brought the report that Jesus was coming, that a blind man had been healed just outside the city and that a great crowd had gathered. For months Jesus had been in Transjordan and now He was coming through Jericho. Zakki immediately responded by going out to catch a glimpse of Jesus. He was drawn irresistibly by his need, by his yearning and by the Holy Spirit. All other things could wait. This was now his primary purpose and he would redeem the time.

II. HIS PERSPECTIVE

A. DISCOVERY

But when Zakki reached the center of Jericho, he found a great crowd which was hostile to him and which was ready to express its hatred. He attempted to look but was unable and was quickly repulsed. We read that he was "of little stature" which expresses his frustration in his inability to see. Yet all of us are little in ourselves. We need perspective, vision, the eternal view, God's view. We need to get somewhere where we can see the world and the world can see us. Zakki was determined to get that perspective.

B. DETERMINATION

The brain which made him rich came to his rescue. He saw a sycamore tree with a projecting limb and, to the best of his ability, scrambled up to it and held onto that limb. It was an undignified, incongruous position but was evidence of his sincerity and his humility. From there he witnessed the panorama of the crowd, the individuals, then in the distance the disciples, and beyond them Jesus walking, but stopping to heal, speaking a word of teaching, singling out an individual to be blessed, and he was enthralled with the sight. The pleasure he took in it made him forget all about the dinner and his engagement. He was absorbed in studying Jesus, in listening and watching. He forgot all about himself. It is like one who discovers the gospel for the first time and reads it with eager hunger.

C. DESTINY

It was thus that he was situated when Jesus passed under the limb of the sycamore tree and stopped and looked right up into his face. Zakki found himself looking into the eyes of Christ, the eyes that had led Matthew to leave the receipt of customs, the eyes which later were to cause Peter to go out and weep bitterly. As he looked, Zakki saw himself. He saw what he had been and what he could be. In those profound pools, all of his life was mirrored. Then, it was if a horoscope was being revealed to him. He was utterly lost. Just then he heard his name called and he realized he was being invited to come down. Christ knows your name. He knows all about you, and the same invitation goes to you. He said, "Come down; for today I must abide at thy house." Thus Christ is ready to face you, to change you and to conquer you. What would you do if Jesus came to your house for dinner today?

Zakki hastened to respond. He delayed not. He let nothing hinder him. He immediately called Jesus, "Lord." His was an instantaneous conversion such as happened with Paul, and such as has happened with countless others. The evidence of it was that he declared, "The half of my goods I give to the poor." This was proof of a loving, generous heart. The new perspective which he had gained transformed his view of possessions and things.

Then he added, "If I have taken any thing from any man by false accusation, I restore him fourfold." The law required that one-fifth was to be added in restitution, but Zakki was ready to restore fourfold. It is evident that he had a new heart, a new outlook, a new testimony (Lev. 5; Ex. 21:1). Let there be no lack of preaching on restitution in Christian circles in this day.

III. HIS PRIVILEGE

A. HE WALKED IN COMPANY WITH JESUS, HIS LORD, BEFORE ALL HIS ERSTWHILE ENEMIES

Jesus and Zakki walked together to Zakki's house. Zakki must have been oblivious to all others and to all else. Such gave rise to the complaint of people, "He eateth with publicans and sinners," for Jesus had gone to be guest with a man who was a sinner.

B. He received the approbation, "a son of Abraham"

This seems to imply that Zakki was saved in the Old Testament sense, but now he became a true believer and was changed. Jesus said, "This day is salvation come to this house." Not only had salvation come in the person of the Saviour, but also in Zakki's personal salvation. For him, it was now a completed work. He was saved.

C. He was host to the Lord

We read nothing in this story about the service in Zakki's home at the meal, about the state of the guests, about the food, but only about the change in Zakki. It is obvious that they were joyful for it says of Zakki that he "received him joyfully." One imagines what the conversation may have been. Surely Zakki would draw out of Jesus the teaching concerning law and grace, new life and work, beginning and growth. This was only the inception of his fellowship with Christ. It is possible that Jesus stayed only for the meal, but it is probable He stayed for the night. It was just fourteen miles or six hours' distance from Jerusalem, and the probabilities are that the next day He went to Bethany and to Simon's house. What a night Zakki spent with Jesus.

D. He illustrated the fact that Christ came to save the lost

This was Christ's own affirmation often reiterated. He is come to save all the lost. Do you know you are lost? If you do not know that you are lost, publicans and harlots will enter the kingdom before you.

CONCLUSION: THE TRANSFORMED HOME

If Christ came to dinner at your home today, what would He change? Your attitude, your speech, your mannerisms, your relationships, your prejudices, your niggardliness? If you are a believer, He will be at your table in fellowship with you. Therefore, let it be a table of joy, of blessing, of fellowship and of action which is pleasing to Him. If Jesus could change Zakki and his home, He can also transform your home. Christ became poor for us, that we through His poverty could be rich.

4

A DINNER LOOKING TOWARD THE CROSS

Saturday — Fourth Day

Text: Matthew 26:7. "There came unto him a woman having an alabaster box of very precious ointment, and poured it on his head, as he sat at meat."

Scripture: Matthew 26:6-13

Worship centers in the crucified, resurrected and glorified Lord. Women were very prominent in the events clustered about the crucifixion, burial and resurrection of our Lord. The women sympathized with Jesus on the way of sorrow. The women, including Jesus' mother, her sister Salome, Mary of Cleopas and Mary Magdalene, were at Calvary. Women also stood afar off, witnessing the crucifixion. The women went to the tomb to watch Jesus buried and the women went to the tomb on Easter morning to anoint the body with spices.

In addition to the above mentioned ones, Joanna is also mentioned. But where was Mary of Bethany, so intimate and friendly with the Lord Jesus? She is unmentioned and is notable because of her absence. It is possible that she could have been included in the "many women" but she is so prominent that it seems she would have been named before Joanna, a very obscure character.

We are not to confuse Mary of Bethany with Mary Magdalene as some do, or with the woman of Luke 7:37-50 who washed Jesus' feet and anointed them with ointment. The latter is a calumny upon Mary of Bethany and there is no reason to identify Mary Magdalene with the woman of the streets of Luke 7. The reason that Mary was not present was because the Jewish authorities determined "to put Lazarus also to death" (John 12:10) because many people believed on Jesus because of Lazarus' resurrection from the dead. Consequently, there is every reason to believe that the tradition, which says that Mary and Martha fled from Jerusalem with Lazarus to Cyprus, is true.

But in substitution for her worship of Jesus at the time of the crucifixion and resurrection, Mary performed an extravagant act of worship.

The place was Bethany, the village of Mary and Martha which was so familiar to our Lord Jesus, although the home used was the home of Simon the leper. Bethany was situated just over the top of the Mount of Olives toward the descent to Jericho and the Dead Sea. Here Jesus had come at the Feast of the Tabernacles to enjoy the hospitality of Mary and Martha. Here Jesus had come to raise Lazarus from the dead. Here Jesus was to lodge during the last week of His ministry.

The occasion occurred on the last Sabbath of our Lord's life. On the afternoon of the Sabbath, Simon the leper made a feast for Jesus in his home. The disciples were guests, Lazarus was an honored guest, Simon was the host, and Mary and Martha helped prepare the meal. Crowds of people milled about outside of the gates and the walls hoping to get a glimpse of Lazarus who had been dead but was raised by Jesus from the dead.

In the midst of the conversation the attention of all was drawn to Mary. She had slipped out and returned with a box of very precious ointment, had slipped up behind Jesus, had broken the alabaster box, poured the ointment over His head and then taken the remnant to His feet, anointed His feet and then washed them with her hair. The aroma and fragrance immediately filled the room and the attention of everyone was drawn to Mary as she knelt at Jesus' feet, wiping them with the hair of her head. The disciples were indignant and their indignation was expressed by Judas who asked, "Why this waste? For this ointment might have been sold for much, and given to the poor." The comment is made by John that they were not interested in the poor but that Judas had made his statement because he was a thief.

Jesus immediately recognized the spiritual insight of Mary and the purpose with which she had done the deed. He said, "In that she hath poured this ointment on my body, she did it for my burial." Mary had comprehended Christ's thrice-repeated announcement of His coming death and resurrection. She understood what none of the disciples had grasped, namely, the nature of His kingdom, the imminence of His death and the deity of

His person. She knew that death could not hold Him. Knowing that she would not be there for these events, intuition told her that this was the last time that she could worship Him in the flesh so she gave her most precious gift to Christ.

The Lord pronounced His eulogy upon her, "Wheresoever this gospel shall be preached in the whole world, there shall also this, that this woman hath done, be told for a memorial of her." Her act had meant a great deal to Him. He knew what lay ahead. He foresaw the triumphal entry, the days of teaching, the last fellowship with His disciples in the upper room, the betrayal by Judas, the denial by Peter, His suffering in Caiaphas hall and before Pilate, and finally His death on Golgotha. He knew that He would endure the pains of hell itself on our behalf and at this moment an act of understanding sympathy and loving worship was given to Him which renewed His courage and His purpose.

I do not think that it is a great act of imagination to believe that He foresaw the spiritual praise, honor and glory which would rise to Him in the ages ahead from the redeemed by His death. Isaiah 53:11 tells us that He saw the fruit of His suffering and was satisfied in the cost which He paid. How much more in this extravagant act of worship did He receive a down-payment on the love, consecration, sacrifice and service of millions like her. In this act of Mary we learn three wonderful truths.

I. OUR PRECIOUS LORD IS WORTHY OF OUR MOST PRECIOUS WORSHIP

A. HOW PRECIOUS IS HE TO US?

Peter tells us, "Unto you who believe He is precious." Yes, His life is precious. There is an infinite value because He was God in the flesh. It is perfectly proper to worship the pre-existent One who partook of human nature and who made atonement for our sins upon the cross. He was precious unto the Father and called by Him His beloved, His delight, His express image by which He revealed Himself. He is precious also to us as the foundation of our faith, as the means of our righteousness, and as the hope of our future destiny.

His blood also is precious. It is the one means of redemption, of the remission of sins and of the remedy for our corrupt nature (I Pet. 1:19.)

His Spirit is precious. The Holy Spirit given to us by Him is our assurance of forgiveness, of life and of inheritance as the sons of God. Yes, we must conclude that Jesus is very precious to us.

B. WHAT PRECIOUS WORSHIP SHALL WE GIVE HIM?

Are we willing to give Him our life, that is, ourselves? He deserves the whole heart, soul and mind of man. He wants our entire being, no less. Since He gave Himself for us He has a right to expect this of us (Rom. 12:1, 2). We may very well break the alabaster box of life in worship of Him.

Will we give Him our substance? After all, it belongs to Him. If He needs it, shall we withhold it from Him? The ointment which Mary gave was very precious. It was worth 300 pence, or the equivalent of the labor of a man for 300 days, yet she gladly gave it to the Lord.

Will we give Him our service, no matter how hard, sacrificial or trying it may be? Thus missionaries have served Him through the years. Capable doctors are expending their lives in far-off areas of the world, all for Jesus' sake, though they are unsung and unhonored in this world.

C. HOW OTHERS CONSIDER OUR EXTRAVAGANCE IS INCONSEQUENTIAL

Whatever great thing you may do for Christ, or whatever sacrifice you may make, it is no extravagance. There will be misunderstanding of it by some, there will be criticism by others, there may be even tensions within our own families due to the fact that we are giving our life and our money to the Lord and to His work. Nevertheless, He deserves it and He has a right to expect it. If we have grasped the spiritual nature of the kingdom and if we understand His purposes and have sympathy with Jesus' teaching as it was given in His resurrection, nothing will be too precious for Him.

II. OUR SACRIFICE IS THE MEASURE OF OUR WORSHIP

A. LET IT NEVER BE FOR RECOGNITION

Whatever we do for Christ to express our worship, it must never be for show, for impression or for power. We must not take the avenue of the harlot or the false bride, namely Tyre, but we must be as the true bride, Jerusalem, who does not need to advertise herself. What she does is not for glory. The consecrated self-giving of a church or of an individual commends itself according to God's standards, not in comparison with other churches or other individuals. The question is, Of what are we capable? Have we rendered according to the benefits we have received?

B. Let it be the measure of our love and devotion and desire to extend His sovereignty and Kingdom

The Lord said, "If ye love me, keep my commandments." In His commandments He laid a task upon the Church to evangelize the world and to teach all things whatsoever He had commanded us. The part we take in this task will correspond to our love. The response which we make to His commandments will reveal the sincerity of our affection.

C. Let us give in accordance with what we have

When God gives it is "according to His riches" (Phil. 4:19) not out of His riches. The principle is exactly the same for us. We are to give abundantly and liberally and hilariously according to what we have received. As God commended the giving of the widow's mite, so also He knows what we will give.

III. OUR MEMORIAL IS IN THE SOULS FOR WHOM CHRIST DIED

A. For most servants there will be no memorial here on earth

Few servants of the Lord will be catapulted into fame. There will be some Livingstones, Careys, Taylors, Moodys and Grahams but for most of us the faithful acts of worship, service and self-denial will go unsung by the multitudes. We are familiar with many people who would do great sacrificial things if they could be eulogized and memorialized, just as many would have done exactly as Mary did if they had known that they would thus become immortal.

B. For the true Christian the great reward is the commendation of the Lord

Jesus said that our Father seeth in secret and if He seeth in secret He will reward us openly. Some day we may hear, "Well done, good and faithful servant!" Whatever we do, God is not unmindful of our labors of love (Heb. 6:10).

C. For sharing in soul winning, a crown awaits you

What have you done to bring the world to the feet of Jesus in worship (I Thess. 2:19; Dan. 12:3; Prov. 11:30)? If you have ever done anything extravagant for yourself and excused yourself for it, ask yourself if you are now willing to do something extravagant for Christ. What Mary did at this dinner party you may also do for Christ.

GLORYING IN THE CROSS

GLORYING IN THE CROSS

Introduction

The cross is the center of the Christian religion. How essential it is that we are able to read the law of Moses with illumined eyes so as to discover the prefiguration of the cross and to understand how God was able to forgive the sins of men before the accomplishment of atonement and still remain just and holy. In examining the cross in the prophets, one immediately is impressed with the fact that the death of Jesus on Calvary was inevitable. It could not have been circumvented. Hence, there could not have been an offer of a kingdom to the Jews which would have embraced their acceptance of Him as a king and the omission of His death upon the cross. Such a theory would invalidate all of the prophetic word of the sufferings of Christ.

The Psalms above all of the Old Testament writings present the spiritual experiences of the Messiah in His sufferings and thus become the source of spiritual succor to believers who pass through trials or who identify themselves voluntarily with the sufferings of Christ.

It is essential for the preacher to recognize, understand and preach the place of the cross in the believer's experience. To allow the cross to remain as a forensic, declarative or judicial event without transferring its meaning to the believer's own life is to fail in our preaching of the heart of Christianity.

Since so much of the New Testament, and the Old in fact, is centered around Calvary, Calvary should take the place of pre-eminence in our interpretation of the life, death and resurrection of Jesus Christ.

1

THE CROSS IN THE LAW

Text: Hebrews 9:22. "And almost all things are by the law purged with blood; and without shedding of blood is no remission."

Scripture: Hebrews 9:13-28

The blood of Christ is equivalent to the cross of Christ where His blood was shed when it is mentioned in the Scripture. The "blood of Christ" is mentioned in the New Testament nearly three times as often as "the cross" of Christ, and five times as often as the "death of Christ." The term "blood" is in fact a chief method of reference to the sacrifice of Christ, particularly in the context which defines its efficacy. In Colossians 1:10 the phrase, "the blood of the cross" is used. In other places "the blood of Christ" and "the cross" are used jointly (Ephesians 2:14ff). Always the connotation of the cross is the shedding of Christ's blood, and hence the meaning of blood in the Old Testament is a forerunner of the cross.

In the Old Testament the blood was given as a means of atonement for the soul (Lev. 17:11), hence it was forbidden to drink blood or to eat flesh with the blood in it (Gen. 9:4; Lev. 17:3-7; Deut. 12:15; 16:20-28). When the hungry Israelites ate flesh with the blood in it, after Jonathan's great victory over the Philistines at Beth-aven, it constituted a sin (I Sam. 14:32). In the Old Testament we learn that physical life is God's creation and belongs to Him, especially if it is the life of man which is made in God's image.

Both animal and human life could only be taken by divine permission. When an animal was to be slain to be eaten, the blood was to be poured out unto God. When a human life was to be taken, it was only under the authority of God in a fulfillment of the law of God. When blood of men was wrongfully taken, it was required by God. Thus the Lord instituted capital punishment for manslaughter (Gen. 9:5, 6). Whenever human blood was wrongfully shed and unrequited, it corrupted the land (Num. 35:33; Psalm 106:37,38). Innocent blood could only be put away from Israel by expiation (Deut. 19:11-13). All of this pointed to the cross of Christ.

I. THE PRINCIPLE INVOLVED

A. THE SHED BLOOD OF ANIMALS WAS GIVEN BY DIVINE APPOINTMENT TO BE USED TO MAKE ATONEMENT FOR SIN, TO EFFECT EXPIATION AND CLEANSING

The first preaching of the gospel in Genesis 3:15 implied the shedding of blood for the remission of sin. Adam and Eve were clothed in the skins of animals and Abel was accepted because he came in the appointed way, namely with the sacrifice of a lamb. Thus, from the very beginning, God taught that it was essential to have the shedding of blood for the remission of sin. In all the repulsive blood sacrifices of the Old Testament we may see a preparation for the death of the Lord Jesus upon the cross. Past sins, committed before the death of Christ on the cross, were covered by this blood until the expiation by Christ might be made (Rom. 3:25).

B. SUCH LIVES LAID DOWN IN DEATH BY THE SHEDDING OF BLOOD HAD VALUE AS AN EXPIATION

Expiation was not made by the blood of the guilty, requiting his sin, but by the blood of a guiltless substitute, a lamb without blemish and without spot. This was the exchange of a ransom for a life, otherwise forfeit because of sin. The lamb, or bullock, or pigeon died in the place of the sinner.

C. THE SYMBOL OF THE GREAT SACRIFICE IN THE SHEDDING OF CHRIST'S BLOOD ON THE CROSS FOR A MAN

Christ was the lamb of God, "who taketh away the sin of the world," (John 1:29). Peter tells us that He was without blemish and without spot (I Pet. 1:19). The curse of death on Christ came not because of His own deeds. He perfectly obeyed the law of God and could have gone directly to heaven without death, as Enoch was translated or Elijah was taken up into heaven. But He chose to die, to pour out His soul, to shed His blood as a substitute for man. The cross, therefore, is the antitype of all that was foretold and foreshadowed in the law by the blood sacrifices.

II. THE PASSOVER ILLUSTRATION

That there was no remission of sin without the shedding of blood was clearly illustrated by the Passover. In conjunction with that ritual, God said, "When I see the blood, I will pass over you" (Ex. 12:13) .

A. THE SINFUL PEOPLE NEEDING REDEMPTION

In Egypt the Israelites were ignorant, idolatrous and iniquitous. They were in danger of judgment and were liable to death. When they were called to become God's people it was necessary that they be cleansed from all the defilements of Egypt. This cleansing was symbolized through the Passover.

B. THE SACRIFICE SUBSTITUTED FOR THEM

A lamb was to be chosen for each family, a lamb without blemish and without spot (Ex. 12:4, 5) . The life of this lamb was taken even though the lamb itself was not liable to death. The blood of the lamb was sprinkled upon the lintels of the doors and the posts of the doors in the form of a cross to provide shelter and protection from the divine judgment. The saving power of the substitutionary death of the animal was expressed by the sprinkled blood. This was a token which God would see. As the inhabitants ate the flesh of the roasted lamb, the blood was effective for their salvation. It had been poured out and it became a type of eating Christ by faith.

C. THE SIGN OF OUR REDEMPTION

Christ is called our passover (I Cor. 5:7) . In an exact parallel it is His shed blood on Calvary which is accepted by faith that gives us forgiveness. Christians, therefore, are to purge out the leaven of malice and wickedness and keep the feast with unleavened bread of sincerity and truth, namely, consistent lives.

III. THE PRECEPT INSTITUTED

The fact that there was no forgiveness except through the shedding of blood is illustrated also by Leviticus 16, the Day of Atonement.

A. THE RITUAL OF THE DAY OF ATONEMENT

The high priest who was to observe the Day of Atonement himself had to be cleansed by the offering of a bullock as a sacrifice for himself and his house. Then, being holy, he was able to offer the sacrifice. It was unnecessary for Christ to do this for He was holy and needed no atonement for Himself. Then the high priest took two goats. One was put to death and his blood was offered on the Mercy Seat for the people to make an atonement. Over the head of the other the sins of the people were confessed and it was released in the wilderness as a scapegoat, or a symbol of the separation of the sins from the people. Then the remnants of the slain goat were burned without the camp after his blood had been sprinkled upon the horns of the brazen altar seven times. This also was a perfect illustration for the satisfaction reconciling the sinner to God and the removal of his sins from him.

B. THE REAL ATONEMENT OF CALVARY

When the Lord Jesus died for us He did not offer a repeated sacrifice but a completed and finished one. It was "once for all." It was not with His blood that He entered into heaven but through His blood, that is, His death. Thus He became our advocate, granting forgiveness and release. Not for Himself did He suffer without the gate but for you and for me. "Neither by the blood of bulls, and goats, but by His own blood He entered once into the holy place having obtained eternal redemption for us." (Heb. 9:12) .

C. THE REMEDY FOR SIN IN THE CROSS

By the death of our Lord Jesus on the cross "once in the end of the world He hath appeared to put away sin by the sacrifice of Himself" (Heb. 9:26) . By this sacrifice He perfected forever them that are sanctified, namely, those whom He represented (Heb. 10:14) . By His atoning death on the cross He saves those who believe, whom He represented on Calvary.

INFERENCE

The new covenant of grace, of forgiveness and of release of sin is a covenant sealed by blood. Just as blood was used to establish the first covenant (Heb. 9:18-21) , so the new covenant is sealed by the blood of Christ's death on the cross (Matt.

26:27, 28) . The blood of Christ, through His death on the cross, established a new covenant by which transgressions of the old were forgiven. Now "the blood of the everlasting covenant, make you perfect in every good work to do His will, working within you that which is well pleasing in His sight through Jesus Christ" (Heb. 13:20, 21) .

2

THE CROSS IN THE PROPHETS
MONDAY — SIXTH DAY

TEXT: Luke 24: 25,26. "O fools, and slow of heart to believe all that the prophets have spoken: Ought not Christ to have suffered these things, and to enter into his glory?"

SCRIPTURE: Luke 24:13-27

The witness of the prophets is appealed to as evidence of the necessity of the cross by the Lord Jesus Christ and later by Peter in his preaching and later by Paul in his preaching. Consistently the expectation of Calvary was derived from the teaching of the prophets.

A. THE PHENOMENON OF PROPHECY

Prophecy is established upon the basis of revelation. Only God can foretell the future and can suggest the knowledge of future events to men. This is frankly supernatural and pre-supposes the fact that God does disclose Himself and His will to men. He may use a voice, or dreams, or visions, or the height-ened sensibilities of man to suggest the truths or the facts which He wishes to reveal but the source must be God. If there is no revelation, there can be no prophecy.

Prophecy also involves inspiration. The individuals who were to receive God's revelation had to be inspired by the Holy Spirit. Only God could enable these men to receive and to record the revelations of His plan. Prophecy also includes inscripturation of the revelation. This depends upon the work of the Holy Spirit overseeing the writing of the prophets so that the re-sultant scripture was the Word of God. These things are all involved in the phenomenon of prophecy.

B. THE PERSON OF THE PROPHETS

Peter declares "Holy men of God spake as they were moved by the Holy Ghost" (II Pet. 1:21). This declares that the

44

prophets personally were holy men. They were sanctified in character by a deep religious experience which prepared them to endure the suffering attendant upon the prophetic ministry and to appreciate the prophetic revelation. Thus, Isaiah received his deep spiritual experience recorded in the sixth chapter of "the Holy One" of Israel.

Peter implies that the prophets were obedient men, "They spake as they were moved." The message which God revealed to them was not always easy to give and many of the prophets would have preferred not to have had the responsibility of giving it. This was true especially of Jonah who fled from the task of preaching repentance and judgment to Nineveh. Also, of Jeremiah who did not desire to prophesy but excused himself with the statement, "I am a child." Peter also tells us that these were chosen men. Thus we learn that prophecy was a gift from God and not an achievement of the striving of the individual. The oral prophets such as Elijah and Elisha spoke as they were moved but theirs was an oral prophecy whereas Moses, Samuel, David, Amos, Hosea, Isaiah and others were the writing prophets. All were chosen men of God.

C. THE PREDICTIONS OF CHRIST'S SUFFERINGS

Peter also tells us that it was impossible for these prophets to understand the meaning of their own prophecies which the Spirit did signify when it testified beforehand the sufferings of Christ, and the glory that should follow (I Pet. 1:10, 11). Such a fact in itself was an evidence of the supernatural nature of prophecy. Had men invented their prophecies, they would not have laid such emphasis upon the suffering of the Redeemer; rather, they would have thought of Him as a glorious, powerful King. It was even difficult for the disciples of the Lord Jesus to grasp this fact when Jesus foretold His imminent death and after His death the cross was an offense, a stumblingblock (Matt. 16:21, 22; 17:22, 23; I Cor. 1:23; Gal. 5:6). Revelation and inspiration alone are sufficient to account for these accurate pictures of the Crucified One given in the prophets. As we have examined the cross in the law of Moses, let us also examine it in the prophets.

I. THE CROSS IN ISAIAH

There are several references to the humility and suffering of the Messiah such as chapter 42:1-3; 50:6, 7; 61:1, 2; 63:3, but the great passage describing the suffering Saviour is Isaiah 52:13-53:12. This passage is interpreted by the Orthodox Jew as applying unto the suffering of the nation Israel but a careful study of it will reveal that it is not to the nation but to an individual servant of God, namely the Messiah, to whom the Scripture is referring.

A. GENERAL MEANING OF ISAIAH 53

Christians may be certain of the meaning of the passage because it is twice referred to in the New Testament under the inspiration of the Holy Spirit. The first is in Acts 8:32-35 where Philip expounded this chapter to the Ethiopian eunuch and preached unto him Jesus. The second is in I Peter 2:24 where Peter quotes the 53rd chapter of Isaiah as justification from the Scripture for his teaching of the vicarious atonement of the Lord Jesus Christ. Hence, we must accept this chapter as a description of the passion of our Lord.

B. INTRODUCTION TO THE PROPHECY (ISA. 52:13-15)

Here we have (1) identification of the Servant in verse 13, (2) the amazement of men at the marking of the visage of the Servant of the Lord from suffering in verse 14 and, (3) the foreseen conversion of kings and nations through the achievement of the Messiah's sufferings. Needless to say, this is one of the grandest passages in all the Scripture and one most precious to evangelical Christians.

C. THE DESCRIPTION OF THE PASSION AND SUFFERINGS OF THE MESSIAH

Here we have an uniquely accurate and appropriate description of what was done to the Lord Jesus Christ. We have (1) the sufferings of loneliness described in verses 1-3, (2) the sufferings of sickness described in verse 4, (3) the sufferings of sin described in verses 5 and 6, (4) the sufferings of oppression and conflict described in verses 7 and 8, (5) the sufferings of death described in verses 9 and 10, and (6) the sufferings of atonement for sin described in verses 11 and 12. In the light of the New Testament interpretation of this passage, we may definitely say there is no clearer picture of what the Saviour did for us than this 53rd chapter of Isaiah.

II. THE CROSS IN DANIEL

A. HOW THE VISION WAS GIVEN TO DANIEL

As one of the holiest men of the Old Testament, Daniel carried the burden of his exiled people. While he was fasting and praying in behalf of his people, he was studying the writings of Jeremiah (Dan. 9:2; Jer. 25:11, 12) and learned that the captivity of Israel was to last seventy years. On the encouragement of this Scripture which he believed, Daniel set himself to seek the Lord by prayer, supplication, with fasting and intercession.

Vicariously he repented of the sins of his people which is expressed in a prayer that has formed the pattern of some of the great liturgies of the church (Dan. 9:3-19). How long Daniel continued in this ministry of intercession, we do not know, but in due season Gabriel was sent to him with a message that at the beginning of his supplication the commandment came forth for him to reveal the matter of the future of his people and to have understanding of the vision (Dan. 9:20-23).

B. THE VISION OF WHAT THE MESSIAH WAS TO ACCOMPLISH (Vv. 24, 25)

Gabriel revealed that the Messiah would (1) finish the transgression, (2) make an end of sin, that is, bring forgiveness, (3) make reconciliation for iniquity, (4) bring in everlasting righteousness, (5) seal the vision of prophecy, (6) anoint the Most Holy, and (7) restore a remnant to Jerusalem.

C. THE VISION OF THE MEANS OF ACCOMPLISHING THIS

All this was to be accomplished through the death of the Messiah who was to be "cut off" but not for Himself. What words could describe Calvary better than these? His death was to be for others "not for Himself" and following this the destruction of Jerusalem was to be connected with the rejection of the Messiah and His achieved ministry. Daniel was very accurate in his foresight and proclamation of the sufferings of the Messiah.

III. THE CROSS AND ZECHARIAH

A. ZECHARIAH'S UNUSUAL GIFTS OF PROPHECY CONCERNING THE MESSIAH

This prophet foretold the entry of Christ into Jerusalem on an ass (Zech. 9:9), the selling of Christ for thirty pieces of silver (11:13), the glory of the coming Messiah as King, God and Lord (14:1-21).

B. ZECHARIAH'S VISION OF CALVARY

In the midst of his prophecies, Zechariah declared that the wounds in the hands of the Messiah were wounds that He received in the house of His friends (13:6). This was literally fulfilled in the upper room supper and fellowship of Jesus with His disciples. Zechariah also declared that the sword of justice would be sheathed in the heart of the shepherd so that the sheep would be scattered. The Lord Jesus even quoted this on the night before His crucifixion as applying to Himself (Matt. 26:31, 67, 68). Here we see that through the Holy Spirit Zechariah had in mind the very things which would occur to Christ before His crucifixion.

C. ZECHARIAH'S UNDERSTANDING OF THE CHRIST'S INFLUENCE ON ISRAEL

This prophet, through the inspiration of the Spirit, grasped the divine revelation that the Messiah was the one who would have been pierced (Zech. 12:10) and that He would be looked upon as such by Israel which would result in their sorrow and mourning, the contrition of repentance, the accompanying effect of which would be their conversion (Rom. 11:26).

CONCLUSION

Thus it is evident that the crucifixion, death and resurrection of Jesus Christ were inevitable. Jesus said, "Ought not Christ to have suffered." If prophecy is based upon the revelation of God and God's revelation is based upon His eternal decrees, then it was necessary that prophecy be fulfilled in the death of Christ upon the cross.

3

THE CROSS IN THE PSALMS

Text: Luke 24:44. "These are the words which I spake unto you, while I was yet with you, that all things must be fulfilled, which were written in the law of Moses, and in the prophets, and in the psalms, concerning me."

Scripture: Luke 24:36-48

A large portion of the Psalms deals with prophecy and all that we said concerning the prophets in "The Cross in the Prophets" may be said at this point. The prophecies contained in the Psalms involved divine revelation, the inspiration of the Holy Spirit and the inscripturation of those revelations under the oversight of the Holy Spirit. Thus, as we examine the Psalms, we also find predictions of both the sufferings and the glory of the Messiah for Jesus opened their understanding that they might understand the Scriptures, including the Psalms, in their prophecies concerning Him, and the necessity of His sufferings and His resurrection give us clear authority for so understanding this portion of the Scripture.

As we examine the sufferings of Christ in the Psalms, we find that there are many minor references in the Psalms to this, that there are some major Psalms completely dedicated to His sufferings and that there is a complete picture of the misery of Christ as He went to Calvary contained in the Psalms.

I. THE MINOR REFERENCES TO THE SUFFERINGS OF CHRIST IN MANY PSALMS

We will be able to mention only a few of these for the Messianic prophecies in the Psalms are prolific. Some of them contain promises given specifically to the Messiah to assist Him in meeting His temptations and sufferings. In witness of this there is the 91st Psalm which gives the promise of His preservation from plagues, the promise of His being kept by angels, the promise of treading on the dragon himself. The Christian should remember that such Messianic promises primarily apply unto the Saviour and it is only as we are in the Saviour and as we appropriate our position in the Saviour that we can claim these promises for ourselves. Promiscuous appropriation of Messianic promises can give a false hope of security to the believer.

A. PSALM 2:1, 2

Here we have a picture of the raging of the heathen, of the vain imaginations of the people of God, of the opposition of kings and rulers against the anointed of the Lord. That this applied unto the life and death of our Lord Jesus is declared by Peter and the Christians in their prayer unto God against the persecutions which were initiated by the chief priests and elders of Israel (Acts 4:23-28). An interesting sidelight on this text in Psalm 2:2 is the translation of the words "take counsel together" in Russian, namely *soviet*. We have a picture here of kings and rulers sovieting against the Lord: such they did during His earthly life and such they will do through history.

B. PSALM 34:20

In the midst of this wonderful Messianic Psalm we have the declaration that not one bone of the Messiah should be broken. This also was taken by John and applied to the death of Jesus on the cross and His piercing by a spear so that they would not have to break His bones as they did those of the thieves (John 19:36). Many were the Scriptures which were fulfilled in Jesus' crucifixion.

C. PSALM 16:10

Here is a remarkable prophecy of the sufferings of death of our Lord and His descent into Sheol but the inability of corruption to have any power over Him. The text was quoted by Peter on the day of Pentecost as applying to the death and resurrection of Christ (Acts 2:26-31) and by Paul in his sermon in Pisidian Antioch in attempting to prove from the Scriptures that Jesus was the Christ and that He should suffer and rise again (Acts 13:35-37).

D. PSALM 40:6-8

Here we have a description of the consecration and obedience
to the Lord Jesus in coming into this world and perfectly fulfilling the will of God. It is quoted by the writer of Hebrews as
illustrative of the conversation of the Son of God when He
emptied Himself and became a man, coming into this world to
do the will of God, which will He perfectly performed so as to
inherit eternal life (Heb. 10:7).

E. PSALM 118:22

Here the Psalmist declares that Christ was the stone which
the builders rejected but which through the Lord's doing has
become a cornerstone or chief head-stone. This is quoted several
times in the New Testament as being fulfilled in the sufferings,
the death and the resurrection of Jesus Christ: by Peter before
the Sanhedrin in Acts 4:13, and again in his epistle declaring
the nature of the church being built upon this stone (I Pet.
2:7, 8). By the above it is easy to see that there are many minor
references to the sufferings of Christ in the Psalms, all of which
could have taken considerable time as the Lord walked on the
road to Emmaus or as He expounded the Scriptures in the
upper room after His resurrection in showing from the Psalms
that the Christ must suffer.

II. THE MAJOR DESCRIPTIONS OF THE SUFFERING MESSIAH IN THE PSALMS

In illustration of this we might take Psalm 22 or Psalm 69.
Let us deal primarily with Psalm 22.

A. THE POSITION OF PSALM 22 IN THE PSALMS

It is good to notice that Psalms 22, 23 and 24 constitute a unit:
Psalm 22 the sufferings of the Messiah, Psalm 23 the ministry of
the Messiah and Psalm 24 the glory of the Messiah. Without
Psalm 22 there could be no Psalm 23 or Psalm 24. They are a
logical sequence and should be studied together. The benefits of
Psalms 23 and 24 have been won by the sufferings of Psalm 22.

B. THE PLACEMENT OF PSALM 22 IN THE MOUTH OF CHRIST AT CALVARY

One of the most familiar statements of our Lord upon the cross
is "My God, my God, why hast thou forsaken me?" This describes an experience which no one else has ever known and no

one ever need know if he accepts the Lord Jesus as his substitute. According to Hebrews 2:14, Christ took part of flesh and blood and tasted death that "through death He might destroy him that had the power of death, that is, the devil; and deliver them who through fear of death were all their lifetime subject to bondage." No man need ever taste death as Christ did on the cross in that God-forsaken experience. Yet it is interesting that these words were taken from the first verse of Psalm 22. Similarly, on the cross the Lord Jesus declared, "I thirst." This was a statement describing His physical, mental, spiritual and social agony. He thirsted for social fellowship, for physical water, for mental sympathy and this, too, was a quotation from Psalm 22:15 which says, "My tongue cleaveth to my jaws." Likewise, when the Lord finished His sufferings on the cross, He declared, "It is finished," which is merely a translation of the very last verse of Psalm 22 which says, "He hath done this." Our salvation was completed and finished on the cross.

C. THE PLAIN DESCRIPTION OF CALVARY IN PSALM 22

From the above quotations it is evident that the words of Psalm 22 were in the mouth and in the mind of Christ while He was hanging upon the cross during His suffering. This reveals that Calvary was foreknown to God, that details of Christ's suffering could be described long in advance because He was the lamb slain from before the foundation of the world. A close description of the sufferings of Christ is contained in verses 6, 7, 8, 16, 17, 18 and those above mentioned.

III. THE MIGHTY MISERY OF THE MESSIAH REVEALED IN PSALM 69

In this last Psalm which we will single out we want you to note:

A. THE SORROWS OF SOUL WHICH OVERWHELMED THE LORD ON CALVARY (vv. 1, 2)

Here the Lord Jesus cries out, as the deep waters of suffering overwhelm Him, to be saved from Calvary. It is a picture of strong crying, of petition with tears unto Him who is able to deliver.

B. THE SEARING HATRED AND PERSECUTION WITH WHICH THE
   SAVIOUR WAS SURROUNDED ON CALVARY (VS. 4a)

It appeared that all those surrounding Him hated Him and
would destroy Him. The multitude was more than the hairs of
His head.

C. THE SINLESS CHARACTER OF THE MESSIAH (VS. 4b)

They hated Him wrongfully. He had done no one any evil
and yet their opposition was intense.

D. THE SHAME WHICH THE SAVIOUR SUFFERED ON THE CROSS
   (VS. 7)

One can never estimate how He felt with the ignominy, with
the nakedness, with the ridicule and with the mockery on the
cross.

E. THE STRANGENESS OF THE MESSIAH UNTO HIS BRETHREN (VS. 8)

One should compare John 7:3-5 with this passage and recognize how that the Lord was repudiated by His own brethren
who did not believe on Him and was thought to be beside
Himself by His own family.

F. THE ZEAL OF THE MESSIAH FOR THE LORD'S WORK (VS. 9)

This verse is quoted in John 2:17 concerning Christ's
cleansing of the temple as a manifestation of His zeal for the
purity of the worship of the Lord.

G. THE SCORN OF THE MESSIAH (VV. 9b-12)

They reproached Him, spoke against Him, they mocked Him
in song. This prophecy the New Testament fully vindicates.

H. THE FORSAKENNESS OF THE MESSIAH (VS. 17)

Even God seemed to hide His face from Him. (The entire
picture of verses 14-20 should be compared with the sufferings
of the Lord in Gethsemane, described in Matt. 26:36-45.)

I. THE BROKEN HEART OF THE MESSIAH (VS. 20)

We are told that when the centurion would take Him down
from the cross He was already dead and when His side was
pierced with the sword, out came blood and water, revealing
that He died of a broken heart.

J. The gall and vinegar given to Him to drink upon the cross (vs. 21)

Because of all this suffering and the victory which He won in substitution for His people, He is able to exercise the prerogatives of both judgment and blessing as described in the remainder of this Psalm, verses 22 to 36.

Thus we see that the Psalmists, as prophets, received a revelation from the Lord and wrote of experiences which they did not understand. Perhaps many of these experiences were grounded in their own relations with men but they went far beyond that and applied unto the Messiah as the Lord Himself declared in teaching His disciples the meaning of Calvary.

4

THE CROSS OF JESUS

WEDNESDAY — EIGHTH DAY

TEXT: John 19:25. "There stood by the cross of Jesus his mother."

SCRIPTURE: John 19:16-37

The cross of Christ is a fact of history. It is indisputable that Jesus of Nazareth died on a cross outside of Jerusalem about 29 A.D. under the Romans. There is no serious question of that fact by any reputable historian with the exception of David Strauss. Almost one-fourth of the narratives of the Gospels are devoted to the events of the last week, especially the crucifixion. Of eighty-nine chapters in the four Gospels, twenty-five are occupied with the passion of the Lord. The interpretation of the cross to mean that Jesus died for our sins is also a fact (which interpretation originated with Jesus); it was presented in the oral gospel (Luke 24:46, 49; Acts 13:38; 3:19-21); and it is found in the writings of the apostles.

The cross was a brutal means of death. It was shameful, ignominious, painful, repulsive and reserved only for criminals. The suffering of the cross was intense. There was the shame of nakedness, the scourging which preceded it, the piercing of the hands and feet by nails, the distension of the limbs from hanging on the nails, the fever which attended the stress on the body, the unusual thirst, the irrationality into which the victim usually succumbed, and finally the broken bones which marked the conclusion of life. In the crucifixion of Jesus there was more than physical suffering involved. If not, we could not understand His aversion, beyond that of other normal men, to the suffering that was to come.

This death of Christ is the basis of our saving faith (I Cor. 15:1-3). When the death of Christ on the cross is joined with the resurrection, that constitutes the gospel. When the facts of this gospel are accepted in faith or received in evangelical obedience they work salvation. Paul says, "By which ye are saved." When a believer wishes to worship God, it must be by way of the cross. He must bow at the cross of Jesus and find access to God through the reconciliation wrought by that cross.

I. THE CROSS WAS AN ALTAR

A. THE UNIVERSALITY OF SACRIFICE IN RELIGION

From the earliest times an altar has always been the center of religious worship. The earliest Syrian altars were of limestone and alabaster, several examples of which are in the British Museum. The Sumerians, who worshipped Zoroaster, made their altars in the form of a truncated cone. The earliest Palestinian altars were circular and made of stone and usually were placed in shady places by springs. Altars represented sacrifice, atonement, gifts of thanksgiving and worship. Often a sacrificial fire was perennially kept burning upon the altar. In contrast with heathenism in which every god had an altar, the early Christians had no altars, only a table on which Communion was celebrated.

B. THE UNIQUENESS OF THIS ALTAR

When Noah worshipped Jehovah he erected an altar (Gen. 8:20). Abraham built his altars (Gen. 12:7, 8; 13:18; 22:8) and so did others of the Old Testament patriarchs. When the tabernacle was erected there was an altar of burnt offering and also the Mercy Seat. No approach could be made to God except by an altar sacrifice. The altar of burnt offering was made of acacia wood, covered with copper and decorated with a horn at each corner. The altar of incense within the holy place where prayers were offered, was overlaid with gold. The Mercy Seat was within the Holy of Holies and also overlaid with gold. In fulfillment of all this typology, the cross became the altar on which atonement was wrought for the entire human race (Heb. 9:13, 14). Christ was "set forth to be a propitiation for our sins" (Rom. 3:25) on the cross as an altar. Thus the cross became the Mercy Seat of redemption where the sacrifice once made was final and never repeated (Heb. 9:26).

C. THE ANTITHESIS TO ANY OTHER ALTAR

Whenever in the name of Christianity the claim is made for the establishment of an altar for a renewed sacrifice, it must be false. This would be to crucify Christ afresh and to put Him to open shame. Because one branch of Christianity believes in the renewed sacrifice in the Eucharist, it has erected altars everywhere, it has made a chancel as a fence to shut off the congregation from the priests and it has reverted to the Old Testament sacrifices. It is a tragedy for a Bible-believing Christian to ape the liturgical branch of Christianity. The forms, the ritual, the mediation of a priesthood have no place in a true Christianity. We have one altar, one sacrifice, one priest and one salvation.

II. THE CRUCIFIED CHRIST WAS THE SACRIFICE

A. THE PREPARATION

All the types, figures and symbols of sacrifice in the Old Testament look forward to the coming of the Messiah. To the Israelites the lamb meant only one thing, a substitute. Thus, Jesus was "the lamb of God who taketh away the sin of the world." This teaching, as we have seen, was enlarged in the symbolism of the day of atonement (Lev. 16), where there was a sacrifice for the priest whereas Christ needed none, there was a confession of the sins of the people and there was a cleansing of the people by the sacrifice of the substitute goat and the release of the scapegoat. In harmony with this, the Lord Jesus testified concerning Himself that "the Son of man came . . . to give His life a ransom for many" (Matt. 20:28), and "I, if I be lifted up, will draw all men unto me" (John 12:24), and "as Moses lifted up the serpent in the wilderness, so must the Son of man be lifted up" (John 3:12). Many times the Lord Jesus said, "The Son of man must be crucified," thus preparing them for His coming sacrifice.

B. THE PROVISION

The substitutionary lamb had to be without blemish and without spot. The character of Christ corresponded to this. He lived in perfect obedience to the law in fulfillment of the Father's will and without the blemish of any sin (John 8:46; Gal. 4:4; Lev. 1:3). This obedience was to an eternal covenant made with the Father. In this covenant God freely gave His Son (Rom. 8:32), the Son volunteered to die upon the cross (John 10:17), and in the fullness of time that obedience was manifested at Calvary, when He was "obedient unto death" (Phil. 2:8). Jesus made satisfaction to the moral demands of divine righteousness. No one else could have done it for all others have sinned and come short of the glory of God. Thus, in Jesus the perfect lamb was provided.

C. THE PASSION

What the Lord Jesus suffered as an innocent victim on Calvary we can never fully know. The scripture declares that He became sin for us (2 Cor. 5:21; 1 Pet. 2:24), that He bore the wrath of God in judgment (Gal. 1:13), that He endured the curse of hell (Eph. 4:12). He did this in order that others might be delivered from the pains of death and hell. Now a Christian may die with a smile upon his lips and with victory in his heart. This is the explanation of the early New Testament martyrs seeking death in the name of Jesus. Those sufferings of the Lord were eternally efficacious for us and our salvation.

III. THE CHRISTIAN'S WORSHIP IS THROUGH THE CROSS

A. ACCESS TO GOD THROUGH HIS BLOOD

This access to the holy and living God is the possession of the reconciled, the forgiven and the cleansed (Eph. 2:13-18). On the ground of the priesthood of Christ, the believer enters into His priesthood. He has a high priest who has passed into the heavens through the blood of His death and thus opens for the believer the privilege of intercession as a priest of God (Heb. 4:14-16). Thus the believer's prayers are based upon a complete atonement and a living Mediator (Heb. 9:26).

B. ACCEPTANCE WITH GOD BECAUSE OF THE DEATH OF THE CROSS

It is the blood of the cross which justifies. The believer is declared righteous by Christ's blood and hence is saved by His life (Rom. 5:9, 10). The blood of the cross cleanses the believer from all defilements of the way (I John 1:7). The blood of the cross is efficacious in preserving the believer from every attack of Satan (Rev. 12:8). Thus, because of this death of Christ through the shedding of His blood, those for whom He died are acceptable with God.

C. ADORATION OF GOD BY CALVARY

God can only be approached, worshipped and experienced through faith in Christ who sanctified the new way into the holiest of all (John 14:6; Heb. 11:6). This death of Christ as the means of our worship of God, is memorialized by the Lord's Supper as the primary act of worship for the believer. This death of Christ on the cross must be the most prominent point of emphasis in the Christian preaching as well as worship. Well may the Christian say, "I am determined to know nothing among you save Jesus Christ and Him crucified."

5

THE CROSS IN CHRISTIAN EXPERIENCE

Thursday — Ninth Day

Text: Matthew 16:24. "If any man will come after me, let him deny himself, take up his cross, and follow me."
Scripture: Matthew 16:13-27

The cross is central to the Christian religion. It was transformed by Christ from a symbol of shame, ignominy and cruelty to a symbol of beauty, love and worship. It is at the center of Christian architecture where the nave and the transept meet. It is at the crown of our spires. It is at the heart of the symbols of Christian worship. Clow said, "In the teaching of Jesus, in the preaching of the apostles and in the appeal of the epistles, the eclipsing topic is the cross and its redeeming sacrifice." By the cross habits are broken, prisoners are released, broken hearts are healed, guilt is washed away, condemned consciences are justified and human nature is renewed.

St. Paul taught that the cross was the source of all blessing. He declared, "God forbid that I should glory save in the cross of my Lord Jesus Christ." In his Galatian epistle the cross takes a prominent place in every chapter (Gal. 1:4; 2:20; 3:13; 4:4, 5; 5:11; 6:14). Every religious movement that leaves out the redeeming cross of Christ ends like a desert river in a marsh, or in Unitarianism. There is no life in a redemptionless Christianity. Revivals are utterly impossible without it. There is never a great conversion without a soul kneeling at the cross. The great need of the world is the preaching of the cross as doctrine and as life. "We preach Christ crucified, unto the Jews a stumblingblock, and unto the Greeks foolishness; but unto them which are called, both Jews and Greeks, Christ the power of God, and the wisdom of God " (I Cor. 1:23).

There are three great messages of the cross, no more and no less. Let us examine them.

I. THE MESSAGE OF SALVATION (ROM. 3:25, 26)

John Bunyan's picture of Pilgrim passing through the wicket-gate and on up the hill toward the cross where he found that his burden was loosed and tumbling down entered into a sepulchre so as to be seen no more, is the common interpretation of the cross. It is one interpretation and the major one but not the only one.

A. EMPHASIS UPON THE CROSS AS A MEANS OF SALVATION BY JESUS

One need only read the Gospels to learn that the Lord placed a great emphasis upon the inevitability of the cross (John 2:19; Matt. 16:21; 17:9; 17:22, 23; 20:18-19; 20:28). The fact of the cross looms large in the thinking of Jesus. The meaning of the cross was explained by Jesus (Luke 24:25, 26). He pointed out to His disciples that it was essential for Him to suffer and enter into His glory and that it behooved Him to suffer and to rise again from the dead the third day that repentance and remission of sins might be preached unto the Gentiles.

The content of the apostolic gospel of the cross as an atonement and as the satisfaction made by the Lamb of God for the people of God was received from Jesus Himself. The one explanation for the unanimity of the New Testament writers concerning the content of the gospel is that they received it from the Lord Himself. He tarried for forty days after His resurrection, teaching them things concerning the kingdom of God. During this time He undoubtedly gave the authoritative interpretation of His incarnation, His life, His death and His resurrection.

B. EXPOSITION OF THIS PHASE OF BIBLICAL TRUTH

We have seen that the phrases, the cross of Christ and the death of Christ, are used synonymously in the Bible. The blood of Christ is mentioned three times as often as the death of Christ and five times as often as the cross of Christ but the content of these phrases is identical. The shedding of the blood of Christ was in atonement for our sins (Heb. 9:22). Hence, in the Old Testament all figures pointing toward the death of Christ showed that the life was in the blood and the blood was given on the altar as an atonement for the soul (Lev. 17:11).

For this reason Abel was accepted by God, for he came in the appointed way through a blood offering. Cain was rejected because he brought the fruit of the ground. For this reason God instituted the Passover to teach the people the necessity of an atonement of blood. For this reason the Day of Atonement was enacted every year as an object lesson to the people of Israel concerning the necessity of forgiveness through redemption.

Therefore, the acceptance of redemption by the cross is a matter of life or death. We either yield evangelical obedience or we are excluded. Thus the cross has become the symbol of objective salvation wrought by Christ. The foremost meaning of the cross is the removing of the guilt of our sin by redemption. The cross reconciled God by a satisfaction made in the meeting of the penalty of sin (Eph. 2:14; Col. 2:14; II Cor. 5:19).

C. EXPERIENCE OF SALVATION THROUGH THE CROSS

Salvation comes by believing that my sins were imputed to Christ on the cross (I Pet. 2:24). This constitutes forensic righteousness in the sight of God. It is justification by faith. It is a declarative truth and it is factual (Rom. 3:25-5:1). Once an individual is justified before the tribunal of God, the flow of regenerative life begins from his union with the Crucified One. This beginning of life for us was purchased and is received through the experience of the cross.

II. THE EXPERIENCE OF SANCTIFICATION (ROM. 6:1-14)

A. THE POSITION OF CRUCIFIXION WITH CHRIST

It is a great truth that when a Christian is justified and born again, he is born crucified. He is joined with Christ in death by the baptism of the Holy Spirit. This is the primary teaching of Romans 6:3-6. It is an aspect of the cross which is overlooked by many Christians. Many are glad to claim forgiveness for their sins but not glad to take the position of death to sin. But it is necessary for us to accept this truth that we are dead to sin, that the old man is crucified with Christ, hence dead to lust, lying, pride, selfishness, ambition, pleasure and other springs of evil. We are not only dead to the law but also to sin. Immediately the justified and regenerated Christian should manifest the attribute of holiness which is received by identification with Christ in death. This is the beginning of sanctification, by identification with Christ's cross.

B. THE POWER OF DELIVERANCE BY THE CROSS

The consequence of union with Christ in death is union with Christ in resurrection life. If we have died with Him, we also shall live with Him. There follows a new beginning with new motives, new desires, new thoughts and new purposes. "If we be dead with Christ, we believe we shall also live with Him," (Rom. 6:8). In this new life the conquest of the motions of sin occur as they attack us. Ye are "to reckon yourselves to be dead to sin," "to let not sin reign in your mortal bodies," and to "yield your members servants to righteousness unto God." Thus the Christian is separated by the cross from the world, the flesh and the devil. This assuming of a place of identification with Christ in death is a critical experience. It necessitates consecration, surrender and a deliberate dedication. It is not done in a moment.

C. THE PLACE OF THE SPIRIT IN THIS SANCTIFICATION

Once a person is crucified with Christ, or united with Him in death, the glorified Christ releases in his life the work of the Holy Spirit. Thus, on Pentecost Peter could declare "who being by the right hand of God exalted, hath shed forth this which ye now see and hear." The crucified and glorified Christ gives unto the crucified believer the Holy Spirit so that he can reverse the condition of life from one of defeat to one of victory. This is all through the Spirit. Whereas in Romans, chapter 7, the personal pronoun *I, me* or *my* is mentioned forty-eight times, in chapter 8 of Romans it is not used at all but instead the Holy Spirit is mentioned nineteen times. This indwelling Holy Spirit renews the life of the believer by fulfilling the law in him, by making him spiritually minded, by quickening his body, by guiding him in the truth, by assuring him of his salvation, and by helping him with his infirmities.

III. THE EXPERIENCE OF SERVICE THROUGH THE CROSS (ROM. 12:1-2)

A. THE PRINCIPLE OF SERVICE

The principle of service is involved in the cross and is often stated by Jesus. He declared that we are to deny ourselves, to sacrifice and to serve if we become Christians (Matt. 16:24; John 12:24; Matt. 20:28). The surrender of self to this principle is the greatest obstacle to our sanctification, our spiritual attainment in love, our exercise of power and our manifestation of holiness. Unless we are willing to dedicate self and take the place of crucifixion and to enjoy new life in Jesus Christ, we cannot render such service. But the scene of contemporary life demands redemptive living and if we are to have any effect upon our age through missions, evangelism or social service, it must be through adopting this principle.

B. THE PATTERN IS CHRIST HIMSELF

Christ set the pattern for such action in saying, "Follow Me." We examine His life of teaching, of healing, of doing good and of ministering until He was so exhausted by the strain that He could sleep in the midst of a storm, and we realize that we do not follow Him. He sealed His teaching of the truth by laying down His life upon the cross. He suffered at the very hands of those whom He served the most. When He was reviled, He reviled not again, but He bare in His body our sins on the tree.

C. THE PRACTICE EXPECTED OF A CHRISTIAN

Christians are to be imitators, followers of Jesus. Our highest objective is to be conformed to His image. Anything less than such a standard is sin. What Jesus did He wants us to do. We have a loss of religious motivation and power when we leave all of this imitation of Christ to the modernist. This is an error of too many evangelicals. They are willing to take the forensic aspect of the cross but not the sanctified or the service aspects of the cross. Whether we like it or not, we as Christians must be identified with Christ's cross.

CONCLUSION

It would seem that if one has the illumination concerning the second and third aspects of Calvary in Christian experience and refuses to apply them, that he also would reveal by this action that the forensic aspect of Calvary has never been applied to him, namely, he is not forgiven.

6

THE BLOOD OF THE CROSS

FRIDAY — TENTH DAY

TEXT: I John 1:7. "The blood of Jesus Christ his Son cleanseth us from all sin."

SCRIPTURE: Ephesians 2:11-17

The Bible places great emphasis upon the blood of Christ. The phrase "the blood of the cross" is taken from Colossians 1:20 and refers to the reconciliation wrought by the death of Christ upon the cross. Sometimes this has been preached in so crude a way that it has caused the truth to become a stumbling block to people. Most people have a natural abhorrence of blood. The constantly repeated Old Testament sacrifices with their rivers of blood when divorced from the New Testament implication of salvation are repulsive to most people.

Care needs to be exercised lest we alienate sensitive spirits on the Biblical doctrine of atonement. We are not necessarily orthodox because we emphasize the blood. The phrase "the blood of Christ" is used metaphorically to represent the death of Christ and the communion of His blood (I Cor. 10:16) speaks of participation in the benefits of His death.

There are erroneous views concerning the meaning of the blood of Christ. Bishop Westcott introduced the erroneous view that the blood shed was the life released. He meant that by Christ's death His life was liberated and made available for men on earth. Actually, Christ's risen life makes effective what He did for us in His death on the cross. But shed blood is not life.

There is also the erroneous view that the blood of Christ saves, and thus some glory in the blood. But the Scripture says that the life is in the blood and that the blood shed is the life poured out as an atonement for our souls (Lev. 17:11). The death of Christ in substitution for us is what saves us from sin (Eph. 1:7). The blood of Christ represents the mystery of His

65

dual nature, for it was the blood of man and yet it was the blood of God (Acts 20:28) which was shed for us on the cross. Therefore all types of Biblical Christianity speak of salvation by the blood of the cross. Hence, it becomes us to analyze the significance theologically of "the blood of the cross" in order to grasp the doctrinal interpretation of the work of Christ on the cross.

I. THE MEANING OF BLOOD IN THE BIBLE

A. REVIEW OF "THE CROSS IN THE LAW"

We have seen in a previous sermon that the Scripture declares the life is in the blood (Lev. 17:11; Gen. 9:4; Deut. 12:15, 16, 20), and that the blood is given for an atonement for our souls. This was taught in the Passover ritual and in the liturgy of the Day of Atonement. We also saw that blood violently taken away from man is required by God (Gen. 9:5, 6). This blood must be put away by expiation or the land is guilty (Deut. 19:11-13).

B. RECOGNITION OF THE NEW TESTAMENT USE OF BLOOD

Blood is used in the New Testament to speak of damage to human life which threatens or results in death. It is possible to resist sin unto blood, that is, to death (Heb. 12:4). The blood of the martyrs will be revenged (Rev. 6:9, 10). And responsibility for blood is to be guilty for one's hurt or death. Thus Judas cried, "I have betrayed the innocent blood" (Matt. 27:2-8). Thus the Israelites cried, "His blood be on us" (Matt. 27:25). Thus also Jesus declared that "all the righteous blood shed upon the earth, from the blood of righteous Abel unto the blood of Zacharias son of Barachias, whom ye slew between the temple and the altar. Verily I say unto you, All these things shall come upon this generation" (Matt. 23:34-36).

Blood is also used in the Bible to speak of the beneficial consequences of death. Thus Paul says, "The cup of blessing which we bless, is it not the communion of the blood of Christ" (I Cor. 10:16). It is also used to symbolize the means of access to God. The Lord Jesus came "through his blood" into the tabernacle in the heavenlies (Heb. 9:11, 12). He did not take the blood into the tabernacle, but through His shed blood in death, He entered into the heavenly tabernacle. It was by His rent flesh and spilled blood that He could enter.

Christians are said to enter into the holiest of all through Christ's blood, namely, through His satisfactory death. Thus they enter into the benefits of righteousness, of intercession and of fellowship. Though the act of the shedding of Christ's blood was completed once in His death, that blood has efficacy to continue to provide inner purification and cleansing for the confessing and repenting believer (I John 1:7).

C. Restoration of the blood to its rightful place in . preaching and worship

Blood was the ransom paid by Christ for our sins. He gave His life (Matt. 20:28; Mark 10:45; I Tim. 2:6; Titus 2:14). Thus the redeemed have been purchased with this terrible price, namely, the blood of Jesus; His life poured out (I Pet. 1:18, 19; I Cor. 6:20; 7:23). Therefore, the song of the redeemed in heaven will be concerning Him who redeemed us by his blood. (Rev. 5:9).

II. THE BLOOD OF CHRIST

A. Taken on in the incarnation

The Bible says that Christ "took flesh and blood." The phrase "flesh and blood" stands for man's living body in its present earthly state indicating weakness in opposition to the body that shall be in the resurrection (I Cor. 15:50; Gal. 1:16; Eph. 6:12; Heb. 2:14). The Word of God became flesh (John 1:14) and blood when He came into this world. Christ assumed our life which had to be kept alive by blood. This was His condition "in the days of his flesh" (Heb. 5:7). Therefore, the phrase "blood of Christ" refers to His earthly life which came to a violent end in His death upon the cross. He had no blood after His resurrection (Luke 24:39).

B. Taken from Him in death

The passion of our Lord included the shedding of His blood in Gethsemane through the scourging in Pilate's hall, by the crowning of the thorns, by the piercing of the nails and by the thrust of the spear in His side. The blood of Christ poured out was the pouring out of His soul in death as the sacrifice for sins (Isa. 53:10). The blood of the atonement was once for all offered upon the altar of the cross or the Mercy Seat as an expiation and satisfaction for our sins.

C. TOKEN OF DIVINE RECONCILIATION

Not only is man reconciled to God through the blood of the cross (Eph. 2:11-17), but also Jew and Gentile are reconciled to each other through the breaking down of the middle wall of partition. Those alienated from God are restored to Him by the blood of Christ, that is, His death. The divided races are re-united in one body, namely, the church, because in His flesh He endured the enmity of the law and abolished it (Col. 2:14).

III. THE CLEANSING OF THE BLOOD

A. REDEMPTION COMES BY FAITH IN THE BLOOD (cf. Rom. 3:25; Heb. 9:12)

Christ made eternal redemption for us through His blood. Just as in the Old Testament expiation was made through the blood of a substitute, so the blood of Christ placed upon the Mercy Seat made atonement for our souls. Thus our consciences are purified from defilement and dead works to serve the living God, all effectuated through the blood of Christ (Heb. 9:16). Through this life poured out, there was a satisfaction of divine justice and holiness so that God might forgive sin. This remission is the taking away of the sins of the people.

B. JUSTIFICATION IS CONNECTED WITH HIS BLOOD (cf. Rom. 5:9)

Justification is a declarative act wrought for us by God as a righteous Judge, declaring us acquitted through the propitiation that has been made by the death of Jesus Christ on the cross. It was a definite exchange of life for life. The death penalty has been met and cannot be extracted again. Our guilt was imputed to Christ and His righteousness imputed to us. Thus there is detailed in Romans 5:1-9 the benefits drawn from this redemption.

C. CLEANSING COMES THROUGH THE BLOOD (I John 1:7)

Figuratively, washing of the blood is the washing of regenera-tion and the taking away of the guilt, the stain and the defilement of sin. This blood is efficacious for daily cleansing from the stains of the journey of life that come upon Christian people. Such appeal to the blood is the claiming of the benefits of Christ's redemption in the daily walk of life.

As the blood of the old covenant was irrevocable, so is the blood of the new covenant which has brought to us the remission of our sins. It has been sealed by the death of Christ and is thus inviolable. He who has been sprinkled figuratively by the blood has received acquittal, forgiveness and life.

7

THE PREACHING OF THE CROSS

TEXT: I Cor. 1:23. "But we preach Christ crucified."
SCRIPTURE: I Corinthians 1:18-25

Preaching the gospel is preaching the cross. Paul declares that preaching the word of the cross is the summary of his gospel (I Cor. 1:17, 18). The cross was the heart of Paul's preaching and ought to be the center of all preaching, for in it centers the wisdom, love and justice of God. Christ crucified is the power of God unto salvation and was the means ordained of God for the reconciliation of the world to God. Samuel S. Zwemer says, "The cross is the pivot as well as the center of the New Testament thought. It is the exclusive mark of the Christian faith . . . the keystone of the arch, the cornerstone of the temple of truth. That this is true is evident from the place that the death of Christ occupies in the Scriptures, in the apostolic message, in the liturgies of the two sacraments as administered by all the branches of the church, and in the earliest as well as the latest hymnody."

There is revelation enough in the cross to occupy our attention through eternity. In it are the depth of love, the greatness of justice, the riches of wisdom and the nature of grace. The riches of power, of life, of truth center in the doctrine of the cross. Let the cross be preached and obeyed, and the problems of man's relationship to God, to man, to sin, to Satan, to death and to eternity will be solved. Let the preacher proclaim the cross and the vilest life may be cleansed, the lowest outcast may be lifted, the most abject sinner may be transformed into a saint.

70

I. THE MAGNITUDE OF THE CROSS

A. WHO THE CRUCIFIED WAS

Christians have always been amazed at the wonder of the person who undertook this awful task of redemption for them. From Christ's own claims and the confession of primitive Christianity, we conclude that God Himself was in Christ reconciling the world unto Himself. The pre-existent, eternal, uncreated, self-existent One condescended in love to assume our human nature for the purposes of our salvation. Thus we conclude that when Christ died on the cross, infinite merit was measured against the demerit of human sin. The Church acknowledges that Christ, having risen from the dead, ascended to the place where He was before the incarnation and continues to be God and Saviour forever.

B. WHAT THE CRUCIFIED DID ON THE CROSS

1. The demand for expiatory sacrifice arises from the character of God as being holy and just, and from the awful nature of sin as a transgression of the divine law. It is essential to the nature of God that sin be punished, for justice can only be satisfied when justice is done. Expiation must be made by satisfaction, not by compromise or cancellation or God could not remain just in the justifying of sinners who believe in Jesus.

2. The divine undertaking meets this demand of the precepts of the law. As a result, Christ endured the penalty of broken law (Rom. 5:12-21; Col. 2:14). Christ was made sin (II Cor. 5:21), and a curse (Gal. 3:13), for His people that they might be declared righteous in the sight of God. Christ became the substitutionary ransom for His people.

3. The death of Christ was the means of God's changing the status of relationship which existed between Himself and sinners by imputing our trespasses to Christ (Rom. 5:6-11; II Cor. 5:11-21). Christ's death vindicates God's justice in forgiving sinners and sets Christ forth as the Mercy Seat where alone sin can be forgiven (Rom. 3:21-26).

C. HOW THE CRUCIFIED DID IT

As a priest Christ came to do the will of the Father. In love and worship of the Father and in love for man Jesus suffered and died. He rendered both an active and a passive obedience to

God. There was no rebellion in the spirit of Jesus from Gethsemane to Calvary. Jesus died in the spirit of devotion. Since there was no remission without the shedding of blood, Christ was strengthened for His baptism with blood. It may be said that He coveted the cross.

II. THE MEANING OF THE CROSS

A. THE RECONCILIATION OF LIFE'S ENMITY

The object of reconciliation in the death of Christ on the cross was the world (II Cor. 5:19). The world was at enmity to God due to sin arising from man's rebellion. Following the fall, the relationship between God and man was different. Man was not acceptable to God and he stood upon a different footing. The endurance of the death on the cross was to deal with this enmity so as to remove it and to change man's relationship to God (Eph. 2:14; Col. 2:14). The author of that reconciliation was God Himself. God did what man could never do. It was God's love which motivated the reconciliation and it was God's justice against which the reconciliation was made. The work did not change God's character but fully revealed the mercy and holiness of God so that they kissed in the cross.

B. THE INTERPRETATION OF LIFE'S ENIGMAS

William Childs Robinson has pointed out the fact that the Biblical interpretation of the cross given in the Word of God is as much a fact as is the event itself. He declares that the intelligent solution of the riddle of the universe may be found in the cross. When we accept it as the means of salvation, it interprets all suffering. "The darkest spot of history is the brightest spot, all the pain, and shame and suffering were for a purpose. Then other tragedies may await His purpose and meaning *(The Word of the Cross)*." Thus Calvary becomes the hill of comfort and the house of consolation.

C. THE JUSTIFICATION OF LIFE'S ERRORS

Sin cannot exist in the presence of righteousness unless there is forgiveness or justification. Man's most important question is "How can I be right with God, for I have sinned?" Sin's forgiveness through mercy, sin's punishment through justice produce a contradiction which cannot be solved but by atonement or expiation. The justification of sinners cannot be done arbitrarily. Sin's penalty must be endured by a substitute. Therefore, through the cross, at the moment God forgives sin, He is the most righteous according to this higher law of morality, namely, the atonement of love. The cross alone joins justification and the righteousness of God.

III. THE MEDITATION ON THE CROSS

William Childs Robinson again says, "There is one note that has never been erased from the Christian Gospel. That note is love. Love is the heart of the Gospel, for the Gospel shows that love is the heart of God."

A. THE SOURCE OF THE LOVE OF THE CROSS

Man personally, historically and socially is wicked, corrupt, defiled and disobedient. No ground for love can be found in man. It was out of the love of the Trinity that there came the love of Calvary. The love of Calvary is a replica of the love that exists in the nature of deity. The Son revealed the love of heaven to this world of woe. Therefore, the message of the Gospel is of the love of God, of the Father in giving and of the Son in obeying through Christ's death on the cross.

B. THE CROSS THE MEASURE OF GOD'S LOVE

In immeasurable love God executed His justice, not upon them who deserved it, but upon Himself in taking the penalty of wrath into Himself. Justice was not denied, but was satisfied. Calvary, therefore, becomes the revelation of His love. That which costs nothing reveals no love. The inconceivable suffering of the cross is in the taking of the penalty of sin into the divine nature. Thus, in accepting that love, all the benefits of Calvary become ours: forgiveness, justification and life.

C. THE EFFICACY OF THE CROSS

Calvary changed the relationship of God to the world from a Judge to a Heavenly Father, the destiny from darkness to light, and the condition from death to life. Calvary poured out the further gift of love in the outpouring of the Holy Spirit which is God dwelling in us and accomplishing His purposes through us. Thus "the love of God is shed abroad in our hearts" (Rom.

5:5) . Calvary changes the hearts of hardened sinners through the ministry of the Holy Spirit who can convict, and convert and change.

Thus by the word of the cross comes your forgiveness, your justification, your life, your way of living in sacrifice, love and service, and your ability to accept the will of God with gratitude and hope. Man lifted the cross in revolt against God, but God made the cross the prism through which His love would flash His eternal attributes in self-disclosure and revelation.

THE SUFFERING MESSIAH

THE SUFFERING MESSIAH

Introduction

The study of the fifty-third chapter of Isaiah in the Hebrew and the New Testament quotations of it in the Greek, or references to it in the Greek, has opened my eyes to an understanding of the sufferings of Christ such as I never received by reading the Synoptics or the Pauline references to them. This prophetic presentation has borne in upon me the full meaning of our Lord's atonement and what He underwent physically, mentally and spiritually on our behalf.

A careful and detailed study of the individual Hebrew words used by Isaiah in this remarkable prophecy will repay the inquirer. We are only able to suggest the great realms of Messianic suffering in these brief outlines. Much more remains to be discovered and expounded.

The apprehension of the resurrection as the seal of God upon these sufferings is the perspective through which we should view them. Perhaps it would be better to begin with the Lord's own words, "it behooved Christ to suffer, and to rise again from the dead" showing how He used the law, the prophets and the Psalms before looking into these prophecies. When we realize that Peter (I Pet. 1:10) declared that the prophets searched diligently what the meaning of their own prophecies was in connection with the sufferings of Christ and the glory that should follow, we may realize how great is our privilege of entering into this understanding.

1

THE SUFFERING OF LONELINESS

Second Sunday — Twelfth Day

Text: Isaiah 53:2. "For he shall grow up before him as a tender plant, and as a root out of a dry ground."
Scripture: Isaiah 53:1-12

Jesus Christ was the loneliest man who ever lived. This is the picture of Him given in Isaiah, chapter fifty-three.

A. The figure of a root out of dry ground

This picture is taken from a desert scene in which there is a decayed root surrounded by a dry, parched soil with no normal expectation of life and yet out of which comes a sudden burst of life. Those who have driven across our great western deserts know what it means to face miles and miles of sand and waste without a sign of vegetation and then suddenly to come upon a tree. This is Isaiah's picture of Christ. Some think that he suggests a withered, frail, weak body, but this is not the point of the comparison at all. Rather it is that there was nothing in Israel, the stock, or in the environment of the land to account for the sudden appearance of such new life, growth and beauty in the person of Christ. He stood absolutely alone, a solitary and inexplicable figure from all human viewpoints. He was not a product of evolution of the religious search of Israel.

B. Christ emerged as the grandest, loneliest figure of the ages

Jesus is like a giant tree towering above the forest. The common trees are lower and companionable, but He is solitary in His grandeur. The higher one rises in character and achievement, the more he is singled out for attack. Against a tall tree the storms beat, and the winds blow. Against a great character, opposition, criticism and hate rage. All those who for principle's sake are out of tune with their age are lonely, solitary and isolated.

C. Other lonely characters who are like unto Christ in this attribute

The greater a man gets, the more lonely he feels. When God gave Moses his last view of Canaan land from Pisgah's lofty height, he was alone. No one was with him when he died, but he was buried by the angels. He had lived beyond all those of his generation except Joshua and Caleb, and even these could not reach the eminence upon which he stood. Elijah experienced the sense of loneliness when in his great struggle against the prophets of Baal he cried, "I, even I only, am left." When Paul came to the conclusion of his life and was in the dungeon in Rome, he wrote to Timothy saying, "Only Luke is with me . . . come before winter." In the proportion that each one of us appropriates the greatness of Christ, we know something of His loneliness.

I. THE PATHWAY OF LONELINESS

A. The loneliness of Christ's person in that age

The age of Christ was prepared for Him negatively in the sense that there was no competition to His greatness. The philosophical world was bankrupt. The great philosophies of Aristotle and Plato were in eclipse. Only stoicism, sophism and epicurism were being offered unto men. In politics, the iron rule of Rome was crushing the sense of liberty and dignity of individual men. In morals, degeneracy and profligacy were almost universal. Even religion was being used as a cloak for immorality and injustice. Thus, a pure, honest, noble and elevated person such as Jesus Christ was totally out of step with His age.

B. The description of His loneliness

Isaiah presents Him as despised, as unesteemed, as rejected, as in sorrow, as burdened, as grieving, as physically marred in His countenance, as ostracized from His fellows, as stricken, as wounded, as oppressed, as chastised, as bearing the iniquity and guilt, as imprisoned, as denied judgment, as cut off from the land of the living. There could be no plainer picture of loneliness than this given by Isaiah concerning the Messiah.

C. THE LONELY SUFFERER

An examination of the life of Jesus reveals this loneliness. His brethren did not believe on Him, nor understand Him. His townspeople repudiated Him and would have put Him to death. The masses of the people followed Him because of the miracles. His own disciples whom He chose and trained were unable to enter into His passion and to sympathize with Him in His suffering. While He ministered, He had no place which He could call His own to lay His head. When He prayed in Gethsemane, He said to His disciples, "Could ye not watch with me one hour?" When he was taken to Caiaphas' hall, all forsook Him and fled. When He was examined by scourging and when He was judged by Pilate, no man stood with Him. When He went to Calvary, He was utterly alone. "Wherefore Jesus also, that he might sanctify the people with his own blood, suffered without the gate. Let us go forth therefore unto him without the camp, bearing his reproach" (Heb. 13:12, 13). No one stood with Him, or understood Him, or sympathized with Him. He was unutterably alone.

II. THE PERSUASION OF LONELINESS

A. TO ACCOMMODATE ONESELF TO THE SINFUL MOB

Loneliness is one of the greatest sources of temptation to sin. It is easy to do evil when evil offers companionship and when righteousness offers loneliness. Many persons will excuse their temporary deflection from righteousness or indulgence in sin by the words, "I was so lonely." Loneliness brings the temptation to lower the standard, to come down to the level of the masses, to compromise. Many are those who have fallen before this temptation. Yet Christ never accommodated Himself to those who wished to do evil.

B. TO BE DISCOURAGED AND GIVE UP

It is hard to stand alone, to endure criticism, to accept opposition and yet to cling to our principles. Even the great Elijah was willing to give up. He asked that he might die, for he believed that he had failed. Loneliness sometimes brings doubt as to the value of what one is doing. If no one else sees our objectives, if no one else casts his lot with our struggle, we are sometimes led to question the value of our own judgment.

Solipsism leads to such indecision, and discouragement leads to sin, to give up the standards, to surrender the struggle, to succumb to temptation.

C. TO ABANDON THE CAUSE OR THE GOAL

Only a stout heart with great courage can overcome the pressures of loneliness so as to continue the struggle. For this reason our prayers ought to be with missionaries who stand utterly alone in the midst of heathenism, of false religions, of immorality, of disease, of an alien culture. No wonder there are casualties in the lists of our missionary workers. Every Christian ought to read *To the Golden Shore,* the story of Adoniram Judson and the almost infinite difficulties, sufferings and opposition faced by one single missionary. For years he was completely alone in his evangelization of the Burmese. How easily loneliness could have caused him to give up, as it did others.

III. THE PAIN OF LONELINESS

A. ISOLATION

Man is naturally a social being who loves the approval and the social intercourse of his fellow men. Alone, man dreams. When another person enters, he begins to think. Hence, isolation makes for loneliness, and this loneliness is often felt in the midst of the teeming cities of our day. No man knows the number of lonely people who live in the midst of the masses of our cities.

B. DIFFERENTIATION

The parable of the ugly duckling is the story of many people. No one likes being different, whether by being compelled to wear a different kind of clothing from his fellows, or being crippled, or being placed in different kinds of circumstances. I know one otherwise very firm Christian who refused to go to a certain social occasion because he did not feel he had the proper clothes. To be set apart is to be observed, to be judged, to be talked about, and this people do not like. Involved in this is the problem of sending Christian children into unchristian environments where they cannot do the things that other people do and where their sense of differentiation is intensified.

C. OPPOSITION

It is hard enough to brave the storm in company, but to stand against it alone brings pain to the human spirit. The old adage,

"Misery loves company" is true and happiness often comes from company, or at least from a sense of sharing. One man can stand only so many blows before he falls.

IV. THE PALLIATIVE OF LONELINESS

A. PRAYER

Jesus Christ found the antidote for His loneliness in prayer. Thus we find Him praying before the break of day, at His meals, after others had retired, sometimes through the night seasons and in long vigils in the wilderness. Always He practiced ejaculatory prayer. This gave Him an immediate consciousness of God in every crisis of life. He who prays is never alone. When someone expressed a fear to John Henry Newman that he must be lonely in his old age, he replied, "Never so little lonely as when alone." And Lord Byron wrote, "In solitude when we are least alone."

B. UNION WITH GOD

The Lord Jesus Christ in life had His sense of union with the Father. He said, "as the Father and I are one." In like manner, we may have union with God through Jesus Christ. As Christ is formed in us through the Holy Spirit, the Father and the Son take up their abode within us. We are always conscious that He understands our sufferings because He has suffered in all points like as we have. Thus, a sense of fellowship results which is the antidote to loneliness.

C. THE CHURCH

God has made provision for the social need of man as well as for his need of salvation. This is given in the redeeming agency of God, namely, in the Church. In the Church, we have fellowship, we have communion, we have understanding, we have common labor and common objectives. In the Church, we find that we are a pilgrim people bound for a better country.

CONCLUSION

A true Christian will be willing to share Christ's loneliness. He will go with Him without the camp, bearing His reproach.

2

THE SUFFERING OF SICKNESS

Monday — Thirteenth Day

Text: Isaiah 53:4. "Surely he hath borne our griefs, and carried our sorrows: yet we did esteem him stricken, smitten of God, and afflicted."

Scripture: Isaiah 53:1-12

Was Jesus Christ a sick man? Many ancient Jews derive from this text the thought that the Messiah would be leprous, that He would actually take sickness into His body, that He would be a weak individual. The Italian school of art depicts Him as emaciated, disfigured and unnatural. Most of us are repulsed by that picture of Christ and yet it may be nearer the truth than Sallman's head of strength as a picture of Christ.

Today we find ourselves wanting a strong man, an attractive Christ, a physically perfect specimen. And there is reason to justify such a belief. But the deeper we go into this narrative which describes the Lord Jesus Christ, the more we are forced to at least make room for the possibility of the ancient view. This text leaves no doubt in its teaching that Christ Jesus lifted, carried and removed our diseases and sicknesses, that He endured our mental anxieties and that He was smitten as with a plague. This was exactly the meaning placed upon this text by Matthew (8:17) and by Peter (I Pet. 2:24). Then let us examine the text.

I. THE SUFFERINGS OF SICKNESS ENDURED BY CHRIST

A. What does Isaiah teach when he said, "he hath borne our griefs"?

1. "Hath borne" or nasa *in the Hebrew, or* ferei *in the Greek, means to bear.* The word means to take up, to lift, or to raise.

The word is used in Genesis 7:17 in describing the flood. It says, "and the waters increased, and bare up the ark." The word may be used to lift up the hand, or the head, or the eye. Hence, it comes to mean to bear, to carry, as an infant in arms, or a tree its fruit. Hence, it comes to mean to take on oneself the suffering due to sin. Here we have the idea of lifting, of taking up and of sustaining a burden. When applied to diseases, it must mean that Christ lifted them up and carried them away. By His power, He removed them.

2. *What burden is borne?* The word "griefs" is a Hebrew word, *chaley,* which means sickness, disease, anxiety and affliction. There is no reference to sin, but only to physical suffering. It is translated as sickness many times and is never used for sins (Deut. 28:61, 7:16; II Chron. 21:15; I Kings 17:17; Eccl. 6:2; II Chron. 21:18, 16:12; Exod. 15:26). Out of ninety-three times used, it is only once translated "sins" by the Septuagint but is usually translated "body disease" or "infirmity." The word "sorrow" refers to pain, sorrow, or grief of mind rather than of body. It stresses anxieties and distresses of the mind. This properly means that He took on Him the mental sorrows of men. We do not believe that this means Jesus was mentally unbalanced, or insane, or demon-possessed because He carried these sorrows. Nor do we believe He was leprous or sick because He carried our diseases. He must have carried them as a doctor carries those of a patient or as a mother carries those of a child, by relieving them.

3. *Esteemed "smitten of God."* This means that He was plagued, that He was struck in judgment as sudden destruction smites (I Sam. 6:9; Job 19:21; Gen. 12:17). The people of Jesus' day thought that He was smitten of God for His own sins, but the text tells us that He was smitten, abandoned, cursed by God for us and our sins.

B. How does the New Testament interpret this text?

1. *Matthew 8:17 renders the word "griefs" by the Greek word meaning infirmities.* This leaves no doubt that when the Lord Jesus healed diseases, He was fulfilling the text of Isaiah. Matthew gives the correct translation of the Hebrew word used by Isaiah. Lightfoot declares, "The Jews considered this passage as referring to bodily diseases." Matthew goes farther and he uses

another Greek word to refer to sorrows, just as the Hebrew does, and it is a word meaning mental anxiety. Thus Matthew gives illustrations both of physical and mental healings before referring to the fulfillment of this text. Matthew did not adduce this text as applying to sins which are dealt with in the rest of Isaiah 53, but correctly to sicknesses which Jesus was healing at that particular time.

2. I Peter 2:24. Peter here refers to this same text but applies it to Christ bearing our sins, perhaps in the broader sense of including our sicknesses and our mental illnesses. We may conclude that in the afflictions and sorrows of Christ, He took upon Himself the sufferings, the sorrows and the sicknesses of the world so as to bear them away. Part of them He removed by a direct miracle, part He removed by removing the cause, that is, the taking of sin upon Himself. He was the burden-bearer.

C. CAN WE PRAY FOR HEALING?

There is a danger in teaching that healing is in the atonement. This danger lies in the fact that if people pray for the healing of the body and do not receive it, when they believe it is in the atonement, that they are led to doubt also that their sins are forgiven. Nevertheless, Matthew and Isaiah place sicknesses and anxieties on the same level with sin, and we are taught to pray for healing from them. It is best for us to determine our position with care and then, on a Biblical ground, pray for deliverance from these sicknesses and anxieties in accordance with the divine will. The final deliverance of the body will not come until its redemption at the Second Coming of Christ. In the interim, we may be healed or we may not, according to God's will.

II. THE SUFFERING UNDER SICKNESS

A. TERRIBLE DISEASES BEFORE WHICH WE STAND BAFFLED

The medical profession continues to conquer one disease after another. The last notable case was that of polio. And no doubt sooner or later, cancer will thus be conquered. And yet, we must die and for one cause or another, the body will deteriorate and finally some organ will fail and we will cease to live in this world. Heart ailments, nerve ailments, paralysis, palsy, cancer and other things still take their great toll.

B. MENTAL ILLNESSES OF OUR DAY

Statistics are telling us that mental illnesses are claiming more victims than physical illnesses, so that hospitals have more mental patients than they do physical patients. Moreover, the increase of suicides from fear, anxiety and worry is great. If we understand this text properly, we believe that the antidote for such anxieties and illnesses lie in the work of our Lord Jesus Christ.

C. IS THERE ANY HELP FOR A SICK, SUFFERING AND PLAGUED WORLD?

Our bodies are not yet redeemed from death. Death will hold control over them physically. Yet Christ has perfectly redeemed them and this redemption will be fully applied to us in the Second Coming and the "redemption of our bodies." Moreover, our afflictions may sometimes be permitted for the sake of the kingdom of God as was Paul's thorn (II Cor. 12:9) and "our light affliction . . . worketh for us a far more exceeding and eternal weight of glory" (II Cor. 4:17). These sicknesses may not be judicial or even vicarious, and if they are not, they **may** very well be healed by the Lord.

III. THE SUCCOR TO US IN SICKNESS

It is interesting to note that in Hebrews 4:15 and 2:17, 18 we are promised succor through our High Priest, the Lord Jesus Christ, because He has been touched with the feeling of our infirmities, the very infirmities of which Isaiah speaks. That succor may come to us in the following ways:

A. THROUGH MIRACULOUS POWER LIKE THAT WHICH HE MANIFESTED ON EARTH IN THE GREAT HEALINGS WHICH HE PERFORMED.

He is the God of Elijah, of Paul, and He can do for us what He has done for them.

B. THROUGH STRENGTH OF FAITH ENABLING US TO BEAR CALAMITY AND AFFLICTION WITH JOY

We have the promise, "as thy days, so shall thy strength be." We have the encomium pronounced by Paul and Peter for those who suffer, and the exhortation to rejoice in such suffering because of the corresponding blessing.

C. Through the comfort of the sympathetic Christ.
　　(Heb. 4:15).

　　He has been touched with the feeling of our infirmities and is moved with compassion and thus can sympathize with us and succor us. The gifts of grace, love and mercy are available for our souls. The Lord Jesus will be with us and will succor us in the midst of these trials. Then when we suffer, we are to look to the Lord on Calvary who is the great sufferer.

3

THE SUFFERING OF SIN

TUESDAY — FOURTEENTH DAY

TEXT: Isaiah 53:6. "All we like sheep have gone astray; we have
turned every one to his own way; and the Lord hath laid on
him the iniquity of us all."
SCRIPTURE: Isaiah 53:1-12

The universality of the Christian message is emphasized by
this text which begins with the word "all" and ends with the
word "all." It can only mean that all men are under sin and
wrath, and that divine mercy can be had upon all (Rom.
11:32). Salvation like the Bible is addressed to all men and it
is available to all. This includes you. Whatever this text says
is said to you. The text is used of God to bring men to a saving knowledge of Jesus Christ. Get a repentant sinner on his
knees with this text before him and it will not be long before
he is rejoicing in the knowledge of salvation. The text tells
what Christ did for you when He died on the cross.

Chiang Kai Shek, president of Free China, once was a prisoner of the Communists when he was treating with them in
reference to a unified China. He bore witness that during this
time, it was the power of the cross and the knowledge of the
sufferings of Christ that made him do what was right. He was
so overwhelmed by the love of Christ that he was unwilling
to compromise his convictions.

I. THE SUFFERINGS CAUSED BY SIN

"He was wounded for our transgressions, he was bruised for
our iniquities."

A. THE WAY OF THE TRANSGRESSOR IS HARD

The text describes sin as going astray or as turning everyone
to his own way. The comparison is between men and sheep.

Sheep may be lovable and helpless, but they are also stupid, and they are prone to wander. The figure of sheep as representative of people is often used in the Bible (Ps. 23; John 10; 21; Jer. 23). A dog or a horse will rarely wander or become lost, but a sheep needs perennial supervision. When the Scripture tells us that there is none righteous, no not one, that all have sinned and come short of the glory of God, it is simply telling in other words what Isaiah said when he declared that "all we like sheep have gone astray."

Sin may have a pleasure for a season (Heb. 11:12), but it turns out to be toilsome business, wearisome work and full of sorrow. Sin always returns to one. Moses said, "Be sure your sin will find you out." Thus the sins of Jacob's youth returned to plague him in his old age. Thus the sins of Samson resulted in his grinding in the prisonhouse. Thus David in the tower of Ammon heard the news that the young man Absalom was dead and saw the sword of judgment glittering in his own house. His sin had returned to him.

Moreover, sin brings pain. George Bernard, who wrote "The Old Rugged Cross," once told how a young man whom he knew had committed suicide. He was engaged to marry a lovely girl but just before getting married, he allowed some of his friends to prevail on him to go out for a fling, and he contracted a dread disease. His conviction was so heavy that he took his own life. For this reason, the Scripture says, "The wages of sin is death" and "He that soweth to the whirlwind shall of the whirlwind reap destruction."

B. THE WOUNDS MADE BY TRANSGRESSIONS

Sin causes sorrow to be inflicted upon our loved ones. I knew a civil service employee who had pilfered funds that were committed to his trust until finally he was discovered. He had a lovely family, but the disgrace of his being dismissed from his position and being threatened with a prison sentence left his family brokenhearted. I know a young student who had great possibilities and a fine mind but who succumbed to temptation, brought his father to an early grave and his mother into the depths of sorrow. There are no such things as solitary sins. We hurt others by our selfishness and by our waywardness. When we turn to our own way, as Isaiah describes sin, we are pursuing our own interest, forming our own plans, gratifying our own pleasures regardless of the good of others. This makes us dissocial.

The universal problem was attacked by the utilitarians by attempting to add penalties to antisocial actions so as to make it more pleasurable to be social than to be antisocial. This is one way to attack the universal problem. The sorrows of the world are directly traceable to sin and selfishness, greed, ambition, discontent and avarice. Sins never affect us alone.

C. THE WILLINGNESS OF CHRIST TO BE WOUNDED

Isaiah says, "He was wounded for our transgressions." This is a remarkable prophecy that details the sufferings of Christ in His passion. It is clear evidence of the inspiration of Isaiah for he wrote as if he saw the entire crucifixion. Let us review these things as Isaiah described them. The word, "wounded," means to perforate or to pierce. This literally applied to the painful infliction of positive wounds upon the body of Christ in His hands, His feet, His head and His side. But it also may apply to such things as the denial of Peter and the kiss of Judas. These were as effective in their wounding as the crown of thorns, the scourge, the nails and the sword.

The word, "bruised," means to be broken to pieces, crushed. The Lord Jesus was crushed down by calamity and overwhelmed by mental and physical sufferings.

The word, "stripes," means welts or bruises and is sometimes translated to mean blueness or bruised. Our term is "black and blue." This is the result of a beating or scourging, leaving such stripes with blood collected under the skin. The Lord Jesus had thirty-nine such stripes laid upon Him in the scourging which was administered in Pilate's judgment hall. All this He suffered as our representative. Throughout the idea is suggested and stated that it was not on account of any sin of which He was guilty that He suffered, but for the sins of others.

II. THE SUFFERING COMPENSATING FOR SIN

Isaiah speaks of "the chastisement of our peace . . . the Lord hath laid on him the iniquity of us all . . . he was wounded for our transgression."

A. THE VICARIOUS NATURE OF THE SUFFERING OF CHRIST

Surely the New Testament doctrine could not be stated more clearly than it was by Isaiah (II Cor. 5:21; Rom. 4:25; Heb. 9:28; I Pet. 2:24). The ground and motive of the Messiah's suffering was given here as for our sins. That includes my sin. He was my substitute. His sufferings on the cross were for me. The fact that my sufferings may be vicarious are in a much lesser sense for they are not redemptive as were those of the Messiah.

B. THE TRANSFERENCE OF OUR INIQUITY

The word "laid" means to impinge upon or to strike. The analogy is of rushing upon a foe to overwhelm him. It represents a meeting or a concurrence. Our sins met on Him, overwhelmed Him and prostrated Him. He was struck by the burden of our sins. Christ was the suffering Lamb taken in substitution to die for those whom He represented. There is a nice question here as to whether this was an exact transference of the amount of our guilt, or a token transference, or a mere accommodation. Whatever it was, the Lord Jesus Christ made a sufficient satisfaction for all.

C. THE CHASTISEMENT DUE TO SIN

The chastisement or the punishment by which our peace was effected was laid upon Christ. He took what we should have had to endure. Therefore, He "is our peace" (Eph. 2:14; Rom. 5:1). The nature of this chastisement was similar to what a parent inflicts to correct the faults of a child. It was remedial for us but not for Him. His sufferings had a moral influence over us. They were not for His personal correction but for our correction. Chastisement was only one phase of His suffering. Satisfaction in punishment was also present. He compensated for our transgressions. He bore our iniquity or guilt, and He took in His body the enmity of the law which should have fallen upon us. He suffered as if He were guilty of sin.

III.　THE SUFFERINGS CURING SIN

A. THEY SATISFIED JUSTICE FOR GUILT

In the sufferings of Christ, eternal justice was met and satisfied. The demands of the broken law of God were met. Forgiveness could now ensue while God remained just and the justifier of him who believeth in Christ Jesus (Rom. 3:25). The assurance of justification is thus given to the believing sinner whose sins have been judged in Christ and whose position is now identified with Christ.

B. THEY PRODUCED PEACE BY RECONCILIATION (EPH. 2:14ff).

Peace follows justification and reconciliation with God. There is no continued enmity between God and man. God is appeased. God is reconciled. God is ready to forgive. The knowledge of this reconciliation through the sufferings of Christ is the central experience of the Christian faith.

C. THEY EFFECTED HEALING

Isaiah says, "with his stripes we are healed." This is a healing which is spiritual. It produces soundness of soul. In quoting this, Peter makes it refer to pardon and forgiveness (I Pet. 2:24). As a result, the believer is in the care of the Shepherd and Bishop of his soul. The recovery can be complete. There will be soundness and health through Christ. Hence, the Benediction: "Unto him that loved us, and washed us from our sins in his own blood, and hath made us kings and priests unto God and his Father; to him be glory and dominion for ever and ever. Amen."

4

THE SUFFERING OF OPPRESSION

WEDNESDAY — FIFTEENTH DAY

TEXT: Isaiah 53:7. "He was oppressed, and he was afflicted, yet he opened not his mouth: he is brought as a lamb to the slaughter, and as a sheep before her shearers is dumb, so he openeth not his mouth."
SCRIPTURE: Isaiah 53:1-12

Jesus was oppressed. So are many people in the world, especially minority people.

One thinks of the oppression that existed as a result of war. There were six and one-half million war prisoners in camps at the close of World War II, some five million of whom never returned home again. They were pressed into slave labor until their strength wasted away. There are still millions of forced laborers in the slave camps of Russia. Some estimates run as high as fifteen million. The stories of oppression which came from incarcerated neutrals, from captives at war and from missionaries reveal a long tale of oppression. There are always certain oppressed minorities in every form of economic society, but this is especially accentuated during a time of war.

One people above all others have been oppressed in history, namely, the kindred of our Lord Jesus, the Jews. One persecution after another has followed them. They have been humbled, harrassed and driven from place to place. Many have been separated from their families, uprooted from their homes, caused to live in terror, and millions have been killed. During the Nazi persecution, at least two million were slain, and some place the figure as high as five million. This oppression will go on until the Jews return to Palestine.

The knowledge of the oppression of the people of the world takes from any truly Christian soul much of the enjoyment of the liberty, prosperity and blessing which he has. It is a help to be able to turn to an understanding of the life of Christ when considering this subject. The knowledge of His oppression and sufferings will assist us in bearing ours. Certainly it reveals that in this world we will not be able to end all oppression and injustice by force and law. Something deeper must be the answer.

I. THE PROPHETIC PICTURE OF OPPRESSION AND SUFFERING

Isaiah declared, "He was oppressed, and he was afflicted . . . He was taken from prison and from judgment."

A. COMPULSION

The word, "oppressed," means to be "driven, urged and impelled." The word is used in the Deuteronomic law concerning a creditor and a debtor. Said Moses, "Every creditor that lendeth aught to his neighbor shall release it; he shall not exact it of his neighbor or of his brother." Thus the word referred to the exaction of taxes, of tribute, of loans or of ransom. It is used to describe the action of Pharaoh-necho in exacting gold and silver from Jehoiakim (II Kings 23:35). It is used by Zechariah to refer to conquerors of the land (9:8). In Exodus 5:6, it refers to the Egyptians, who oppressed the Israelites. It means oppression in the sense of urgency, vexation and ill treatment.

Thus Christ was hurried from judgment to judgment, was mistreated by Herod, by the soldiers, by Pilate, then was urged along the Via Dolorosa and finally driven to the cross. It is a picture of vexation from all quarters. The extremity of injustice fell upon Him. He was afflicted mercilessly and was even beaten by Caiaphas' attendant.

B. CONFINEMENT

The word translated "prison" means confinement, "a closure . . . constraint, oppression, vexation." This is a description of violent restraint rather than imprisonment. Thus Christ was violently detained. It is remarkable in that Christ was not imprisoned. He was only secured under guard and was bound (John 18:24). In a literal sense, Christ was taken by violent restraint.

C. JUDGMENT

This refers to a judicial decision and refers to His trial, not His own decisions or His own power of thought. When this is quoted in Acts 8:33, it says, "In his humiliation his judgment was taken away." They denied to Jesus the right to true judgment. This was true in the Sanhedrin of the Jews and also in the court of the Romans.

On several counts, the Jewish trial was illegal. First, the great Sanhedrin could not meet after nightfall. Second, there could never be a unanimous decision exacting the death penalty for one of the members of the Sanhedrin had to be the defender of the victim. Third, a man could not be condemned on his own testimony. Fourth, the death penalty could never be pronounced in the same session in which the evidence was heard. On all of these counts, the Sanhedrin violated its own laws in the judgment of Christ. Christ was taken away to be put to death under a form of law which the court itself had violated. The procedure is a description of an oppressive and unrighteous trial.

II. HIS PATIENCE AMID SUFFERING

Isaiah declared, "Yet he opened not his mouth; he is brought as a lamb to the slaughter, and as a sheep before her shearers is dumb, so he openeth not his mouth."

A. HOW CHRIST FACED OPPRESSION AND INJUSTICE

The gospel narrative of the Lord's attitude under this oppression displays the patience of a lamb. He was quiet, meek and submissive and resembles the sheep being taken to the shearing without any complaint. Thus He was uncomplaining in the midst of His sorrows and of His ill treatment. When He was reviled, He did not revile again. When He was mistreated, He did not fight back. When He was oppressed, He did not resist. Thus He went to the slaughter. He knew that death was ahead, but it was for this reason that He had come into the world, namely, to die (John 12:24,31; Matt. 20:28). As He said in the Garden of Gethsemane, He could have called upon twelve legions of angels; He had all power at His disposal. Yet He went forth to die.

B. PATIENCE COMES ONLY WITH TRIBULATION

The glory of Christ's patience is seen in this setting of oppression and suffering. We too can only learn patience under the rod (Rom. 5:3). When you pray for patience, you are praying for tribulation. Therefore, do not complain when it comes. Patience in suffering of any kind will make you like Christ.

C. IS SUCH PATIENCE POSSIBLE TODAY?

Should we also adopt the attitude of nonresistance to evil? Should we take the attitude when we are threatened of committing ourselves to Him who judgeth righteously (I Pet. 2:23)? Or should we revolt against iniquity, use force against evil and fight unrighteousness? The Lord Jesus said that His servants would fight too if His kingdom had been of this world. It is certain that we can never build the kingdom of God on force. Christ had another way, as we shall see. When force is used in this world, it is in the realm of the state and not of the kingdom of God.

III. HIS POSTERITY THROUGH SUFFERING

Isaiah adds the statement, "who shall declare his generation? for he was cut off out of the land of the living."

A. HIS LIFE WAS CUT OFF

His generation means His cycle of life, and this was ended at Calvary. He was cut off but not for Himself. How then will the length of His life be determined? Did all end with His death? No, for Christ had a great posterity through that death. This question may be paraphrased, "Who can express His posterity or number His descendants?" The answer is given in verse ten which says, "He shall see his seed, he shall prolong his days." A spiritual race was born through this sacrificial suffering of Jesus Christ. He was cut off, but His race was not. It became so numerous that no one can declare it. Even the skeptic, Renan, cried out, "Thou hast conquered, O Galilean."

B. CHRIST'S METHOD OF ENDING OPPRESSION WAS BY MULTIPLYING HIS SEED

Isaiah said, "He shall see his seed, he shall prolong his days." The Lord Jesus later said, "Except a corn of wheat fall into the ground and die, it abideth alone: but if it die, it bringeth forth much fruit." He overcame by submitting. He won by accepting apparent defeat. He refused to resist evil and, in the suffering of evil, He redeemed the people. Through such means more than through force, struggle and revolt, the world has been changed.

C. THE ILLUSTRATION

This passage of Isaiah is quoted literally in Acts 8:32, 33 where the Ethiopian eunuch was reading from the fifty-third chapter of Isaiah as he rode through the desert on his way to his own country. This precise passage is what he was reading when Philip joined himself to the chariot. The natural question of the eunuch was, "of whom speaketh the prophet this? of himself, or of some other man?" Then Philip preached unto him Jesus, the Lamb of God, the innocent One, the meek One, the suffering One who died on the cross to atone for our sins. The result was that the Ethiopian eunuch immediately believed and became a convert. He said, "what doth hinder me to be baptized?" He was one of the first of the vast number converted through the sufferings of Christ. May the Lord give us grace so that by patient submission, we too may conquer. Thus we will be like unto Christ.

5

THE SUFFERING OF GUILT

Text: Isaiah 53:10, 11. "Yet it pleased the Lord to bruise him; he hath put him to grief: when thou shalt make his soul an offering for sin, he shall see his seed, he shall prolong his days, and the pleasure of the Lord shall prosper in his hand. He shall see of the travail of his soul, and shall be satisfied: by his knowledge shall my righteous servant justify many; for he shall bear their iniquities."

Scripture: Luke 23:39-42.

Isaiah tells us that the suffering of the Messiah was divinely appointed. "It pleased the Lord to bruise him; he hath put him to grief."

A. God was pleased with the sufferings of Christ

Does this startle you, shock you, amaze you? This goes farther than saying that God would permit Christ to suffer. There is no suggestion here that God is pleased with the sufferings of the innocent, nor must we infer that Christ was guilty and thus that God was pleased at His suffering. There is no suggestion of any direct agency of God in causing the suffering, but there is the suggestion that the fact was acceptable to God. The thought is that God was pleased with what Christ suffered because it was a work of love, because by the pleasure of the Lord, that is, the salvation of many, prospered.

Christ voluntarily submitted to suffering to gain eternal redemption for His people. This was a tremendous demonstration of love. Thereby Christ exhibited the divine attributes of justice and mercy as they could be shown in no other way. God was disposed to save, but He could only save sinners consistent with His holiness. Christ effected pardon and cleansing for an innumerable company of sinners by His own sufferings.

97

B. GOD'S PURPOSE WAS FULFILLED IN THESE SUFFERINGS

The eternal plan of God included the cross as a means to the salvation of mankind. This eternal plan was not frustrated. The man Jesus did His part, terrible though it was. Thus He may be called "the Lamb slain from the foundation of the world." Because of this great truth, the sins of multitudes who had lived and died before Christ came to earth were overlooked or were covered (Rom. 3:26; I Pet. 1:19; John 1:29). We may conclude that the cross was embraced in the eternal plan of God. As such, it was often foretold through the prophetic word.

C. GOD'S PLEASURE TO CALL OUT A PREDESTINED PEOPLE OR CHURCH PROSPERED IN CHRIST'S HAND

St. Paul declares in Ephesians 1:5, 9 that the salvation of a people or the constituting them the sons of God was "according to his good pleasure." God's benevolence, wisdom, holiness and grace are demonstrated in Calvary. No wonder He was well pleased with His Son who fulfilled His part in the covenant of redemption (Matt. 3:17, 17:5; John 12:28).

I. THE EXPIATORY NATURE OF THIS SUFFERING

Isaiah said, "thou shalt make his soul an offering for sin." This is a satisfaction for guilt.

A. THE SOUL OF CHRIST AN OFFERING

The marginal reading here is, "Jehovah shall make his soul an offering." It is certain that the soul, that is, the person of Christ, was made an offering. In the creation, man became "a living soul" (Gen. 2:7). In the person of Christ were the nature of God and the nature of man, so that He was the perfect sacrifice or offering for sin. The word "sin" is literally a sin-offering. The word may mean guilt or blame, or it may mean a sin-offering or sacrifice for guilt, that is, an expiatory sacrifice, one which appeases God. The Bible tells us that the person of Christ became sin, guilt, trespass (Gen. 26:10; Num. 5:8; II Cor. 5:21). Christ became sin for us. Our sin was nailed to the tree in the body of Christ (I Pet. 2:24). With the shedding of Christ's blood, His soul was poured out and atonement was made. Atonement was not accomplished by the perfect life which Christ lived but by the death that He died. Hence, the emphasis upon the blood of Christ in the New Testament (Matt. 26:28; Rev. 1:5; Rom. 5:8; Heb. 9:22) .

B. THE SUFFERING OF HIS SOUL IN THE HOUR OF THE SIN-OFFERING OR ATONEMENT

It is clear that on the cross Christ suffered the wrath of God against sin, the opposition of God's holiness against evil, the pains of hell and the forsakenness of a damned soul. It was the dread of this that brought His struggle in Gethsemane. It was the fact of this that was foreseen at the time of His transfiguration when Moses and Elias prepared Him for His decease. It was the knowledge of this that caused His temptation in the wilderness at the beginning of His ministry. The full guilt of a condemned soul was Christ's lot as a sin-offering.

C. THE SATISFACTION TO JUSTICE IN THE DEATH OF HIS SOUL

When Jesus died upon the cross, an infinite satisfaction was made sufficient enough for you and for all men. It was not a token or an accommodation, but it was a sufficient satisfaction for all. Jesus made a complete discharge of our debt through bearing our curse and freeing us from the law's demands. It was an expiatory satisfaction appeasing God, reconciling God, affecting God toward man so that pardon and restoration could be given. A mighty gulf separates the death of Christ from the death of the martyrs of all ages. Wonderful though their death may have been, they were never a satisfaction for sin.

II. THE JUSTIFICATORY PURPOSE OF THIS SUFFERING

Isaiah said, "by his knowledge shall my righteous servant justify many; for he shall bear their iniquities." The Lord Jesus not only made a satisfaction for guilt, but He did it in substitution for sinners.

A. THE GOSPEL "THE KNOWLEDGE OF HIM"

It is by the knowledge of Christ that justification comes. We must be acquainted with Him and with His plan of salvation. Thus it is important to learn all about Him, His person, His doctrines, His character, His history, His death and resurrection, and His present power. Only by knowing this experientially can man be justified. Knowledge itself is not salvation. There is a clear difference between saving faith and historical faith, but great is the privilege of making Christ known (Rom. 10:10-16). This is one of the keys to the kingdom (Matt. 16:20, 18:18, 28:18).

B. JUSTIFICATION "TRUST IN HIM"

Just as we must hear the Gospel, so we must also believe it for justification. Isaiah says, "he shall justify many," not all. There is no universalism in the Gospel. The death of Christ was sufficient for all but it is applicable only to those who believe. Those are justified whose iniquities were imputed to Christ. Believing, men are declared righteous and are admitted to God's favor as righteous. The difference between those who are so admitted and those who are not rests in faith. Justification is always connected with faith (Rom. 5:1).

C. RIGHTEOUSNESS "FORGIVENESS IN HIM"

We hear the gospel, we believe it for justification, we accept it to become righteous. Through this we are declared righteous as Christ was — justified and acquitted. He became sin in our place. We become righteous through the imputation of His righteousness. In one case, the sin and guilt were imputed. In the other case, the righteousness and justification were imputed. He took our place under the stroke of justice. We assume His standing of righteousness in the sight of God. Through this teaching of substitutionary atonement, we derive the greatest truth of Christianity, namely, justification by faith.

III. THE SATISFACTORY RESULT OF THIS SUFFERING

Isaiah said, "he shall see his seed . . . he shall see of the travail of his soul, and shall be satisfied." Christ effected salvation for His people.

A. HIS DEATH NOT IN VAIN

The promise is, "he shall see his seed and prolong his days." The highest promise to the patriarchs of old was of a great posterity. The promise of God to Christ was that He would give Him a people, a seed, many spiritual sons and daughters, that His life would be multiplied in theirs. The multitude of believers on earth and in heaven testify to the fulfillment of this promise (Heb. 12:27).

40578

B. HIS SUFFERINGS TAKEN FOR THE RESULT

Isaiah said, "He shall see of the travail of his soul." This is the picture of childbirth. The Scripture clearly says that when Zion travails, her children shall be born. Christ labored, suffered, went into the valley and shadow of death for the birth of His Church, in fact, He saw it prophetically. Just as He suffered, so Zion must suffer if her children are to be born (Isa. 66:8).

C. HIS JOY OVER THE EFFECT OF HIS REDEMPTIVE WORK

Isaiah said, "He shall be satisfied." This suggests the greatness of the number who shall be saved by Christ's suffering. There are yet uncounted multitudes who must come. The compensation for Christ's sufferings on the cross must be comparable to the harvest that comes from the toil of sowing seed. We may be sure that heaven will resound with His praises. The first trophy of that multitude to come was the penitent thief on the cross. On the cross, the Lord Jesus cried, "I thirst," but the promise was that He shall be satisfied. Even on the cross, that penitent thief brought Him satisfaction, joy and compensation for His sufferings.

CONCLUSION: THE REPRODUCTORY POWER OF HIS SUFFERING

Isaiah said, "he shall prolong his days." The conversion of sinners has projected the influence of Christ into the future. Have you added to the cycle of His days by your obedience to the faith? Are you of His seed? Are you justified and acquitted? Has your evangelical obedience brought Him satisfaction for His sufferings?

6

THE SUFFERING OF DEATH

Friday — Seventeenth Day

Text: Isaiah 53:9, 12. "He made his grave with the wicked, and with the rich in his death . . . he hath poured out his soul unto death."

Scripture: Isaiah 53:1-12

This text gives the concluding description of Christ's sufferings and also suggests something of His victory and triumph.

A. The testimony of the sinlessness of Christ

Isaiah declared, "he had done no violence, neither was any deceit in his mouth." The propositional conjunction translated "because" is the Hebrew *al* meaning "although." It connects this clause with the whole series of descriptions of the Messiah rather than applying to His burial alone. Christ had by no injurious conduct of His own provoked His contemporaries to handle Him thus. He in no wise deserved such suffering. His was a lovely life of doing good, of healing the sick and depressed, of comforting the needy. Hence, the poor always heard Him gladly. Such a life convicts those who live selfishly and indulgently, raising their hatred and enmity. As it was then, so it is now. The New Testament totally confirms this prophetic testimony of the sincerity, holiness, guilelessness and purity of Christ (I Pet. 2:20-22; John 8:46; 18:38). What Christ endured, He endured on account of us, not for Himself.

B. The treatment which was accorded Him

In spite of the sinlessness of Christ, this is what they did to Him. They despised Him, they rejected Him, they esteemed Him smitten of God when He was crushed under their calamity, they wounded Him, they bruised Him, they hurt Him with stripes, they oppressed Him, they denied Him a righteous trial, they killed Him without knowing that all this was making His soul an offering for sin. That such a description could be given in minute detail as to His appearance, rejection, manner of death, being pierced and buried is a most wonderful testimony to the inspiration of the Bible. Only God could tell this for no mere coincidence could bring about such a prophecy. This likewise establishes the mission and person of Christ as genuine. No impostor could control providence, the free action of men and also subject himself to such humiliation in order to make this picture appear true. That Jesus is the true Messiah is proved by the nature of His sufferings.

C. THE TEST WHICH GOES EVEN FARTHER IN THE FINAL PROPHECY
     CONCERNING HIS DEATH

It was the intention of those who killed Him that His burial should be with the wicked. They sought to insult Him even in death by burying His corpse with criminals. The Hebrew verb "to give" means to show intention. By design, they meant to place His grave with the wicked, with Barabbas, with the thieves, with the ignominious whose legs were broken and were put in a criminals' field. The text does not designate the persons who so designed. Hence, it must be taken impersonally as meaning His grave was appointed with the wicked. However, an interposition occurred so that the design was prevented and the course changed, and He was with the rich in His death.

The word for death is actually "after death, that is, the grave." As we know, this prophecy was fulfilled by Joseph of Arimathea (Matt. 27:57-60). This rich man buried Jesus in his own new rock-hewn tomb after he had wound Him in fine cloth and had anointed Him with a hundred pounds of spices. No false prophet could have ever foretold such a detail as this, and no pretender could ever have fulfilled it. Christ's death in history is the great fulfillment of this Messianic prophecy which could apply to nobody else.

I. THE EXPERIENCE OF DEATH — HIS FINAL HUMIL-
    IATION

Isaiah said, "he was cut off out of the land of the living."

A. HIS DEATH "HE WAS CUT OFF" (cf. Dan. 9:26)

This suggests a sudden termination in the midst of His labors and activity. Thus in the thirty-third year of Jesus' life, as He began His prime years, they took Him and blotted Him out from the land of the living. Death is the great destroyer whenever it is met. Death cuts off. What is beyond death is the unknown. We must accept it in faith. Suddenly a child is killed by an automobile, a man is struck by lightning, a soldier is missing in action — then what? When Jesus was cut off, He said, "Into thy hands I commit my spirit."

B. WHY HE DIED

Paul said, "he . . . became obedient unto death, even the death of the cross." The wages of sin is death. Jesus Christ came into the world to die, to take the penalty of sins upon Himself. "He bare the sins of many" and "the Lord laid on him the iniquity of us all." Hence, the death of Christ was His predestined hour, as He said, "For this hour am I come." He took upon Him the curse of the law and He was obedient unto death (Gal. 3:13) .

C. HOW HE DIED

Jesus was obedient "even unto the death of the cross." He was "crucified." His revulsion experienced in Gethsemane was from the shame of crucifixion. He despised the shame (Heb. 12:2) . He dreaded the cup which He would drink. The agony of crucifixion is terrible. Any first-class religious encyclopedia reveals unto us the detailed steps of suffering in this mode of death. But greater than the physical suffering was the great agony of the wrath of God. It was this that broke the heart of Jesus Christ so that He literally died of a broken heart.

D. FOR WHOM HE DIED

We read that Jesus tasted death for every man (Heb. 2:14) and that He died for all men (I Tim. 4:10) and that He bore the iniquity of us all (Isa. 53:6) . All who face the dread spectre of death, especially the wrath of God in judgment, may have that terror removed by knowing that Christ died for us. Through Him, death becomes a walking through the valley and shadow, but not alone (Ps. 23) . Knowing that Christ died for you, how can you reject Him?

II. THE EXPERIENCE OF TRIUMPH — EXALTATION

Isaiah declared, "Therefore will I divide him a portion with the great, and he shall divide the spoil with the strong."

A. A PREDICTION OF THE MESSIAH'S TRIUMPH

Isaiah describes Him as a prince, a conqueror, a victor cele-
brating a triumph in which the spoils are displayed. From this
picture the Jews thought the Messiah would be a political
deliverer. Even the disciples of Christ said, "we had hoped."
Yet we may be certain that His triumph will be among the
great of the earth, for He has a portion with the mighty and the
strong. There is appointed to Him a spiritual triumph directly
proportionate to His sufferings. Thus He said to His disciples,
"It behooved Christ to suffer and to enter into his glory." Christ
is the great victor. No power, however formidable, can with-
stand His truth. It will effect the spiritual conquest of the world.
Therefore, Paul places Him over all principalities and powers
and dominion and princes (Col. 2:15; Phil. 2:11; Col. 1:20).

B. A PROPORTIONATE REWARD FOR HIS SUFFERINGS IS HELD IN HIS EXALTATION

The Scripture says, "Wherefore God hath highly exalted
him." In consequence of Christ's great sufferings, He is exalted
to the highest place of honor. The cause of this exaltation is
given in His pouring out His soul unto death in voluntary
sacrifice, in His being numbered with transgressors, in His
bearing the sins of many, in His making intercession for
transgressors. There is a direct relation of this redemptive ministry of Christ and His sovereign power. When He finished His
work of sacrifice as High Priest and entered into the Holiest of
all, it was with the knowledge that His atoning blood was
sufficient to grant mercy for sinners. It was necessary for Him to
toil, suffer and die in order to bring about this triumph. As He
Himself said, "It behooved Christ to suffer." Beyond Christ's
present intercession, there is nothing more He can do for men.
There is no more sacrifice for sin. Those who reject this reject
all share in His triumph and glory.

C. HIS PERSONAL COMING WILL NOT BE TO WIN MEN BUT TO JUDGE THE QUICK AND THE DEAD

Those who are not moved by His sufferings, death and intercession will never be saved. What He did, He did for men now,
and it must be accepted now (II Cor. 6:2). There is no other
advocate. There is no other way. There is no other sacrifice
for sin.

CONCLUSION

How will you treat this Man who so wonderfully fulfills this prophecy? How do you face these remarkable facts? It is impossible to present the vicarious atonement of the suffering Saviour more clearly than by these words and this history. This truth should bow you down with grief for what your sins did to Him and cause your heart to glow with love and adoration to God who has given such a Redeemer and to the Saviour who was willing to pour out His soul unto death for you.

7

IT BEHOOVED CHRIST TO SUFFER

TEXT: Luke 24:46, 47. "Thus it is written, and thus it behooved Christ to suffer, and to rise from the dead the third day: and that repentance and remission of sins should be preached in his name among all nations, beginning at Jerusalem."

SCRIPTURE: Luke 24:36-48

This interpretation of the sufferings of Christ was from resurrection ground. We ought never to forget that when we celebrate the cross, when we remember His sufferings, when we preach on a suffering Saviour, we are doing it from resurrection ground looking backward to the cross and the finished salvation.

A. THE SCENE IN THE UPPER ROOM

This occurred on the first resurrection day. The disciples had gathered in the upper room to review the events of the day. They had the report of the women that Jesus had risen from the dead. They had investigated the tomb and found that the body was gone. They had the testimony of Peter that the Lord had appeared unto him, and finally they had heard the excited report of Cleopas and another disciple to whom Jesus had appeared on the road to Emmaus. Their discussion included suggestions, explanations, interpretations and questions.

B. THE APPEARANCE OF JESUS PERSONALLY

In the midst of this, Jesus appeared to them personally. They were filled with fear, uncertainty and terror. They doubted their senses in spite of what they had already heard. Thus we have the emphasis of Jesus upon His body. He said, "Behold my hands and feet," and He showed them His hands and feet which had the prints of the nails in them. He even invited them to handle Him and see that He was flesh and bone. Then He asked them, "Have ye any meat?" and participated in eating fish and honeycomb, revealing something of the implications of the resurrection body. It was while they were in the midst of the joy of this reassurance that He gave them the interpretation concerning His suffering.

C. THE INTERPRETATION OF AND EMPHASIS UPON THE CROSS BY THE RESURRECTED LORD

Jesus reminded them of the words He had spoken to them while He was here upon earth concerning the necessity of His sufferings, His being crucified and His dying (Luke 18:31-34; Mark 10:32; Matt. 16:21-24, et al). He recalled to them the Scriptures which had to be fulfilled in His suffering, death and resurrection, opening the law, the prophets and the Psalms. Then He revealed to them why He had to suffer in order to bring in the forgiveness of sins. Here we believe in the source of the harmonious content of the Gospel in all the preaching and teaching of the apostles. They received their interpretation of His life, His death and His resurrection from Christ Himself. As for me, I am content to take my doctrinal truth from Jesus' own lips as the interpretation of the cross given while the disciples were still asking why must He die.

I. THE FACT OF CHRIST'S SUFFERING

The Lord Himself declared, "It behooved Christ to suffer," that is, it was necessary for Him to suffer.

A. CHRIST SUFFERED THE LIMITATIONS OF THE INCARNATION

It was part of His suffering to give up His position in heaven, His glory, His majesty and His authority to come to earth. Paul describes it as an emptying of Himself, a humbling of self (Phil. 2:6ff). It was part of His suffering to take permanently into His being human nature and a human body (Heb. 2:14). We must never forget that Christ is forever the God-man and has humanity now in His being. Then He subjected Himself to all the sufferings of earthly existence such as hunger, thirst, weariness, pain, loneliness, sorrow, burden, trial and everything that men must suffer. Thus we see Him in the poverty of Bethlehem, in the labors of Nazareth, in the condition of having nowhere to lay His head. All this was part of His incarnation.

B. Christ Suffered the Contradictions of Men

The Pharisees contradicted Him because He rejected their narrow, limited interpretation and application of the law. Witness the long Sabbath controversies and the hate of this group of people. The Sadducees contradicted Him because He repudiated their naturalism. Often they joined with the Herodians who opposed His political influence. The priests contradicted Him. There was Caiaphas and there was Annas, the high priests, and there were all the subordinate priests who mistreated Him. There was their illegal trial at night which violated the requirements of their own Sanhedrin, and, in conjunction with it, the smiting, the spitting and the berating of Him. There was the contradiction of rulers such as Pilate and Herod who mocked Him, scourged Him, crowned Him, made Him carry His cross, and finally crucified Him. All that men do was done to Him. He was made a little lower than angels for the suffering of death. Yes, Christ suffered the contradictions of men.

C. Christ Suffered at the Hands of the Devil

We find that in the wilderness temptation, the devil came to Him and tempted Him. He came face to face with the devil in Gethsemane, and the manifestation of darkness, of sweat, of agony and the cup of suffering revealed the presence of His archenemy. On Calvary came the final struggle with the prince of darkness who was permanently defeated (John 12:31, 14:30; Heb. 2:14; Col. 2:15). In this conquest, He overcame all powers of evil as a result of which His triumph was celebrated. But we must remember that Satan tempted Him, afflicted Him and harassed Him in a way such as we can never understand even in our darkest trials. When we read in the Old Testament of the affliction of Samson, it is but a prefiguring of the Satanic affliction of Christ.

D. Christ Suffered the Wrath of God

Wrath in deity is holiness in motion against sin. This wrath of God is poured out against all ungodliness and unrighteousness (Rom. 1:18). The cumulative wrath of God upon all the sins of mankind which was withheld and stored up because of the forbearance of God was poured out upon Christ. All of His wrath against violence, impurity, dishonesty, lying, stealing, wrongdoing, plunder, rape, etc., of the ages was expended upon the Christ (Rom. 3:25). When Christ cried, "My God, my God, why hast thou forsaken me," He was experiencing the acme of the divine judgment upon sin. It was then that His divine heart was brought to the breaking point. We shall never understand all that transpired on Calvary, and, thanks be to God, we never need to understand it through the experience of that judgment. We simply know that we are delivered from the wrath of God. All this Christ suffered and it is epitomized by the cross.

II. THE FRAMEWORK OF CHRIST'S SUFFERING

The Lord Himself said, "Thus it is written" and "All things must be fulfilled which are written in the law of Moses, in the prophets, and in the Psalms, concerning me."

A. THE LAW

We have already pointed out how the law gave the promise of atonement and deliverance from sin (Gen. 3:15), how it was necessary for this atonement to be wrought by blood (Lev. 17:11; Heb. 9:22), how a value was placed upon the blood in the preparatory teachings of the Old Testament so that life could not be taken without the authority of God, blood could not be drunk, and taking of human life must be requited, etc., how that a lamb was used as a substitute for a sinner (Ex. 12:1-13; John 1:29; I Pet. 1:19), how the curse of the law ended in death (Gal. 3:11-13), how the Passover was the symbol of the Lord's death, how the atonement was prefigured in the liturgy of the Day of Atonement, and how every sacrifice that was brought to the brazen altar looked forward to the death of Jesus Christ upon the cross.

B. THE PROPHETS

We have already examined Isaiah's picture of the suffering servant (Isa. 43:1-4; 53:12, 61:1, 2). We have seen how Daniel described the work of the Messiah and also the termination of His life (Dan. 9:20-23). We have seen Zechariah's minute picture of the events pertaining to the coming Messiah. And we know that Jeremiah likewise looked forward to the Lord our righteousness and His rejection.

C. The Psalms

As the Lord taught, we have seen that Psalm 22 was a detailed description of His sufferings on the cross, that He even quoted the words of the Psalm when He was hanging on the cross. We have examined Psalm 69 and seen that again we have a picture of Calvary both in its sufferings, its victory and its resultant influence. We have seen it in the minor Psalms where there were many, many references to the crucifixion of Christ. All these things were literally fulfilled on the cross and Christ's sufferings there.

III. THE FORGIVENESS WROUGHT BY CHRIST'S SUF-FERINGS

A. Forgiveness

It has been the hope of men through history to win their own forgiveness. How happy we ought to be to know that it is finished, that God is satisfied, that wrath has been carried, that justice can exact no more, that Christ died once and for all. The veil is rent, the sacrifice ended and there is forgiveness of God. This is the heritage of every believer as acquitted, justified and forgiven.

B. Favor

The beauty of the Christian faith is that God is reconciled, is favorably disposed, is approachable and that man has obtained His favor through the death of Jesus Christ on the cross.

C. Full salvation

Thus full salvation or deliverance from the habits of sin, victory over the practices of sin and power to live without sin may be preached unto the nations. All this is prerequisite for repentance on the part of an individual. Jesus suffered and died that men may repent and thus receive the forgiveness of sins, not in the future but now. This was the purpose of the cross.

QUESTIONS ASKED OF JESUS.
THE LAST WEEK.

QUESTIONS ASKED OF JESUS

THE LAST WEEK

Introduction

Many things occurred during the last week of the life of our Lord. There is a period of silence, however, during several days when we do not know what occurred. In the early part of the week we have the records of His controversies with the various political and religious parties of His day, such as the Pharisees, the Sadducees and the Herodians. These were naturally enemies of one another but they were all united in their opposition to Christ and in their attempt to entrap Him so that they may have wherewith to accuse Him and to cause Him to be put to death.

The answers Jesus gave to the questions asked Him during the last week comprise some of His most powerful teaching with the most profound implications for both the Christian truth and for the conduct of our lives. We examine it with an open mind, we seek to understand it by the power of the Holy Spirit in the analogy of Scripture, and we stand ready to apply it to our personal experience.

The series might easily be amplified to include other questions asked Jesus at other times in His ministry and recorded in the Synoptic Gospels. Jesus not only had the answer but He was the answer.

1

ART THOU A KING?

Text: John 18:37. "Art thou a king then? Thou sayest that I am a king."
Scripture: John 18:28-19:7; Luke 19:12-44

Jesus is king. The Scripture leaves no doubt about the kingship of Jesus. He affirmed, "I am a king."

A. The parable of the nobleman who went to get a kingdom (Luke 19:12-27)

This parable was given to His disciples because they thought that the kingdom of God should immediately appear. It declares clearly that Jesus was of noble birth and had a right to the kingdom but was not exalted into it as yet. During the interim some would accept His authority and some would not. To all His servants He gave talents with the commandment to occupy until He should come. When He shall come in the authority of His kingdom He will demand an accounting of all of His servants within the kingdom and will judge those who would not have Him to reign over them.

B. The triumphal entry into Jerusalem

Immediately following this parable the Lord fulfilled prophetic Scripture concerning the Messiah by riding into Jerusalem as a king. Thus Solomon had ridden into Jerusalem accompanied by Nathan when Adonijah had wished to establish himself as king. Jesus' entry was in humility without the pomp of military power or worldly glory, yet by it He took the step which identified Himself with the Messiah, showing Himself to be a king. The absurdity of any claim to material power through this triumphal entry is self-evident.

C. THE QUESTION OF PILATE, "ART THOU A KING?"

After Jesus had been apprehended, had been tried by the Sanhedrin and had been delivered over to Pilate, He was examined (John 18:33-19:11). The most important question Pilate asked Him from a political viewpoint was "Art thou a king?" He wanted to know if He was a spiritual and heavenly king or a material and earthly king. This would determine Pilate's attitude toward Him as the representative of the ruling power. The answer to this question will also determine His followers' attitude toward the world and the establishment of an earthly kingdom. In response, Jesus definitely affirmed that He was a king. That settled that question but it did not settle the kind of king He was. Therefore we look at the qualifications of His statement. He said, "My kingdom is not of this world." Since the kingdom of Christ is spiritual, his servants will not fight to establish it on earth. His kingdom is one of righteousness, peace and joy in the Holy Ghost (Rom. 14:17). He said "The kingdom of heaven suffereth violence, and the violent take it by force" (Matt. 11:12). He also said, "The kingdom of God cometh not with observation" (Luke 17:20). Thus we may conclude that His kingdom is spiritual, that He is a king, and that the kingdom of Christ or of God should be preached.

I. THE PREACHING OF THE KINGDOM OF GOD IN CHRIST

A. THE APPEARANCE OF JOHN WITH A MESSAGE, "THE KINGDOM OF HEAVEN IS AT HAND"

The Israelites expected on the ground of Old Testament prophecy that there would be the establishment at Jerusalem of the kingdom of the Messiah at which time all their enemies should be subdued and they should enter into a time of millennial blessing. This was the expectation (Luke 19:12) which caused Christ to speak the parable of the nobleman who went for a kingdom. The Israelites sought a kingdom but they failed to grasp the moral requirements necessary for that kingdom, hence they themselves were tested in the presentation of the person of the King, even Jesus. He came doing mighty works, signs and miracles, yet they hated and rejected Him saying, "We will not have this man rule over us." It was Pilate who brought Jesus forth unto the Jews and said, "Behold your king" and they cried, "Away with Him . . . Crucify Him." Pilate responded, "Shall I crucify your king?" and the chief priests answered, "We have no king but Caesar." Yet when Jesus was crucified Pilate had inscribed above His cross the statement, "Jesus of Nazareth, the King of the Jews."

B. THE EARLY MESSAGE OF JESUS

When Jesus came preaching, like John the Baptist He cried "Repent: for the kingdom of heaven is at hand" (Matt. 4:17). Whatever kingdom was announced and offered in the preaching of John the Baptist and of Jesus, it could not have been in contradiction with the prophecies of the suffering Messiah and of the inevitability of His crucifixion which were given in the Old Testament. It was necessary for Christ first to be rejected and die. Calvary was the purpose of God through eternity and it had been clearly revealed in the Scriptures (Luke 24:26, 27; 44, 45, 46).

To understand the announcement of the kingdom of heaven is at hand as an offer of the temporal establishment of God's kingdom when God had foretold through the prophets that the Christ would be crucified, is irrational. There was an interval between the coming in humility and the coming in glory prophesied in the Old Testament which had to be fulfilled (Isa. 53:1-12; Dan. 9:26). That the seventy, and the disciples and the multitudes misunderstood the nature or form of the kingdom which was offered was most natural. It was not the kingdom of glory of the Son of man, but the kingdom of the heavens in a spiritual sense which was offered to them.

C. THE MESSAGE OF PAUL CONFIRMS THIS

After the crucifixion and resurrection of Christ, the kingdom of God was preached by St. Paul wherever he went (Acts 20:21-27; Acts 28:28). His teaching in the epistles confirms the record of his preaching as given in the book of Acts (Col. 4:11; Gal. 5:19-21). Therefore, we conclude that the form of the kingdom offered to the Jews in the person of Jesus Christ inaugurated at the crucifixion and exaltation of Christ and preached by St. Paul was spiritual. Contemporaneous with this is the kingdom of Satan, or of darkness, which is opposed to the kingdom of light, or of Christ (Acts 26:18). The spiritual nature of the kingdom does not exclude other and future forms but it clarifies the present form.

II. THE PHASES OF THE KINGDOM OF GOD IN CHRIST

A. ONE KINGDOM THROUGHOUT ALL DIVINE REVELATION

The Bible is a logical book as is any other book and when the word *kingdom* is used in different chapters of the gospel of Matthew, like chapter 3, chapter 5 and chapter 13, it means one thing — it means exactly what it says. The content of a word does not change in the course of a single book without an explanation of that change. If we were to define the kingdom, it would be "The rule of the heavens, that system which is heavenly in contrast to all that is earthly." It embraces the whole order of rule inaugurated in the glorification and coronation of Christ. In this realm Christ is King. All authority is His (Matt. 28:18). The throne of that kingdom is the cross from which Christ rules the hearts and minds of men (Ps. 47).

B. THE FORMS OF THIS ONE KINGDOM

The kingdom of God is the largest term and embraces all the redeemed from eternity to eternity. This kingdom can be entered only by the new birth. When the Lord Jesus conversed with Nicodemus concerning the new birth, He said, "Art thou a master of Israel, and knowest not these things" (John 3:10). The Lord expected Nicodemus to understand that new birth had been required in the Old Testament for one to enter the kingdom of God. Every member of the Church who has entered by the new birth is a member of the kingdom of God. Thus, we are not only born into His kingdom but we become citizens of His kingdom or of His commonwealth. Of this kingdom of God there are various forms. There was the theocratic form of the Old Testament, there is the present form in the church and there is the future form of the kingdom of glory, or of God's Son. This is the time when the Old Testament prophecies and expectations will be fulfilled (Isa. 2:2-5; 11:1-9; 35:1-10, et al). During this period there will be but one period for Satan will be removed and bound. This is the kingdom which Christ, as the nobleman, went away to receive and having received it of the Father, will rule over it in power.

C. THE CHURCH AND THE KINGDOM

The Church is not synonymous with the kingdom but its members are in the kingdom of God. The conception of the Church is a higher one than of the kingdom. In the Church we are the sons of God, not merely citizens of the kingdom. We have assumed the divine nature. The destiny of the Church is the highest of all God's redeemed people. It is the fullness of Him who filleth all in all (Eph. 1:21-23).

III. THE PRINCIPLES OF THE KINGDOM OF GOD IN CHRIST

A. MANIFESTED WITH CHRIST'S COMING AND EARTHLY MINISTRY AND SET UP AT HIS EXALTATION

The kingdom was at hand during our Lord's ministry in His own personal authority. It could be said to be among them. It was not the restoration of the kingdom to Israel, however, for that was to be yet future. The cross merited the extending to Christ of His kingdom. Satan was defeated, perfect obedience was yielded to the law of God, satisfaction was made to God's holiness and a people was purchased. All this was that in His kingdom should be manifested the moral and spiritual features and holy principles as they were made known by the King Himself.

B. THE STANDARDS OF THE KINGDOM ARE GIVEN IN THE SERMON ON THE MOUNT

As Jesus taught He implied that when I am accepted as King, My subjects shall live thus and so. Thus, the Sermon on the Mount becomes the ethical standard for the believer and becomes the perfect law of His kingdom. It takes the religion of the Lord Jesus into the heart and not into external matters alone.

C. THE PROGRESS OF THE KINGDOM SEEN IN THE PARABLES IN MATTHEW 13

Here the scope is the world, not the Church; it is Christendom and not the Church alone. Christ begins by revealing Himself as the sower and ends by coming to set up His kingdom. He speaks of the value of the redeemed, of the purchase of the Church, of righteous together, of the growth in corruption in Christendom, of the value of the redeemed, of the purchase of the Church, of the separation between the good and the bad at the end time. The chapter reveals no conversion in this age, no perfect Church organization, only a kingdom to be purged.

CONCLUSION

The answer to the question, "Wilt thou restore the kingdom?" is that the time and seasons are in the divine power. Our task is to occupy until He comes.

2

WHAT SHALL BE THE SIGN OF THY COMING?

MONDAY — TWENTIETH DAY

TEXT: Matthew 24:3. "And as he sat upon the mount of Olives, the disciples came unto him privately, saying, Tell us, when shall these things be? and what shall be the sign of thy coming, and of the end of the world?"

SCRIPTURE: Matthew 24:1-14

The immediate answer of Jesus to this question was, "Take heed that no man deceive you. For many shall come in my name, saying, I am Christ; and shall deceive many." The history of deception and error on the subject of the second coming of Christ is stupendous. It is so overwhelming that it sometimes turns people away from any consideration of the literal and imminent nature of that coming. They connect all teaching concerning the second coming of Christ with fanaticism and with error. Periodically, individuals who become deeply interested in this subject are led astray into date setting. This is particularly true of those who left the direct teaching of the Scripture and began to calculate dates on the basis of the great pyramid. Then there are those sects of the Christian religion who teach that Christ has already come again in the person of their leaders. It is to be expected that Satan will counterfeit a great Christian truth which is an incentive to holiness, to evangelism and to missions. A welter of error connected with this truth bears witness to the activity of the great deceiver.

I. SIGNS WHICH ARE GENERAL AND DO NOT BE-TOKEN CHRIST'S COMING

The Lord Jesus then mentioned numerous signs which are general to the age, which may be more intense at one time than another, and which, when they occur, do not warn us of the second coming. Some Bible interpreters identify these general signs with the four horsemen of the apocalypse described in Revelation 6: The first riding a white horse and going forth conquering and to conquer, which is a description of the gospel of Jesus Christ; the second, riding a red horse having power to take peace from the earth, which describes war; the third, riding a black horse with a pair of balances in his hand, describing famine; the fourth, riding a pale horse, and his name being death. To the four horsemen was given power to kill with the sword, with hunger and with death.

A. WAR

The Lord Jesus specifically warned us that there will be wars and rumors of wars but the end is not yet. Throughout this whole age we may expect wars to occur in spite of all the efforts of men to promote peace by conference, by council and by agreement. This is due to the depravity of man and to the control of the nations by Satan (Eph. 2:1, 2). Christians must give their full support to all movements toward peace which are commensurate with the recognition of the perverted and depraved condition of mankind. We must recognize that we cannot have heaven in a place that is ruled by the prince of darkness. The Lord's admonition is that we are not to be troubled when wars are in progress or when we hear rumors of new wars or when we face the possible catastrophe that comes from them. A Christian security can never rest in any man-made peace but only in the Lord Himself.

B. NATURAL CATASTROPHE

The Lord foretold famine. Famine in a nation that has a constant farm surplus so that the government spends hundreds of millions of dollars a year to buy up the surplus and a million dollars a day to store it, seems impossible. Yet, half the world is living in famine conditions constantly. There are a billion people that rarely, if ever, rise above the subsistence level and there are literally hundreds of millions of people who never go to bed with their hunger satisfied.

The Lord Jesus warned of earthquakes. Such earthquakes have occurred throughout history but they are becoming more and more intense in these latter days. California, Turkey, Chile, Greece and other places have been periodically smitten by these terrible earthquakes. The Lord Jesus foretold pestilence. Some civilized areas of the world have cholera, typhus, smallpox, bubonic plague and other pestilences. Even the most civilized countries were struck by the terrible plague of the influenza and they have up until the present suffered from plagues of polio. We are persuaded, however, that Jesus meant not only diseases but also harrowing experiences of many kinds, such as crime, social conflict, revolution and race division.

C. THE PREACHING OF THE GOSPEL

During this entire age the gospel must be preached and will be preached. The Lord Jesus said that this gospel of the kingdom shall be preached unto all the world for a witness unto all nations. In the book of Revelation, in chapter 5:9 and 7:9, we read that the redeemed will come from all tribes, kindreds, tongues and nations so it is evident that this work of preaching the gospel will go on until it is accomplished. Thus when revival comes or when a great religious movement occurs, it is not necessarily a sign of the endtime.

D. THE CONSUMMATION IS NOT BEGUN BY THESE

Jesus has warned us that terrible wars do not initiate the end of the age. Civilization may utterly collapse, the leadership of nations may change and yet Christ may not return. It is conceivable that the world revolution of Communism may even take place and the end not occur. These may only be foretastes of sorrows which are to come.

II. SIGNS WHICH SHOULD AWAKEN BELIEVERS TO WATCH

The Lord Jesus warned that after these beginning sorrows "they shall deliver you up to be afflicted and shall kill you and ye shall be hated of all nations for my name's sake."

A. THE PERSECUTION

Some think that this passage is specifically Jewish and refers to anti-Semitism in the world. If that is true, more anti-Jewish feeling and persecution has existed in our day than in any day in history. Russia was noted for its pogroms against the Jews before the Bolshevik revolution. Germany reportedly massacred in one form or another at least two million Jews during the

Nazi regime. England, America and France are not without their anti-Semitism even today. If, however, the Lord here is referring to the persecution of Christians, it may very well be fulfilled in such terrible persecutions as are occurring under the atheistic regime of Communism. This, he warned, could be sufficient to deflect believers from their faith and that endurance under opposition was necessary for salvation. He did not teach that we are saved by endurance but that he who is saved will endure as an evidence in the midst of everything he suffers. Christians and Jews both have suffered intensely under persecution in our own generation.

B. THE PREACHING OF THE KINGDOM

If we revert back to the questions asked by the disciples we find it is hard to distinguish between the three, but the implication is that the answers of the Lord refer to the end time of the present order, the termination of the period of grace or of the Holy Spirit or of the gospel. The task of the Church during this dispensation is the preaching of the gospel of the kingdom unto all nations. That the kingdom is spiritual and not material is clear from Jesus' own teaching, especially in His testimony before Pilate. All regenerate persons belong to the kingdom which is the spiritual commonwealth of God. There is no promise here of the Christianization of the world but of the evangelization of the world. Many who having heard will not believe. The preaching of the kingdom is the preaching of the doctrines of the gospel so that individuals may repent and believe, thus being regenerate so as to share in the kingdom of God. A careful comparison of the use of the kingdom of God and the kingdom of heaven in Matthew and Luke will show that they are interchangeable and that the kingdom is spiritual.

C. THE PARALLEL OF CONDITIONS TO THE DAYS OF NOAH

In this address (verses 37-39) the Lord compares the conditions in the days of His coming to the conditions in the days of Noah. He speaks of lewdness in the marriage relation, of the widespread wickedness in the world, of the withdrawal of the Holy Spirit from working among men, of the imminence of the terrible judgment of God, of the salvation of the Church out of that condition even as Noah was saved out of his day.

III. SIGNS WHICH WILL TAKE PLACE AT THE COMING

A. The conflict over Palestine resulting in the abomination of desolation

It seems clear that the center of history in the period preceding the coming of the Lord will be Palestine. Wars, conflicts and troubles may arise in other parts of the earth but preceding the coming of the Lord there shall be a concentration of such trouble in the area of Palestine which the Lord described as "the abomination of desolation . . . the holy place." Only a blind man would fail to see that when two-thirds of the oil reserves of the world are located in the Near East, it is more and more becoming an object of desire unto the major nations of the earth. The conflict for the control of the Near East is a distinct possibility in our own day. Russia is moving into this area, the western powers desire to control this area, and the Arab nations desire to play one against the other.

B. The tribulation on the earth

The Lord Jesus promised that in the latter time great tribulation would occur such as had never existed in the history of the world. Undoubtedly, the outpouring of the vials of wrath described in the book of Revelation refers to this time. The whole earth will be involved in the suffering. Men debate in our day as to whether the Church will be taken out before this tribulation or during this tribulation or after this tribulation. It is certain that the Church will not suffer any judgments of the wrath of God but it is also uncertain that the Church will ever escape the wrath of men for antichrist will make war with the saints. Let no Christians divide one from another on this subject. Let them prepare for the coming of the tribulation preceding the coming of Christ.

C. The unmistakable coming of Christ

The Lord said that immediately after the tribulation of those days He should come. He will come like lightning. Every eye shall behold Him. He will come with power and glory, with thousands of His saints. He will come to judge the nations and to begin the golden era.

CONCLUSION

Be ready. Readiness means having a life filled with the Holy Spirit. It means having oil in our lamps and not a mere profession of Christianity. Readiness implies righteousness, the desire that one's life shall please Christ. Readiness implies service so that one may hear, "Well done, good and faithful servant," when the Lord comes. With such readiness we may look for Jesus, the bright and morning star, and hope for His coming.

3

SHALL WE GIVE TRIBUTE TO CAESAR?

TUESDAY — TWENTY-FIRST DAY

TEXT: Matthew 22:17. "Tell us therefore, What thinkest thou? Is it lawful to give tribute unto Caesar, or not?"

SCRIPTURE: Matthew 22:15-22

Among the numerous questions asked Jesus during His last weeks of life was this question, Shall we give tribute to Caesar? It was propounded by the Pharisees in collaboration with the Herodians. The Pharisees desired to entangle Jesus in controversy so as to entice Him to say something which would incriminate Him so that they could accuse Him and have Him put to death. These enemies of Jesus were unremitting in their labors to remove Christ from the scene. Their zealous opposition puts to shame our lukewarm support of Him.

The Herodians were members of one of the parties of the Jews which had gone over to the service of the temporal king Herod. They had sought their own personal advantage and they were hated by their fellow countrymen. Herod Antipas was governor of Galilee and he desired to be king over all the realms of Herod the Great. In the eyes of the Herodians Jesus was dangerous because He claimed to be a king and thus might become a rival claimant to the throne of the Jews. The Pharisees felt that these Herodians would be excellent witnesses in court if they heard Jesus denounce paying of tribute, hence the conservative Pharisees who were natural enemies to the Herodians, were willing to cooperate with them in order to get rid of Jesus. Often the phenomenon is seen of natural enemies uniting to overthrow a common enemy. This they did in reference to Christ.

In the preface to their question they bore a contemporary testimony to Jesus declaring that they knew that He cared not for any man but taught the way of God in truth. Spoken by them it was flattery and wickedness because its intent was to entrap Him but it probably reflected the ideas of the people who were saying the same thing. What they actually said was true, "We know that Thou art true, and teachest the way of God in truth, neither carest Thou for any man: for Thou regardest not the person of men." This was a noble encomium pronounced by the enemies of Christ. Finally they came to the question which had large implications for the Messiah. The Jewish hope was that the Messiah whom God had promised would deliver them from the yoke of Rome to establish them as a sovereign people with great prosperity and blessing. They looked for a return of the theocracy in which the state and the church were united. The relationship of the Christian to the state is a question which needs to be faced by us in the modern world. Shall we also give tribute to Caesar?

I. THE REVITALIZATION OF THIS QUESTION IN THE WORLD TODAY

A. THE SERIES OF CRISES FOR THE CHURCH TODAY

The Church is not granted the liberty and independence in every state which it has in America, nor does the individual have the accompanying freedoms which he enjoys in America. Communist Russia allows no liberty for Church activity. The Church is totally subservient to the state. There can be no teaching of religion to the young, no evangelization of the unconverted, no preaching in the form of indoctrination. The Russian church has sunk to a practice of liturgy for those who are already Christians. The voice of the Church on ethical, social and political problems and questions is silenced. For twelve years the world witnessed a similar subservience of the Church in National Socialist Germany and from 1933 to 1945 both the Roman Catholic and the Protestant Churches were regimented and suppressed so as to be made subservient to the totalitarian state. German foreign missionary work ended. German liberty to preach the Bible, its implications for the home and the state, was curtailed. Pastoral opposition to the state ended in commitment to a concentration camp. The Church was suppressed. On the other hand, we witnessed the opposite reaction in Spain where a church monopoly exists so that there are terrible persecutions of all who do not align themselves with the state church. Here is a throwback to the old medieval relation of the church domination of the state. Against such a condition the people of Mexico revolted and broke the church monopoly of politics and control of education. In all these cases there is involved the question, Shall we give tribute to Caesar?

B. THE SERIOUS QUESTION IN EVERY CASE

The question in mind is, Shall the Church be put to tribute to the state, or shall the Church control the state with a religious monopoly, or shall the state and the Church exist on equal terms? The claim of the medieval popes to the power of both the sceptre and the sword exercised by the Church through hundreds of years has now reacted adversely and in some areas has brought about the state dominance of the Church. Even in societies where the Church and state are divorced, the increasing influence of the state over the individual through old age pensions, labor laws, minimum wages, Social Security, unemployment insurance, government control of education and other social legislation, the state is exercising unusual control over the individual. The espousal of such left-wing social theory by many of the leaders of the Church has brought the Church into a new subservience to the state.

C. THE SERIOUS POSITION OF THE CHRISTIAN

The individual Christian must come to a conclusion as to whether he will accede to the general tendency and drift of the day or whether he will stand opposed to it. When individual Christians in Nazi Germany stood against the tide, they were liquidated or incarcerated in concentration camps. When Christians stand against the state control of life in Russia or China or any of the Communist puppet states, they too are liquidated. There has always been a terrible cost of opposing the powers that be. Sometimes this is a loss of liberty and other times it is a loss of life. St. Paul, in Romans 13, has clearly taught that the powers that be are of God and they are established for the restraint of evil so that the believer is to give obedience to such powers. This is a general rule of political life. However, the inherent right to revolt exists within the Christian teaching. Peter's testimony before the Sanhedrin (Acts 4:19, 20) still applies to Christian life. We must obey God. If the authority of the state conflicts with the authority of God, the believer must give

his supreme allegiance unto God. Yet we are to remember that
the kingdom of our Lord Jesus Christ is not the kingdom of this
world as He clearly witnessed to Pilate (John 18:36) .

II. THE RESPONSE TO THIS QUESTION WILL REVIVE OR KILL THE CHURCH

A. GIVING TRIBUTE TO CAESAR ALONE MEANS THE DEATH OF THE CHURCH

When the Church becomes subservient to the state, its purpose
for existence is gone. The Church was established as a witness to
another worldly society, to a kingdom which was not of this
world, yet the secular and temporal nature of the Church is the
emphasis of the message of a large sector of the Church today.
Insofar as it deteriorates to such a level, any debating society can
perform the same function. It is this end which is purposed by
the Communists and which was purposed by the Nazis. Peter's
answer to the authorities of his day must be the spirit and
power of a particular church today.

B. GIVING TRIBUTE TO GOD ALONE WITHOUT SOCIAL RESPONSIBILITY MAKES THE CHURCH USELESS

On the other hand, we are not to think that the Church is to
speak in a nebulous way about the other world, the spiritual
life and the things of faith. Its message must minister to the
masses and its clergy must be interested in the present life of its
people. The accusation has been made that the Church is an
organ of class expression. This is a Communist line and it is
sometimes repeated by misinformed people today. Therefore the
Church must with a prophetic voice evaluate the ethical implications of social actions and pronounce upon those ethical and
eternal implications. The Church of the Middle Ages attempted
to escape its worldly responsibility through aestheticism and it
failed. God has put us in the world and we must face worldly
problems.

C. GIVING TO GOD HIS TRIBUTE AND TO CAESAR HIS TRIBUTE IS THE ONLY SOLUTION

Personal religion, or a right relationship to God is the only
power and resource to change individual lives and thus to
change society. Religion is a mighty working power in individual

life. The application of religious conviction to the social scene is an imperative. We cannot cast the world to the dogs nor to the swine. It is too precious. We are obligated to make it the best possible world. We must express our convictions in community life. We are in the world although we are not of the world.

III. THE RESCUE OF THE CHURCH FROM CAESAR'S DOMINION

A. BY RETURNING TO ITS FIRST PURPOSE AND LOVE

It is not necessary that the Church should abandon all efforts to change society but it should do so through the Biblical means of exalting the Lord Jesus Christ and proclaiming the Biblical message to the masses. The gospel deals with the souls of men and with eternal truths. The Church is the pillar and ground of that truth.

B. BY GOING TO ITS KNEES IN PRAYER

Let the Church revive its practice of prayer. Prayer is an expression of faith in what God is and what God can do. In response to prayer a revival of true religion can occur in which we seek the will of God among men.

C. BY RESTORING THE SEEKING NOTE TO THE CHURCH'S PREACHING

Unless the Church returns to its evangelistic mission and its teaching ministry, it will fall upon perilous times. Men are lost and they need a Saviour. The gospel offers new life and a transformed way of life here. The mission of the Church is to seek men who are lost and alienated from God. Let the Church and its members bear the image and superscription of God. This is the best way of impressing itself upon the world. Render unto God the things that are God's and unto Caesar the things that are Caesar's.

4

WHOSE WIFE IN THE RESURRECTION?

WEDNESDAY — TWENTY-SECOND DAY

TEXT: Matthew 22:28. "Therefore in the resurrection whose wife shall she be of the seven? for they all had her."
SCRIPTURE: Matthew 22:23-33

This question was asked by the Sadducees. The Sadducees were to be distinguished from the Pharisees and the Herodians. The Herodians rejected Jesus because His kingdom was otherworldly. The Sadducees rejected Jesus because He performed acts which violated their principles of naturalism. They took the position of certain naturalistic scientists of our own day who reject all possible miracles and all supernatural. The Pharisees rejected Jesus because He broke their customs and made Himself to be God.

The Sadducees' doctrine was the exact opposite of that of the Pharisees. The Pharisees believed in angels, immortality, heaven and in a physical resurrection. Their trouble was not their content of doctrine but their hypocrisy (Matt. 23). The Sadducees denied any supernatural force at work in the world today. They rejected the physical resurrection, the existence of angels and of spirits. Hence, they worked out this dialectical question concerning the resurrection which they thought was irrefutable. A good illustration of the difference between the Sadducees and the Pharisees is found when Paul is tried before the Sanhedrin. When he perceived that one part were Sadducees and the other Pharisees he cried out: "I am a Pharisee, the son of a Pharisee: of the hope of the resurrection of the dead am I called in question." When he said this such a dissension arose between the two parties that no decision could possibly be reached (Acts 23:6-10).

Jesus warned His disciples to beware of the leaven of the Sadducees. This leaven is the deadly poison which is an antidote to Christian work today. It is paralleled in the essence of modernism. These Sadducees clung to a moral life but they rejected the power thereof. Paul described it, "A form of godliness denying the power thereof." Our purpose is to examine the answer of Jesus to these ancient liberals or modernists. We could very well call this question "Jesus and the Modernists."

I. THE DIFFICULTY OF THE MODERNIST

A. HIS HONESTY

At times we have heard Bible believers impugn the honesty of a modernist in his questioning of the Bible or the teachings of the Bible. Rather than resorting to the device of calling the modernist dishonest, it would be better for us to resort to evidence and proof which would solve the problems of the modernist. A modernist is one who approaches the Bible with his preconceptions either of naturalism or an evolutionary philosophy. The modernist honestly does not believe in the phenomenon of prophecy, therefore he redates certain books of the Bible to make the prophecies after the event. He does not believe in the miraculous. He does not believe in the essential deity of Jesus Christ. He does not believe in the resurrection of the body. Modernism is rationalism applied unto the Christian religion. The way to meet this is on the presupposition of a consistent theism, a thorough doctrine of revelation and an approach to the evidence given in the Word of God itself.

B. THE ILLUSTRATION OF THE SADDUCEES' QUESTION

In the Old Testament we have the story of Ruth and Boaz. Boaz became the kinsman-redeemer of Ruth who had lost her husband by death. It was the law of the Old Testament that when a man died without children, his brother should take his wife and raise up children unto his dead brother's name. Hypothetically one can see how that the illustration of the Sadducees was true. I knew a woman who successively was wife to four brothers of the same family. Each one died and finally she herself survived the fourth one. Now, the question of the Sadducees was, whose wife should she be in the resurrection? These Sadducees did not believe in a resurrection of the body and a continued existence of the personality and so they thought in this case they had irrefutable evidence that such a resurrection was impossible.

C. MODERN OBJECTIONS BROUGHT TO THE DOCTRINE OF THE RESURRECTION

Today men argue that the chemical elements of the body could not be reassembled, that a resurrection of the body is totally unnecessary, that there are insuperable difficulties involving age, limitation, recognition, etc. Bible believers do not stumble upon these questions for they know that if Jesus Christ arose from the dead and if God is the kind of God the Bible tells us He is, that He can overcome all of these difficulties.

II. THE SEAT OF THE DIFFICULTY
The Lord Jesus exposed these Sadducees on three counts.

A. SELF-DECEPTION

He said, "Ye do err." The error of the Sadducees was culpable because they could have known better. They had the entire Old Testament revelation and in the case of Abraham alone they had a figure concerning the resurrection in his belief that God could raise Isaac from the dead (Heb. 11:19). They were illustrations of self-deception in humanity. Paul outlines this in Romans 1:21-23. Care should be exercised even by so-called Christians that when they have the source of knowledge open to them in the Bible, they are not deceived or led astray. It is easy to err, especially when the prince of deception, the devil, is seeking to lead us astray.

B. IGNORANCE

Jesus said, "not knowing the scriptures." Evidently these Sadducees had not mastered their own Old Testament Scriptures. Peter tells us that the rulers of the Jews crucified and delivered Jesus up to death through ignorance (Acts 3:17) and therefore that they ought to repent of those deeds done in ignorance. Paul declares that they did it "because they knew him not, nor yet the voices of the prophets which are read every Sabbath day" (Acts 13:27). Because an act was done in ignorance does not mean that it loses its wickedness or that ignorance will lessen the punishment. If there is any characteristic of the modernist it is his utter disregard of the Scripture. In our day a new movement called Neo-Orthodoxy has appeared which similarly disregards the authoritative teaching of the Scripture. It has reaffirmed many of the Christian beliefs but it does so without deriving those beliefs from an authoritative Bible. Such would also be condemned by Jesus.

C. DISBELIEF IN THE INTERVENTION OF DIVINE POWER

Jesus said, "not knowing the power of God." The Sadducees did not believe in the power of God which raised Christ from the dead and which can quicken us (Eph. 1:19). A divine power had clearly been revealed in the flood, in the destruction of Sodom and Gomorrah, in the return of the Israelites from captivity, and yet the Sadducees did not believe it. Likewise, the modernist does not believe in the available power of God today. On all these counts the Sadducees were culpable and their religious kindred are culpable today as well.

III. THE SOLUTION TO THE DIFFICULTY

A. THE FACT OF THE RESURRECTION

The Lord Jesus said, "In the resurrection they neither marry, nor are given in marriage." The Lord definitely taught the resurrection (John 5:29-31). Throughout the Bible we have a clear affirmation of the coming resurrection of the body (Dan. 12:1, 2; I Cor. 15:1-58). The argument in I Corinthians is not advanced to prove that Jesus Christ rose from the dead but is advanced on the ground of the resurrection of Jesus Christ to prove the resurrection of the believer. This is a clear Pauline doctrine. Christ's raising of the dead is represented as His last work to be undertaken for the salvation of men before they enter into their eternal status of bliss. That the resurrection body will be different from the present body the Bible affirms, but that it will also have an identity with the present body we cannot doubt.

B. THE CONDITIONS OF THE RESURRECTION

The Lord declared that there would be no giving or receiving in marriage in heaven. We do not doubt but that there will be full memory and continuation of fellowship and love in heaven such as has been on earth but the redeemed family relationship will transcend all earthly family relationship. The eternal state will be one of spiritual communion that transcends any earthly relationship we have ever known. This does not imply that we shall either forget our earthly relationships or shall repudiate them, but a higher arrangement and relationship shall exist in heaven.

C. THE RESURRECTION IS NOT TO BE CONFUSED WITH THE PRESENT HEAVEN

Verses 31 and 32 clearly declare that the dead now are living with Christ although they have not yet been resurrected. The tomb of Abraham, Isaac and Jacob is in Machpelah, in Hebron. Their bodies are still there, yet they are declared by Christ to be living. The New Testament makes plain that death marks the departure from this life into the presence of Christ (Phil. 1:21-23; II Cor. 5:1-9). There is no room in the New Testament for the theory of the sleep of the soul.

CONCLUSION

The Sadducees and rationalists can give no hope concerning our lost loved ones and their condition after death. The Bible can give us that hope. We are convinced of a living God, of our living departed loved ones and of the future resurrection of the body. All this, however, will be the heritage of those who have known the power of God which quickened Christ from the dead and now quickens us from spiritual death (Eph. 2:1-6).

5

WHICH IS THE GREAT COMMANDMENT?

Thursday — Twenty-third Day

Text: Matthew 22:35, 36. "Then one of them, which was a lawyer, asked him a question, tempting him, and saying, Master, which is the great commandment in the law?"

Scripture: Matthew 22:34-40

This was the last question the world asked of Jesus as a teacher. Some questions were asked Him at the trial and some questions were asked Him by His disciples but no more by His enemies of His contemporary day. This ended the questions which men asked Him concerning the problems of the day. It is possible to be so absorbed in what Christ taught about problems so as to miss Him personally.

A. The question of the Pharisees

The interest in Jesus of the three main parties reveals the importance which He assumed before them during this last week of His life. He had answered the Herodians masterfully so that they marvelled, left Him and went their way (verse 22). He had answered the Sadducees so that they were astonished at His reply to their question (verse 33). Now the Pharisees were represented by a scribe (Mark 12:28) who had been listening and from the viewpoint of one who had accepted the Scripture and the supernatural, asked for an exposition of the law. The scribe might well have been Nicodemus.

B. The Pharisees were the most sympathetic to Jesus of the hostile groups

Some of the Pharisees believed on Jesus after He had raised Lazarus from the dead (John 11:45). Many of the Pharisees believed on Jesus after His resurrection (Acts 6:7). This inquirer had an understanding which would prepare him to accept

Christ. Now he tried Him in order to make proof of Him, to ascertain whether He should believe or not.

C. THE FINAL QUESTION WHICH YOU MAY ASK BEFORE PUTTING YOUR TRUST IN HIM

He is the highest and the best and is worthy but you hesitate before taking the final leap. So it is with many and we trust that these answers will satisfy them so that Christ may become the great answer for them or for you. With this man the question concerned the relationship to the law as a basis for righteousness.

I. THE GREAT QUESTION, "WHAT IS THE GREAT COMMANDMENT IN THE LAW?"

A. THE LAW, OR TORAH

The law was the great source of light, of wisdom and of salvation to the Jews. Devout Jews sought to live blamelessly by the law. Such were Zachariah and Simeon and Saul himself. The law was God's revelation and was holy and just and good. The law was ordained unto life but became a means unto death. Jesus never opposed the law; He brought out the true meaning of the law. But the law had become a great burden in the hands of the Jews. They were unable to obey all the laws of the Torah and thus they had no sense of salvation or of having attained unto righteousness. Few transcended the righteousness of legality and attained to the righteousness of heart which was by faith, therefore few were truly sons of Abraham. If one commandment could be singled out which would state this means of righteousness before God, men would be happy. Hence the question.

B. THE LAWYER'S QUESTION WAS, "WHAT SHALL I DO TO INHERIT ETERNAL LIFE?" (Matt. 19:16; Luke 10:25)

Here were scribes and lawyers, religious men who did not have a certainty of salvation. They had kept the ten commandments in an external sense. They had been moral, religious and earnest but they were still unsatisfied. They represent hosts of men and women who follow Jesus today, who accept the Sermon on the Mount as the standard of their religion but who do not have any knowledge of salvation.

C. THE LONGING TO DO SOMETHING

As soon as men think about salvation and the law, they want to do something. This marks human life universally. They want to develop a new social system, or a new philosophy, or hold a conference to effect a new means of achievement. Thus works find their way inevitably into religion and we have a religion of works for salvation, trusting in character, in merit, in achievement. This is the error of all non-Christian religions. On the basis of the commandments we confine ourselves to works or to religious exercises.

II. THE GREAT ANSWER

A. THIS DO AND LIVE

In Luke's narration of this interview he quotes Christ as saying, "This do and thou shalt live" (Luke 10:28). The answer of Christ is that those who are to be justified by works must keep the law. This is a way of salvation. If anyone will keep the law, he will be saved. The law is a manifestation of the covenant of works which exists between God and men. The law has two parts: The first tablet consisted of four commandments which were Godward; the second tablet consisted of six commandments which were manward. Normally, when Jesus responded as He did to the rich young ruler, He quoted only the commandments that dealt with men. If a man does not keep God's commandments to his fellowmen, how much less will he keep his obligations to God. Though the law is the means to life, no man has ever kept the law except the Lord Jesus Christ.

B. THE SUMMARY OF THIS LAW GIVEN BY CHRIST

The Lord Jesus summarized the law in the word "love": love for God and love for his fellow men. On this agree the teachings of Paul and of John (Rom. 13:8-10; Gal. 5:14). This interpretation was not initiated by Jesus but is taken directly from Moses who stated both these commandments and is simply a translation of the religion of law and legalism into a religion of the heart as a manifestation of faith.

C. THE INTERPRETATION OF THIS GREATEST COMMANDMENT

The covenant of works, or the law, is thus fulfilled by love which embraces God and our fellow men. This is a revolutionary

power, strong as any physical force or armament. It is a philosophy which can transform the world. It is the only hope for a
decent world in which to live. Such love which can be illustrated
by the parable of the Good Samaritan (Luke 10:29ff) is the
great need of the world.

III. THE GREAT DECLARATION

According to Mark, Jesus replied, "Thou art not far from
the kingdom of God" (Mark 12:34).

A. UNIVERSAL RECOGNITION OF THIS TRUTH

When the Lord Jesus summarized the law with the two great
commandments, the scribe said, "Thou hast truly said." Men
assent unto the truth of the philosophy of love. They know that
God does not want sacrifices and burnt offerings but obedience
and love. The necessity for burnt offerings as a prototype of
Calvary was due to the lack of the life of love and a lack of
righteousness (Mark 12:32, 33). The most which God requires
under the gospel is a heart-obedience which is initiated by
repentance and faith. This is called evangelical obedience.

B. ONE WHO ACKNOWLEDGES THIS COMMANDMENT IS NOT FAR
FROM THE KINGDOM BUT IS NOT IN

Dean Alford says, "This man had laid hold of the principle
in which the law and the gospel are one." All he lacked was to
take the means of entering the kingdom of God. Here was a
man who stood at the door but who had not entered. He was
close in understanding but he was not in through trust or faith.
All this man needed was to enter through Jesus Christ, the door.
He knew his lack and he desired to have eternal life. Now he
needed the committal of faith.

C. THE ONE AND ONLY WAY INTO THE KINGDOM IS BY THE NEW
BIRTH, THROUGH THE CROSS AND NOT BY THE LAW

If this were Nicodemus, a learned rabbi, we know just how
near the kingdom he was, for he later entered. If he was some
other scribe or rabbi we do not know whether he ever entered
or not. The step by which this understanding soul should enter
was a spiritual, personal and direct committal to Jesus Christ.

CONCLUSION

Has the answer of Calvary become yours? Do you believe on Christ as the righteousness of God, the Saviour, the law-giver and the one who satisfied the law in His atonement? In Him your question will be answered.

6

WHAT THINK YE OF CHRIST?

FRIDAY — TWENTY-FOURTH DAY

TEXT: Matthew 22:41, 42. "Jesus asked them, saying, What think ye of Christ? Whose son is he?"

SCRIPTURE: Matthew 22:41-45; Mark 12:35-37

Essentially the question is put the same in all the synoptics. It was the response of Christ to the questioning of the Pharisees, the Herodians and the Sadducees. He said, "What think ye of Christ? Whose son is he?" They answered, "David." He then said, "How then doth David in spirit call him Lord. . . . If David then called him Lord, how is he his son?" Jesus was asking their opinion concerning the Messiah. Their inability to answer Him reveals the devastating nature of His logic about the Messiah, to all of which He Himself conformed, proving that He was the Messiah.

A. THE DUAL NATURE OF CHRIST AS MAN AND GOD IS HERE SET FORTH CLEARLY

The universal doctrine of the Church and the Bible is that Jesus Christ was perfect deity, was perfect humanity, had a single personality in two distinct natures. Rationalism has always attempted to solve this mystery by denying either His deity or His humanity or by subordinating one to the other. An examination of Paul's preaching reveals that he consistently presented the Old Testament teachings concerning the Messiah and then proved that Jesus of Nazareth was the Messiah. The person of Christ is the center around which all else moves in Christian doctrine. Without Him our faith is futile.

B. THE DEITY OF CHRIST IS THE SUPREME SUBJECT OF THE BIBLE

The Old Testament foretells the Messiah to be God. He is described as the angel of God with divine attributes and prerogatives (Gen. 16:7-13; 22:2-12; Ps. 22, 45, 110; Micah 5:1-5; Isa. 9:6; Mal. 3:1). The New Testament plainly demands submission of the mind to such truth. It proclaims Jesus of Nazareth, the man approved of God, as pre-existent, as creator, as redeemer, as sovereign and as judge. The New Testament requests men to believe on Him and to worship Him. Moreover, the Lord Jesus Christ claimed such a position. He claimed to be God (John 9:35-38; 10:30; 5:18; Matt. 26:63, 64; 28:20). This nature of Christ was recognized even by His enemies (John 8:59; 10:33; Matt. 26:65). It was because of that claim that they opposed Him. And the claim was accepted by His friends (John 20:28; Matt. 16:16; Gal. 1:2; Rom. 1:3, 4).

C. THE DENIAL OF THE DEITY OF CHRIST IS PREVALENT TODAY JUST AS IT WAS IN JESUS' DAY

These Pharisees were not ignorant but unbelieving. They rejected Him and they were soon to cry, "Crucify Him." Christians are often asked in our day to make common cause in religious work, religious education, and week-day education with those who openly deny His deity. They should face the riddle of this question asked by Christ. It will force them to decide either for or against Christ.

I. JESUS IS OF THE LINEAGE OF DAVID — A MAN

The answer to the question, whose son is He, as David's, is correct. On this answer Christ built His argument. The Messiah is a descendant of David.

A. BORN TO A WOMAN

In the annunciation made to Mary, Gabriel declared, "That holy thing which shall be born of thee shall be called the Son of God" (Luke 1:35). To the shepherds the angels announced, "For unto you is born this day in the city of David a Saviour, which is Christ the Lord" (Luke 2:11). Thus "when the fullness of time was come, God sent forth his son, made of a woman, made under the law" (Gal. 4:4). The genealogies trace the Christ back to David. There was no doubt in the scribes' minds that Christ was to be of Davidic descent. When the wise men sought the king of the Jews at Jerusalem the scribes told Herod that He was to be born in Bethlehem (Micah 5:2). The promise was made to David through Nathan that the Christ would come of him (II Sam. 7:12, 16; Ps. 89:34-37; Ps. 110). Christ came into the world like any other child, although His conception was supernatural.

B. BORN OF A VIRGIN

No doubt is left by the Scriptures as to the fact that the Messiah was to be born of a virgin (Isa. 7:14; Matt. 1:18; Luke 1:27). The Greek word, *parthenos,* can only mean virgin. Under inspiration it is applied to the Hebrew word of Isaiah 7:14. Christ's coming was the result of the creative act of God, the overshadowing of the Holy Ghost (Luke 1:35). Hence, He was to be more than a man. He was intensely human but He was intimately divine. It was this claim to deity that made the scribes turn viciously against Him. The fact that Jesus did not proclaim His virgin birth does not militate against His deity. The mother of Jesus knew the facts and she was among those who believed on Him as the Son of God. The virgin birth was the only means by which David's son could become David's Lord.

C. BORN A KING

The son of David was to be a king, to sit on David's throne (Luke 1:32; Matt. 2:2). This was David's own hope based upon the promise of II Samuel 7:12-16. Under inspiration we have Messianic Psalms applying to this kingship of David's son (Ps. 45 and 110). It is interesting that Jesus said David wrote Psalm 110 and that it was inspired "by the Spirit" and that it is Messianic, all of which is denied by certain critics today. The fact that the people would take Jesus and make Him king by force (John 5) and that Jesus refused it, shows that His kingdom was spiritual. The kingdom of Christ will surpass David's kingdom as the Lord did surpass David as a man. It is a spiritual and an eternal kingdom.

II. JESUS IS DAVID'S SON

David said, "The Lord said unto my Lord," and this he said by the Holy Spirit.

A. THE MEANING OF LORDSHIP

David uses the same word for Jehovah and for his own son. The New Testament declares that Jesus is identified with the

Lord (Luke 22:70; Acts 3:14; I Cor. 2:8; Heb. 10:10-14). Hence, the attributes of Lordship are attributed to Jesus as the Son of God. He is declared to be omnipotent (Matt. 28:18), omniscient (John 2:24, 25), omnipresent (Matt. 28:20) and eternal (John 1:1, 2; Heb. 13:8).

B. THE IMPLICATION OF LORDSHIP

Lordship implies sovereignty and exaltation (Ps. 110:1-3). Historically this was fulfilled in the ascension of Christ. Prophetically it will be fulfilled when He shall appear as the rod of Jesse, or as King of Kings. Lordship implies priesthood (Ps. 110:4). This is being exercised by Jesus in heaven as priest after the order of Melchisedec (Heb. 7-9). Lordship involves judgeship (Ps. 110:5-7). Christ is exalted in heaven and enjoys the right of judging both now and to come.

C. THE TESTIMONY TO HIS LORDSHIP

Christ's life bears witness to His Lordship because He was Lord of Himself, of men, of the forces of nature and of demons. This His miracles displayed. He was Lord of truth as His teaching exhibits. He was Lord of death and life as His resurrection exhibits for He laid down His life and He took it up again.

III. THE DEMANDS OF JESUS AS LORD

A. AUTHORITY OVER MEN'S LIVES

If Jesus of Nazareth is the Christ of God, He has a right to demand that we accept Him as Lord. The crucified Jesus is the Lord of glory and the coming King. This fact constitutes Him the Saviour, gives Him power to forgive sin (Mark 2:5) and to give eternal life (John 10:20). He may demand obedience as our Lord. His law is absolute and becomes the standard for our lives. We must conform to His will as the supreme imperative. The only alternative is a hostile rejection of Christ as did the scribes who received His condemnation in such severe terms. There are just two alternatives for everyone and no more.

B. THE DEVOTION OF MEN'S HEARTS

Christ desires men's love. He said, "If ye were of God ye would love me" (John 8:42). Love to Christ is manifested in the keeping of His commandments (John 14:15). Thus, love should be the source of our good works and our obedience to His will.

C. THE DETERMINATION OF MEN'S DESTINY

Christ as Lord demands the right to determine our destiny. The true believer trusts his destiny to Christ alone. He has no other hope for salvation; there is no other to whom he may go. If his eternal destiny is entrusted to Christ, then surely this also should be true of his temporary destiny. He should submit to His Lordship in life and in death. The time is coming when Christ will sit in judgment upon our destiny (Matt. 16:27; Rev. 22:16; Matt. 7:22, 23).

CONCLUSION

What, then, do you think of Christ? Is He your Lord? You must decide that now. You have light enough so that you will never have an excuse for indecision. Receive Him as your Saviour and God. Acknowledge that the historical Jesus who died on the cross is the Christ of God. Love Him as your Lord. He will guide you, direct you, comfort you, help you and bless you. He will be your Saviour.

7

ART THOU THE SON OF GOD?

SATURDAY — TWENTY-FIFTH DAY

TEXT: Matthew 26:63. "I adjure thee by the living God, that thou tell us whether thou be the Christ, the Son of God."
SCRIPTURE: Matthew 26:57-68

In the Apostles' Creed we declare, "I believe in Jesus Christ, His only Son, our Lord." This is a plain declaration of the deity of Jesus Christ. This deity is declared in all the great Christian creeds. What basis is there for a belief expressed in these Christian creeds about Christ? That question was asked by Caiaphas when, under oath, he asked Christ if He was the Son of God.

A. THE CLIMACTIC SETTING FOR THIS QUESTION

The Last Supper, the high priestly prayer of Christ, the precious private fellowship with His disciples, the prayer season at Gethsemane, the betrayal by Judas and the abandonment by His disciples were all over. Now Christ stood alone before Caiaphas. Truly, Peter was out in the courtyard warming himself by the fire of his enemies and John must have been somewhere about for he gained admittance for Peter, but before the Sanhedrin Jesus stood alone. His trial that night was illegal for the Sanhedrin had no right to meet at night. The witnesses who spoke against Him were false and could not agree in their accusation. The charges against Christ were changed on three occasions and the authorities, who wanted to condemn Him, were utterly frustrated until such a time as Caiaphas, the high priest, put Jesus under oath and asked Him the question, Art thou the Son of God? For Jesus to remain silent in those circumstances would be to deny His deity. He had to speak. There are times for all of us when silence would mean a denial of our Lord. Silence might deliver us from persecution, or ostracism, or trouble, but we would be guilty of denying our Lord.

147

B. THE DOGMATIC AFFIRMATION

There were no higher possible words in which to state the deity of Jesus Christ. Jesus actually quoted the words of Daniel 7:13 referring to the kingdom of the Ancient of Days when He said, "Thou hast said: nevertheless I say unto you, Hereafter shall ye see the son of man sitting on the right hand of power, and coming in the clouds of heaven" (Matt. 26:64). This was only one of many such professions of deity on the part of Jesus Christ. In chapter 8 of John the Lord so affirmed His deity that the Jews accused Him of blasphemy and attempted to stone Him. In chapter 9 of John Jesus asked the blind man whom He had healed, "Dost thou believe on the Son of God?" and then announced to him, "Thou hast both seen him, and it is he that talketh with thee" (verses 36, 37). In John 14 He said to Philip, "He that hath seen me hath seen the Father." In John 17 He assumed and stated in His high priestly prayer that He is equal with God. The Lord Jesus accepted the title "The Son of God" five times and He referred to His ascension to heaven and His return in glory nineteen times. It is no wonder that the priest rent his clothes and accused Him of blasphemy if he believed Jesus made a false claim, for it is certain that He claimed to be Christ.

C. THE DEMONSTRATION OF THIS FACT

The Lord Jesus had shown Himself to be the Son of God during His three years of ministry upon earth as we shall soon demonstrate. If you want to know what God is like, we shall see a picture of Him in the Lord Jesus Christ. What is God? God is infinite in being, wisdom, power, holiness, justice, goodness and truth. As we look at the Lord Jesus do we find that He fulfilled these attributes and requirements?

I. BEING — HIS MAJESTIC PERSON

A. The person of Jesus was so majestic and untouchable that at His word the priests and soldiers who would have apprehended Him in the garden fell backward to the ground, that in Jerusalem His enemies dared not touch Him, and at Nazareth, when His fellow countrymen would have put Him to death, He passed through the midst of them and went His way.

B. The glory of His person was seen in the transfiguration when He was metamorphosed before them, in the walking upon the water as He came to them at the fourth watch of the night, and in the wonders connected with His birth, His death and His resurrection.

C. The self-sufficiency of His person is glimpsed in His containment of silence before His judges such as Caiaphas, Herod and His claims before Pilate. Observation of His person makes us conclude, "Majestic sweetness sits enthroned upon the Saviour's brow."

II. WISDOM — HIS MATCHLESS TEACHING

A. THE SERMON ON THE MOUNT

There is a height to which man's thinking may be led concerning ethical living in human relationships. Even non-Christians give assent to the moral elevation of such teachings. In addition, there is the discourse at Nazareth at which his fellow-citizens marvelled; there is the teaching concerning the mysteries of the kingdom of God under countless parables which presented divine truths in new form. He spoke words of wisdom.

B. THE KNOWLEDGE OF THE OLD TESTAMENT LAW

The scribes and Pharisees spoke with a derived authority from having studied under other great teachers and from quoting other authorities. The Lord used His own authority and placed His words on an equality with the law and with the Word of God. He said, "It hath been said unto you, but I say unto you." Though all groups attempted to entangle Him in His interpretation of the law, they failed, for He was a master of its knowledge.

C. THE REVELATION ABOUT GOD

Jesus spoke with an authority about God which no one else ever had. He declared His identity with God, that the teachings and will of God were His teachings and will, that He revealed God and that He that had seen Him had seen God. Thus, the height of revelation came in the person and teaching of our Lord Jesus Christ. No wonder when the soldiers heard Him they felt they could not arrest Him and concluded, "Never man spake like this man."

III. POWER — MIRACULOUS POWER

A. That Jesus did signs and wonders and miracles was attested by Peter before a multitude on the day of Pentecost and again before the Sanhedrin and was not disputed. These great works declared Him to be the Son of God. He Himself said, "Believe me for the works' sake."

B. THE MIRACLES JESUS DID

The gospel narrative depicts Him as healing disease, stilling tempest, raising the dead, casting out demons, knowing the thoughts of men and exercising supernatural power. Either that gospel picture is totally in error or else divine attributes were manifested in the ministry of Jesus.

C. THESE DEEDS MADE THE PEOPLE WANT TO MAKE HIM KING

It was when Jesus had turned five loaves and two fishes into a sufficient amount of food to feed five thousand that the multitudes determined to make Him King. He Himself told them that they followed Him for the miracles. Such was the attestation of His miraculous power.

IV. HOLINESS — HIS MORAL PERFECTION

A. HIS UNBLEMISHED CHARACTER

There was no sin in Jesus. His judges found no fault in Him. He challenged men to convict Him of sin and they could not. He had the perfect character. He was the Lamb of God who taketh away the sin of the world and to be such He had to be without blemish. He perfectly obeyed the will of God.

B. THE TESTIMONY OF SUCH A CHARACTER

Paul declared that Jesus was declared to be the Son of God by the Spirit of holiness. It was the holiness of His character which attested His moral perfection.

C. THE CONNECTION OF HOLINESS WITH HIS OFFICE OF SAVIOUR

It was the perfect obedience to the law of God and the freedom from all evil that made Jesus Christ the Saviour from sin. What Adam failed to do, Jesus did. "By one man's obedience we are declared righteous" (Rom. 5:17). This also was an evidence of His deity.

V. JUSTICE — HIS MIGHTY PRECEPTS AND JUDGMENTS

A. Jesus' upbraiding of the unrepentant cities of Bethsaida, Chorazin and Capernaum with a pronouncement of judgment upon them, His rebuke of the Pharisees as hypocrites, vipers and whited sepulchers, His indictment of unjust servants by parable reveals the perception of a holy judge.

B. The act of cleansing the temple of the money changers in the name of His Father whose house they had defiled again bespeaks the holy wrath of Christ.

C. The general teaching of judgment, retribution and punishment in parabolic and didactic form reveals the commitment of Jesus unto a holy concept of justice. This, too, showed Him to be God.

VI. GOODNESS — HIS MERCIFUL PARDON

A. Mercy was an attitude of Jesus' life. His treatment of the woman taken in sin, His forgiveness of the woman who knelt to wash His feet, His parable of the Good Samaritan, His treatment of those who opposed Him, all revealed loving-kindness and tender mercy.

B. Mercy was manifested toward the sinner but never toward the sin. To the man at Bethesda's pool, to the woman taken in adultery, He declared, "Thy sins be forgiven thee."

C. Mercy and peace met together in Christ, goodness and justice were revealed in His life and exhibited in the cross. Thus "the goodness of God leadeth you to repentance."

VII. TRUTH — HIS MAGNIFICENT PERSUASION

A. The Lord knew the truth and foretold it. His prophetic words unveiled the program of the ages just as His own person and work fulfilled the prophecy of the Old Testament.

B. CLAIM TO THE TRUTH

Christ not only claimed to know the truth but to be the truth (John 14:6) and He told them that a knowledge of the truth would make them free.

C. THE TRUTH WAS REVEALED IN HIM

He, therefore, who knows Christ knows the truth and has freedom. In religious things it is no longer necessary to seek for the truth for we find the truth in Christ.

CONCLUSION

Thus the centurion who saw the trial and unjust condemnation of Christ, who performed the scourging, who forced Him to carry His cross, who crucified Him, who heard the seven sayings on the cross, who witnessed the events of the earthquake, darkness and fearfulness, and who testified that Jesus was dead, declared, "Surely this was the Son of God." He believed that He was what He claimed to be for He had shown Himself to be the Son of God. Can you say with Thomas, "My Lord and my God"?

JESUS, PRAY FOR US

JESUS, PRAY FOR US

INTRODUCTION

The Apostle Peter tells us that Jesus Christ is our example which may literally be translated "copyhead" (I Pet. 2:21). Paul says that we should be imitators of Him even as He imitated the Lord. One of the best ways to imitate the Lord is in His practice of prayer. A real consideration of the events of Holy Week leads us to Christ's high priestly prayer of John 17 to His prayers in Gethsemane, and to His prayer on Calvary. Certainly, the Lord was a man of prayer. It was while He was praying (Luke 11:1) that His disciples came to Him and asked Him to teach them to pray.

Commonly we talk about the prayer Jesus taught His disciples to pray as the Lord's Prayer. That is not the Lord's Prayer. It is the Disciples' Prayer. He taught them to pray, "Our Father, which art in heaven." The Lord's Prayer is His prayer of John 17 for His people, the members of His Church, as our mediator. In it is communion with an equal rather than a petition to a superior. He declares His will concerning those who have been given Him in the covenant of redemption. In Gethsemane, Jesus prayed for Himself. There He was passing through the temptation and trial preliminary to Calvary. By prayer, He Himself came into perfect submission to the will of God and perfect dedication to Calvary. It was His last temptation to abandon the cross. On the cross, the Lord Jesus Christ prayed for the unconverted, those who sinned through ignorance. It almost could be called His prayer for the world.

Thus we see that Jesus not only prayed, but He taught us how to pray. As we read the Gospels and see Him at prayer early in the morning, at meals, at special times, during whole nights and in times of great emergency, we know that we too must learn to pray.

1

THE PRAYER LIFE OF JESUS

TEXT: Mark 1:35. "And in the morning, rising up a great while before day, he went out, and departed into a solitary place, and there prayed."

SCRIPTURE: Luke 9:18-36

Prayer is a great mystery. How can man have a part in governing this vast universe? How can he be a first cause? How can he have the "dignity of causality?" This is what prayer means in the Biblical sense. Prayer is not merely a psychological exercise, but is something projected into the external world. The Lord says, "Ask me of things to come concerning my sons, and concerning the work of my hands command ye me" (Isa. 45:11).

A. GREAT MEN BEFORE THE GOLDEN ALTAR

The altar of incense was made of gold, or at least covered with pure gold, and it symbolized the approach of men to God through the act of prayer. It stood in the Holy place before the veil which separated it from the Holy of Holies. The incense burned upon this altar permeated the veil and came into the divine presence. Thus the incense of our prayers rises up to the very dwelling place of God. A careful reading of the Bible with an eye fixed upon the prayers which are recorded will show us how Abraham prayed (Gen. 20:17; 18:23-33), how Jacob prayed (Gen. 32:9-32), how Moses prayed for his people (Ex. 32:30-32; Num. 11:2, 21:17), how Samuel prayed for a king (I Sam. 8:6), how David prayed (II Sam. 7:18), how Solomon prayed (I Ki. 8:28-54; II Chron. 6:12-42), how Hezekiah prayed (Isa. 37:5) and how Daniel prayed (Dan. 9:4-20). All these men stood regularly before the golden altar.

B. HUMAN NEED OF PRAYER

Prayer is the most natural act in the world when man feels his insufficiency and impotency. For this purpose, the divine invitation is to "come boldly unto the throne of grace, that we may obtain mercy, and find grace to help in time of need" (Heb. 4:16). What is your own need about which you ought to pray? Confess it, name it, let it lead you to the throne and to say to the Lord, "I need Thee every hour."

C. JESUS PRAYED

The fact that Jesus prayed reveals how real was His human nature and how He actually entered into the life of man through His incarnation. Prayer was the only means of communion with the Father available to Jesus during His incarnate state. We will never fully grasp the mystery of the kenosis or self-emptying of Christ (Phil. 2:5-9). It will be helpful for us to realize the value of prayer to Christ as we recapitulate His prayer life.

I. JESUS' CONSTANT PRACTICE OF PRAYER

A. A PART OF THE DAILY LIFE OF JESUS

The Lord Jesus prayed before the break of day. He sought the face of God early in the morning (Mark 1:35). He prayed at meals. This is shown by His prayer at the multiplying of the loaves and the fish (Mark 6:41), at the Last Supper as He blessed the bread before He broke it, and also at Emmaus where the disciples recognized Him as He prayed (Luke 24:30, 31). Also we find that the Lord prayed before retiring (Matt. 14:15, 23). Thus prayer formed a part of the daily activity of Christ.

B. AT TIMES OF SPECIAL NEED

The Lord not only prayed regularly, but He had special seasons of prayer. He went out into a mountain and prayed during the night (Matt. 14:22; Mark 6:46). It was with this in mind, that He took Peter, James and John into a mountain when He was transfigured before them (Luke 9:38; Matt. 17:1-13). Each of these nights of prayer ended with a great manifestation of power in healing, or in walking on the water, or in exorcising a demon. Likewise, when the crowd pressed upon Him and He was physically exhausted, He withdrew into the wilderness and prayed (Luke 5:16). Thus He was alone praying near Banaeus when the great confession of Peter concerning His deity was made (Luke 9:18).

C. BEFORE GREAT CRISES

Each time that the Lord Jesus faced a crisis in His life, He devoted a considerable period of time to special prayer. Before He undertook His ministry immediately following His baptism, He went off into the wilderness for forty days of prayer (Luke 3:21). Before choosing His disciples, He spent the night in prayer (Luke 6:12ff). Before He met the end of His life, He spent much time in prayer. His prayer was not for Himself alone, as we witness in His testimony to Peter, saying, "I have prayed for thee, that thy faith fail not" (Luke 22:32). The prayer in Gethsemane pertained to His own spiritual need as He faced the cross. The Lord teaches us that the one place to which to go in a critical hour is to the chamber of prayer.

II. THE CLIMAX OF JESUS' PRAYER LIFE

A. HIS GREAT HIGH PRIESTLY PRAYER

This prayer is contained in the seventeenth chapter of John and constitutes a prayer for the Church. Since we are going to expound this prayer, we will only mention here that it contained a statement of His purpose for coming into the world which was predestined from eternity, namely, to give eternal life to those given Him by the Father and to finish the work which the Father had given Him to do. It was a statement concerning those who became His by redemption and who were thus to enjoy union with the Father. It was a statement of His desires for them that they should be kept in the world from sin, that they should be sanctified by the truth, that they may be one with Him as He was one with the Father, and that they may be with Him where He shall be in heaven. This is an evidence of His intercessory ministry for His Church.

B. HIS PRAYER IN GETHSEMANE

Here the Lord Jesus Christ prayed for Himself (Matt. 26:36ff). We read that He went a little farther. No one else could enter with Him into this suffering and trial. He had to bear it utterly alone. Figuratively, there was set before Him a cup to drink. This cup He was to drink upon Calvary and it contained all of the physical suffering, the mental sorrow, the spiritual isolation, the sin, the guilt, the curse, the wrath that man should have borne as a result of his sin. Before He had finished His praying in the Garden of Gethsemane, He had dedicated Himself to the cup, He had surrendered Himself to the will of the Father, and He was ready for Calvary. His own human will was brought into perfect alignment with the will of God.

C. His prayer on Calvary (Luke 23:34)

Here He prayed for the sinners who ignorantly were crucifying Him. This was a prayer for those who did Him wrong out of ignorance. Surely it is a manifestation of perfect love. Apparently, these soldiers were just fulfilling their duty and had no rancor or animus in putting Him to death. Because of this, He prayed that they might be forgiven. If prayer means anything, divine mercy was extended to these soldiers and perhaps to others who were included in the group. It was this theme which Lloyd Douglas developed in the book *The Robe*. We almost think that this prayer could be extended to all who sin out of ignorance. A merciful and just God is interested in such and we may believe that Christ prayed for them. This prayer has inspired similar prayers in many Christians. Thus Stephen prayed, and his prayer helped to convert St. Paul. Thus Tyndale prayed for those who strangled him outside of Brussels. Thus Christians have always prayed for their enemies and for the world.

III. THE CONTINUED PRAYER LIFE OF JESUS

Hebrews says, "Wherefore he is able also to save them to the uttermost that come unto God by him, seeing he ever liveth to make intercession for them" (Heb. 7:25). Paul said, "He maketh intercession for the saints according to the will of God" (Rom. 8:27). John said, "And if any man sin, we have an advocate with the Father, Jesus Christ the righteous" (I John 2:2).

A. The mediatorial kingdom of Christ

At His ascension, the Lord entered His exalted state in which He exercises sovereignty over the lives of His people. Here He will reign in a mediatorial kingdom until His last enemy is destroyed (Eph. 1:22; I Cor. 15:24). He exercises this mediation by intercession. His presence is a constant intercession for those for whom He died. Moreover, the prayers of others are acceptable because of this ministry of our Lord. Through these prayers, He will conquer His enemies, for He prays with and through us (Rev. 6:2-6).

B. THE MEANING OF HIS KINGDOM IN INTERCESSION

As high priest, Christ continues what He did on earth. In His death, He ended all sacrifice and became high priest of a new order, that of Melchisedec. All other mediators are dispensed with due to the mediation of Christ. He constituted His followers a kingdom of priests who need no other mediation but His own.

C. THIS INTERCESSION PROVES THAT HE HAS COMPLETED OUR SALVATION, IT AFFORDS US A FINAL SECURITY SO THAT WE WILL NOT FALL AWAY, AND THROUGH IT, WE HAVE RECEIVED THE HOLY SPIRIT, THE PROMISE OF THE FATHER BESTOWED UPON US AS BELIEVERS

CONCLUSION

His command is to prayer. He said, "Pray ye." Time and time again the Lord said, "Pray, pray, pray, pray." Pray for those who despitefully use you. When you are praying, forgive. Always pray and do not faint. Pray the Lord of the harvest. Follow His example and enjoy communion with the Father through prayer.

2

PRAY THAT WE MAY HAVE ETERNAL LIFE
MONDAY — TWENTY-SEVENTH DAY

TEXT: John 17:3. "And this is life eternal, that they might know thee the only true God, and Jesus Christ, whom thou hast sent."
SCRIPTURE: John 17:1-5

The high priestly prayer of our Lord Jesus is contained in John 17. If I have my choice and am privileged to read any Scripture or hear any Scripture read before I die, I want it to be the seventeenth chapter of John.

A. THIS IS THE LORD'S PRAYER FOR HIS CHURCH

Just as the Lord taught us to pray concerning every possible human need in the prayer entitled "Our Father," so in this high priestly prayer He prays for every possible need of His Church. It is prayed to an equal in communion rather than as a petition of an inferior to a superior. It is classed as a declaration of His will concerning those who have been given to Him in the eternal covenant. Its contents surpass the ability of our finite intelligence. It is one of the most profound and deep passages of the Scripture, so we can only approach it in humility.

This prayer was probably prayed on Solomon's porch after He had left the Upper Room with His disciples and before He reached the Garden of Gethsemane. It was in the interim when He wanted to be alone to teach His disciples before He was to be betrayed by Judas. It was the last quiet hour which He had in intimacy with His own disciples.

B. THIS IS THE LORD'S HOUR

The prayer opens with the words, "The hour is come." As we read the Bible, we are impressed with the certainty of the times pertaining to our Lord. His birth was established (Gal. 4:4), the hour of His second coming is established, and here we learn that the hour of His death was established. The events which befell the Lord Jesus Christ were under the control of a sovereign God and Christ voluntarily offered Himself to the Father's will. Calvary is the central point of all history to which everything looked forward before the event and to which all look backward since the event. Everything hangs upon the cross.

C. This is the Lord's glory

Prayed Jesus, "Glorify thy Son, that thy Son also may glorify thee." The Scripture makes it plain that Calvary was decreed from all eternity, that it was the condition of the fulfillment of the covenant of redemption. The Son covenanted to die upon the cross for a people as their substitute. The Father covenanted to give Him a people through this redemptive act. Hence, the hour of Christ's glory was the hour of His crucifixion and resurrection through which He was able to claim the covenant privileges which were offered to Him by the Father. This is the destiny for which He became incarnate. He had glorified the Father in the revelation which He had given of Him. Now He came to the final step of glorification, namely, the redemptive cross, the resurrection and the ascension following which He would enter into His mediatorial kingdom and His position of power. In this prayer, He expressed His desire for His hour of glory (Luke 24:20), namely, the exaltation which was to be effected by His sufferings.

I. THE AUTHOR OF ETERNAL LIFE

Said Jesus of Himself, "Thou hast given him power over all flesh, that he should give eternal life to as many as thou hast given him."

A. The pre-existent Christ

The statement, "glorify thou me . . . with the glory which I had with thee before the world was" constitutes a claim to eternal glory. Christ here represents Himself as having a glory and returning to it. He never lost sight of His supreme deity even in the midst of His incarnation. This is taught in the rest of Scripture which gives an equality of honor to God the Father and to the Son (John 1:14, 18; Phil. 2:5-11). Here we see that this teaching was instituted by the Lord Himself. He was conscious of this aspect of His nature. He prayed as God in the flesh (vv. 5, 10, 11, 21, 24, 25). The whole prayer is based on this union of equality. As the Father glorified Him, He would glorify the Father. There was reciprocity in service and life.

B. THE INCARNATE CHRIST

Jesus declared, "I have glorified thee on the earth." He had revealed God's attributes in His life. In Him, men saw justice, compassion, holiness, goodness, truth and love. He had perfectly represented God to man (John 14:6). He was sent of God on a mission to man and had made known the communicable attributes of God which now in the presence of men had received a new glory. As Christ resumed His eternal glory, it was no longer as pure deity but now as incarnate deity, or as the God-man.

C. THE AUTHORITATIVE CHRIST

Christ was given "authority over all flesh" in order that He might give them life. Thus He is the mediator of the new creation (Col. 1:17). He demonstrated His mastery of the elements, of demons, of death, of diseases while He was on earth, and now He is to receive His position of mastery so that every knee shall bow to Him (Phil. 2:12). He alone is the minister or mediator of life. He gives eternal life, the kind of life which no man has in his terrestrial existence. It is God's life only and it goes to those to whom God gives it. This is not mere existence, but it is eternal felicitude. This is the right of the Son according to the eternal covenant, that from His position as mediator between God and man and from a heavenly kingdom, He may give eternal life to His own. This life begins in this world as the gift of God (Rom. 6:23; John 3:15, 16) and its full fruition will be in the presence of God forever (Ps. 16:11).

II. THE ASSURANCE OF ETERNAL LIFE

Prayed Jesus, "This is life eternal, that they might know thee the only true God, and Jesus Christ, whom thou hast sent."

A. THE KNOWLEDGE OF GOD IS ETERNAL LIFE

This knowledge does not refer to ideas about God, to intellectual speculation and to mental dialectics. It refers to the experience of intimacy with God, of the knowledge which comes by fellowship, by acquaintanceship, by mystical union. It is the knowledge to which God refers when He says, "Israel whom I have foreknown." The entrance to such knowledge of God is the *summa bonum,* it is life eternal, it is God. This is the perfect purpose of creation.

B. THE KNOWLEDGE OF GOD COMES THROUGH JESUS CHRIST

How can God be known? By searching? By the study of history? By nature? By thought? By experience? According to the Scripture, the natural world is excluded from the knowledge of God. The baffled gropings of men are shown in their clouded religions which fall short of the knowledge of God. The hopeless transmigration of souls revealed in Buddhism, the search for Nirvana, is evidence of this. The Bible makes plain how God may be known. It is our guide, and it declares to us that God is revealed only in Jesus Christ (John 1:18). There is a dark, unknown, unapproachable God revealed in the terrible deeds of hurricane, storm and death, but there is also the aspect of light, goodness and compassion in God, and this was revealed in Jesus Christ. The meeting place of both is in the person of Christ who shows the truth and the mercy, the righteousness and the love of God. To know Christ is to know God. Isaiah said, "By the knowledge of him shall my righteous servant justify many." Acquaintanceship, experience, intimacy with Christ is the only knowledge of God one shall ever have. When we accept Him, we shall have eternal life. This is the Bible answer to the hunger for eternal life. It is gained in the knowledge of Christ.

C. THE KNOWLEDGE OF CHRIST COMES BY, FIRST, AN ASSENT TO THE TRUTHS ABOUT HIM; SECOND, BY FAITH IN THE WORK HE HAS ACCOMPLISHED; THIRD, BY COMMITTAL TO HIM

First, an assent to the truths about Him such as His deity, His finished work upon the cross for our salvation, His mission to reveal God. Second, faith in the work which He has accomplished for redemption. This is to believe on the Lord Jesus Christ. And, third, committal to His person. It is necessary to make a complete trust of our destiny and of the details of life to Christ that we might enjoy mystical union with Him. This is known as evangelical obedience to the Gospel.

III. THE ATTAINMENT TO ETERNAL LIFE

Jesus said, "I have finished the work which thou gavest me to do."

A. The perfect obedience to the will of God

When Christ came into the world, it was to do the will of God. He said, "I come to do thy will, O God" (Heb. 10:5, 6; Ps. 40). He adopted man's position under the law. He took on Him the nature of man, not of angels (Heb. 2:15). He endured temptation, sorrow and the curse of the law (Gal. 3:13). He was a real man. By the accomplishment of a perfect obedience and a conformity to the will of God, He won a right to eternal life for man on the basis of the covenant of works. What Adam failed to do, He did (Rom. 5:18).

B. The prolepsis of Calvary

Now He prayed that "thy Son also may glorify thee." This referred to the cross even though the cross had not yet occurred. Of His redemptive work, only the cross remained. His farewell address was over, and a foretaste of joy enabled Him thus to pray proleptically as though He had accomplished the redemption (Heb. 12:2). Now in prayer, He said, "It is finished," whereas on Calvary, He cried, "It is finished." This was the purpose of His coming into the world — to die. The death of Christ made a full and glorious display of the attributes of God — His love, His justice and His wisdom. Thus eternal life was purchased by the unblemished substitute being the Lamb of God and taking our sin. What had been agreed upon in eternal counsels of God was now to be performed.

C. The predestination of the Father

He referred to "the men which thou gavest me." He prayed with a sense of divine control, giving God the glory for everything. He confessed that He Himself was sent of the Father, that the Father would draw men to Him, that He would give life to all whom the Father sent to Him (John 6:37ff). Grace of life is within the authority granted to Christ for His mediatorial work. He has life to give (Acts 4:12). Therefore we must come to Him.

CONCLUSION

His prayer was for those to whom He had given life, namely, His Church, those who would believe through His name, that they might be kept, be sanctified, be one and be with Him where He is. That is the kind of prayer He is now praying as our intercessor.

3

PRAY THAT WE WILL BE KEPT SECURE

TUESDAY — TWENTY-EIGHTH DAY

TEXT: John 17:11b. "Holy Father, keep through thine own name those whom thou hast given me, that they may be one, as we are."

SCRIPTURE: John 17:6-15

There is a name in which we are secure.

A. THE REVELATION OF THE NAME

Jesus prayed, "I have manifested thy name unto the men" (v. 6); "I have declared unto them thy name" (v. 26). "Father" is the name used in this prayer (vv. 1, 5, 11, 21, 24, 25). Many attributes were known of God in prechristian revelation but not His fatherhood, except His national fatherhood. Though Old Testament believers were doubtless regenerate, they did not have a conception of the fatherhood of God. Men knew His presence, His power, His knowledge, His holiness, His infinitude, but not His fatherhood. Fatherhood was revealed through the Son (John 1:18) who was the only begotten of the Father. In Jesus, we see the love, compassion, tenderness and holiness of the Father revealed. "Father" is the name Jesus taught His disciples to use in contact with God. For them, God was not to be afar off but a father. Every Christian should thank God for that revelation of God.

B. THE REGENERATION THROUGH THE NAME

By this revelation of God's loving, compassionate, suffering, redeeming nature, or name, through Jesus men come to trust God the Father. By regeneration or the new birth alone can men call God "Father." They are not children of God by nature (John 8:44), but only by regeneration. Thus by receiving eternal life through Jesus Christ, we come to know God as Father. We are adopted in the family and have all the rights and privileges of the sons of God.

C. The reward of knowing the name

Jesus said, "I kept them in thy name . . . keep through thine own name." Those who call God "Father," who belong to Him, who have been given to Christ are secure through the keeping power of God. They have been kept, they are being kept and they will be kept through His name. They have a right to that name because of their being born of the Father through the Son.

I. THE GROUND OF OUR SECURITY

Jesus prayed, "They have kept thy word" (v. 6). This is the word of predestination, a word of preaching, and a word of prayer.

A. The word of predestination

1. God's part

God exercises general control and sovereignty over all men through His creation. But His special control and authority is exercised through foreknowledge (I Pet. 1:2; Rom. 11:2) and elective love. God does not have respect to persons nor exercise favoritism, but only manifests His holy good pleasure (Eph. 1:4) with a redemptive purpose. In grace, God gave these people to Christ because of His finished work, and He draws them to the Son that He might save them (John 6:37-41). Here election is stated in simple terms, but its explanation is left for our wonder. We cannot help but ask why Nathaniel (John 1:48) and others were so prepared as to immediately believe.

2. Our part

We must be ready to hear the Word, to believe, and to obey. Jesus said, "They have kept thy word." He also said, "They have received . . . and they have believed" (v. 8). The elective work of God is always joined to the proper response on the part of the believer to the Word. This implies a moral decision as that made by John, Andrew, Nathaniel, Philip and others. There must be a response to the Word.

3. The result is that certain men are given to Christ out of the world (v. 6).

Out of the world, some were separated and allotted to Christ as disciples. The Greek preposition *ek* "expresses that the disciples were among the unregenerate until they became subject to

Christ's elective grace." Jesus said, "they have known . . . all things . . . of thee." This knowledge of the things of God comes by spiritual enlightenment. They received Jesus as Messiah and His Words as the words of God.

B. THE WORD OF PREACHING

Christ prayed, "I have given unto them the words which thou gavest me" (v. 8). Truth taught by Jesus Christ is God's Word and His revelation. The Church of the living God has always so accepted it. His teaching about God the Father, about law, about the new birth, about the kingdom, about the character of the Christian man is final. And of the disciples, Christ said, "They have received them . . . and they have believed that thou didst send me." What made these disciples Christians was their submission to the Word of God in Christ. The same conditions exist today. The Word of preaching is powerful and it must be obeyed. When it was, knowledge was received. Christ prayed, "They . . . have known surely that I came out from thee." There was imparted to them conviction, certainty and trust from the knowledge of Jesus as the Son of God, or Messiah. This certainty should be a part of Christian experience.

C. THE WORD OF PRAYER

The Lord said, "I pray for them: I pray not for the world" (v. 9).

1. His intercession

As priest, interceding is a great part of Christ's work as He prays for His people — for you and for me. This is a continuation of His practice initiated upon earth (Luke 22:32). We have His promise that He will continue to pray for us (John 14:16; Heb. 9:25; Rev. 8:2-6). The pattern given to us in this prayer in which He was so burdened for our security should encourage us to come to Him as He exercises His ministry of intercession. It is a caricature of Christ to present Him as a stern, unapproachable person needing to be mediated by His mother, Mary, or by some saint. We are to come boldly to Him personally.

2. Through His relationship

He said, "For them which thou hast given me; for they are thine. And all mine are thine, and thine are mine" (v. 10).

Unbelievers, sinners, reprobates are not included in the intercession of Christ. What a fearful thing is their state and how
soon they may slip into hell. They have no security. But if they
are once quickened by the power of God (Eph. 2:1-3), they are
included in His intercession. These are the believers, the redeemed, those who are given by the Father to the Son and who
are constantly in the prayers of our high priest. What a sustaining comfort this is to be a child of the Father's love. The
disciples were Christ's by possessive love through the covenant
of redemption, and thus are united to God and to each other in
the brotherhood of faith. The brotherhood of man and the
fatherhood of God on a natural plane is modernist teaching.
It is not Biblical.

3. Through His transformation

Jesus prayed, "I am glorified in them." This reveals that there
is a renewal of character and life so as to glorify God in the
believer. The transformation must begin by the Spirit's work in
the believer now (II Cor. 3:18) but will be final in the glory
which is to come (II Thess. 1:10). The Church, the "all" described in verse 10, will be the "fullness of him that filleth all
in all" (Eph. 1:23).

II. THE EVIDENCE OF OUR SECURITY

Christ prayed, "I kept them in thy name." Of this keeping,
we have an example, we have an exception, and we have the
expectation.

A. THE EXAMPLE

"Those that thou gavest me I have kept," said Jesus. This
refers to the disciples with whom He was physically on earth.
His prayer was for them whom He was about to leave. He had
given them His provision, His instruction and His comfort, but
they would need this much more when He was gone. Thus He
guarded them in the Garden of Gethsemane by saying, "Then
let these go." Thus He guarded Peter from the desires of Satan
by prayer. He withstood the accuser as the advocate of the
brethren.

B. THE EXCEPTION

Christ said, "But the son of perdition; that the scripture
might be fulfilled" (v. 12). Here we have an affirmation that

Judas was lost and he is called "the son of perdition." This should resolve the debate as to whether he was saved through a final repentance. Some wonder whether God had given Him Judas and then He had lost him. Rather, this shows the meaning of the previous clause, "whom thou gavest me." There is no irresistible grace without our keeping God's Word. In John 6:70, Jesus said, "One of you is a devil." Judas was a son of perdition from the beginning. Thus Jesus did not keep Judas. The answer is that Judas was not included in those given by the Father, for all that the Father draws and gives shall be saved (John 6:37-41, 10:28-31), and all such will be kept from apostasy and finally will enter the presence of Christ.

C. THE EXPECTATION

Christ declared, "And now I am no more in the world . . . and I come to thee" (v. 11). This was a prolepsis looking beyond the crucifixion to the resurrection and the ascension. He said, "I was with them . . . I have finished the work," speaking from the viewpoint of His ascension. That was the time of greater need for those who were deprived of His presence. It was His expectation to begin a heavenly ministry of intercession where He would always be praying for His own. Meanwhile, through His intercession, the Holy Spirit would be given to the Church who would do everything as an advocate which Christ had personally done when He was here, namely, teach, guide, enlighten, comfort and empower.

III. THE SPHERE OF OUR SECURITY

A. IN THE WORLD

When the Lord prayed, "keep through thine own name," He was praying for those who "are in the world" (v. 11). The saints must go on "in the world." Christ did not pray for them to be taken out of the world, by death or by translation. He was going but they were to remain. The Lord has a purpose for the saints to fulfill in life, in work, in suffering, and in witness. We must finish that work before we go into His presence. Yet the saints are also "out of this world" (v. 6), that is, separated from the unbelieving mass of men called "the world." This separation is due to the love of God in Christ. Moreover, the saints are not alone "in the world" even though Christ is not in the world.

His spiritual presence and prayers are effective and He is with us in the person of the Holy Spirit. We must live in a world of unregenerate men yet separated from these men.

B. NOT OF THE WORLD (vv. 14, 16)

There is a difference between the believer and the world in motive, in intention, in goal and in activity. The separation is just as real as if the believer had been taken out of the world, for a different spirit motivates him. Any desire to be taken out of the world on the part of the believer is misplaced. Rather, he is to stand in the world without the world being in him. His desire should be to fulfill God's purposes in the world. Probably the destiny of the believer will be comparable to Christ's in the way in which the world treats him.

C. HATED BY THE WORLD (v. 14)

The world hated and rejected Christ. This revealed that the mass of men were not chosen of God or they would have loved Christ (John 8:34). The more like Christ the believer becomes, the more the world will hate him because the life of the believer condemns, pricks and stabs the world's conscience. This antipathy is natural. Thus Christ prayed that the Father would "keep them from evil." The power of the Church to influence the world comes from this fact of the difference between it and the world. The world is condemned, it hates, and yet it is attractive to the Church, and some of those in the world will submit to the gospel. Hence, the Church should never stoop to do the things the world does, but it should be separate from the world and lift the world. Jesus prayed that the Church may be secure in the world, thus having victory over internal and external evil and thereby glorifying the Father on earth.

4

PRAY FOR OUR SANCTIFICATION

Wednesday — Twenty-ninth Day

Text: John 17:17. "Sanctify them through thy truth: thy word is truth."

Scripture: John 17:17-19

It is an overpowering thought that Christ prayed for us. Servants of the Lord are greatly assured in the knowledge that Christian people are praying for them in their great undertakings or their needs. How much greater is it to know that Christ is praying for us.

A. Christ is praying for us (Rom. 8:26-32)

In this passage of Scripture, we learn about the one who prays for us, who is God, who knows the mind of God, who knows all things about us, and who brings our prayers into alignment with the will of God. He is God's gift to us and He guarantees that God will give all things to us which are for our good. He who prays for us has a right to receive everything for which He asks, for His very presence before the Father is a prayer and the reminder of a finished redemption and the ground upon which He makes His petitions.

B. We pray in Christ's name

By Christ, we have access to God, the source of all blessing (Eph. 2:18; John 14:18). But for what do we ask? It may be health, for that is important. It may be prosperity of material things occupies us. It may be other objects of desire in persons, and property and blessing. But there are many and great blessings which are unknown because we have not asked for them. James says, "Ye have not, because ye ask not." Prayers for revival, for awakening, for divine movement in our community, in our families are often unknown because we have not asked.

171

C. WHAT CHRIST PRAYS FOR

If we may judge from this prayer, Christ is concerned about the most important things, the eternal things. He prays for eternal life for His people, for security of those saved, for their holiness, for sanctification, for their oneness with Him and each other and for eternal fellowship with them in heaven. In this passage, we catch the overtones of His intercession, pleading for our sanctification.

I. THE OBJECT OF HIS PRAYER — SANCTIFICATION

A. SEPARATION

Probably the lowest sense of the word "sanctification" is to set apart, to particularize, to designate (Titus 2:14). This has been amply covered in the preceding prayer, where He intercedes for the saints to be "in the world," but simultaneously "out of the world," and "not of the world." They were to become a separate people. The Israelites were a peculiar, a separated people, but they were not always holy. Ezekiel said, "The heathen shall know that I am the Lord, saith the Lord God, when I shall be sanctified in you before their eyes." They did many things which did not glorify the name of God. The actions of the sons of Jacob are a good example of this. They brought the name of their father and of their God into reproach in Shechem. In the light of sanctification's meaning of separation, there is a tendency of people to externalize this business of sanctification to dress, customs, forms of behavior, thus erecting barriers between themselves and others. Jesus did not pray for this.

B. CONSECRATION

This is an important part of sanctification. Christ had consecrated Himself to the mediatorial office and mission of redemption and is an analogy for what the believer is to do when he is "sent" by Christ into the world. Yet even this consecration for an apostolic mission does not exhaust the meaning of sanctification. It is a necessary step but insufficient as an exposition of sanctification. Far more is in the prayer than this. Consecration to the will of God is a prerequisite of sanctification and holiness, but it cannot be equated with it. If Christian experience ends with this step and produces no inner satisfaction, it is insufficient.

C. PURIFICATION

This is the supreme meaning of sanctification. It is the preservation from moral defilement, from moral impurity, and thus the making ready of the saints for their inheritance in heaven. This inner cleansing is the heart cry of the saints. "O, make me clean" (Ps. 51; Isa. 6; Rom. 7). This goes far deeper than the previous aspects of sanctification. It is the positive side of "keep them from the evil." There is internal evil of our sinful natures which leads us into moral defilement and which needs to be purified. This purification is a personal experience of being crucified with Christ so as to be identified with Him in death to sin and in life to righteousness (Rom. 6:3-8).

II. THE MEANS OF SANCTIFICATION

A. GOD

Jesus prayed, "Sanctify them." God the Father, the sovereign disposer of all, has a primary part in allowing trials and experiences to befall us which reveal our need and turn us to Christ. Nothing occurs to us without this good pleasure of the Father.

The Holy Spirit is not mentioned here but is the universal agent of sanctification according to the Scripture. The believer must be baptized with the Holy Spirit and fire. It was this Pentecostal baptism which cleansed the apostles' hearts and empowered them for His work.

The Word is the third agent in sanctification. Union with the incarnate Word, namely, Jesus Christ, brings this cleansing. Understanding of God's truth in revelation is the most powerful medium of self-condemnation, of aspiration, of consecration and of transformation. The divinely inbreathed Scripture is profitable for sanctification (I Tim. 3:16; Ps. 119:9). Sanctification comes by obeying God's Word.

B. EXAMPLE

Christ said, "I sanctify myself." There was an inherent power in the Lord Jesus to live a holy life, to keep morally clean, to obey the whole law. He was different from us for He was the truth. Christians must be sanctified through the operation of the Spirit and obedience to the Word of truth. The inference is that Christ was free from sin so that He could perform His mission of redemption in the world. Without that perfect obedience, He could not have reconciled His people. Yet this example should have a powerful influence over us, for we too are to sanctify ourselves by separating ourselves from sin, by consecrating ourselves to the mission of the church and by purifying ourselves from all filthiness of the flesh (II Cor. 7:1).

C. The steps in sanctification

The Biblical steps are five, no more and no less. First, there is the confession of need which comes from the knowledge of the Word and the knowledge of oneself and his deficiencies. Second, there is the consecration of all. This may be equated with surrender or yielding, but it is a critical consecration. Third, there is prayer for God's filling with the Holy Spirit. The activity is God's and comes in response to prayer. Fourth, there is the faith in the divine promise to give the Holy Spirit to those who pray. And, fifth, there is obedience to the still small voice who speaks to us telling us what to do as we seek God's presence. This is a critical experience, but it is not a once-for-all experience. It enters us upon a quality of life which must be maintained and is maintained in the proportion that we meet the conditions.

III. THE PURPOSE

The Lord Jesus prayed, "As thou hast sent me into the world, even so have I also sent them into the world." One cannot say that this sanctification has no connection with the mission, for it did have a connection. But consecration to the mission is only the end of sanctification. This means several things.

A. Consecration to exemplary living

The believer is a representative of Christ. Christ said, "I also sent them." We stand in Christ before the world bearing testimony, witnessing and working for Christ (John 20:21; Acts 1:8). There is need then for the world to be able to recognize a Christian standard of life in us so that they may learn of Him. Do they see a holy, loving, compassionate God in us? If they do not see Christ in us, our sanctification is imperfect. This consecration necessitates a renunciation of illegitimate and unnecessary things which mar the example of holiness and love (John 15:1-7). If the believer does not purify himself, then it will be necessary for God to purify him for the sake of such a witness.

B. CONSECRATION TO PRAYER

When we are sent ones, we must take upon us the burden of others. Our prayers must be an exercise of the ministry of intercession. Failure to support the dear souls who are dependent upon us, who represent us on the mission field or who are our agents in preaching the gospel resulting in their sickness, their loneliness and their death is a lack in our consecration. Christ sanctified Himself "for their sake." From birth to death, He was set apart. He determined to forego many pleasures and activities, all for our sake. Thus we ought also for the sake of others to consecrate ourselves.

C. CONSECRATION TO WITNESSING

The Lord Jesus established His worldwide program after His resurrection. This is the Church's task now. Our willingness to consecrate ourselves to fulfill this program is evidence of our sanctification. Examine your life. Take inventory. Search your heart and see if you are consecrated to His will in the world.

CONCLUSION

On Pentecost, God answered this prayer for the consecration, cleansing and commissioning of His disciples. May the Lord fulfill it in us by our having a Pentecostal experience similar to theirs.

5

PRAY FOR OUR UNITY

THURSDAY — THIRTIETH DAY

TEXT: John 17:21. "That they all may be one; as thou, Father, art in me, and I in thee, that they also may be one in us: that the world may believe that thou hast sent me."

SCRIPTURE: John 17:20-23

Jesus said, "I pray." Can I say, "I pray?" When I think who it was who prayed, that He spent His time in prayer just before He died, that He prayed for His Church and the objects for which He prayed for His Church as the mediator, it condemns me for my lack of power.

A. HIS PRAYERS WERE FOR YOU, FOR ME AND EVERYONE FROM THAT TIME UNTIL THE END OF THE AGE

He embraced the entire Church in His prayer. In verse 20, He reveals that it was not for them alone, but for those who would believe on Him through their word. This involves all generations, the other sheep of which He spoke in John 10:16, and the generations whom He saw when on the cross He suffered and was satisfied (Isa. 53:11). He prayed for all the converts to come. If you are a believer, He prayed for you. If you are in gospel work, He prayed for all those who will be saved through your witness. This prayer should be dear to all believers because it entitles us to certain privileges and blessings.

B. PARTICIPATION IN THE PRAYERS OF JESUS IS THE RESULT OF OUR BELIEVING THE TESTIMONY OF THE CHURCH

When we believed through the word of witnesses who have gone before, we became the objects of this prayer. When we were baptized into the body of Christ by the Spirit (I Cor. 12:13; Rom. 6:1-3; Eph. 1:13), we immediately became the subjects of Christ's prayers.

176

C. THE PURPOSE OF THIS PRAYER OF CHRIST IS OUR UNITY, OUR ONENESS, OUR COMMUNION WITH HIM AND WITH ONE ANOTHER

This should result in three things: in our having the gift of divine life (John 10:10-16), in our loving God, Christ and one another (John 14:23) and in our being dedicated to the truth so as to speak it in love (Eph. 4:15). Out of this grows the community of the saints as members of the body of Christ.

I. THE PENTECOSTAL FULFILLMENT

A. CONSTITUTING BELIEVERS ONE BY THE HOLY SPIRIT

Pentecost celebrated the sheaf offering unto the Lord in which the individual shocks of grain were bound together in a bundle and offered to God. Acts 2:1 declares that the disciples were all "of one accord" when the Day of Pentecost was fully come. They had come to a unity of life, love and fellowship. They had made confession of their shortcomings. They had made restitution for wrongs within the apostolic group. Their desires and experiences were one. Then, when they became filled with the Spirit, they even counted not their things their own. Thus the Spirit took the individual believers and constituted them one body.

B. ADDING EACH BELIEVER TO THE UNION BY THE BAPTISM OF THE SPIRIT

Pentecost constituted the Church a unit. The disciples were baptized by the Spirit into the body of Christ. Whenever an individual believer is united to the Church, it is by the baptism of the Spirit which may be called being born of the Spirit, being sealed with the Spirit, being indwelt by the Spirit. Thus many were converted in the post-Pentecostal era. Multiplication of power is achieved by unity. If one shall chase a thousand, ten shall chase ten thousand. This is not a mathematical but a geometrical increase of power. Thus the unity of the Church empowered it through the presence of the Holy Spirit. Every man converted today becomes one with all believers in fulfillment of the prayer of Jesus Christ.

C. MAKING AN ORGANIC UNITY, NOT AN ORGANIZATIONAL UNITY

One cannot read this prayer without getting the impression that the unity for which Christ prayed is spiritual. He wanted one that was like "I in them, and thou in me." It was to be as the union between the Son and the Father. This can only be accomplished by the indwelling Holy Spirit who makes us partake of the divine nature (II Pet. 1:3). For this purpose, Christ prayed that the Father and the Spirit would come to and take up their abode with the disciples. Such a spiritual unity will suppress quarrels and divisions.

The modern fragmentization of the Church into denominations, divisions and groups demonstrates the need for a new Pentecostal experience so that men of every race, clime, condition and status may be one in Christ. This is not arguing for uniformity of religious expression or worship or organization. Absolute sameness of opinion in religious faith and practice is contrary to human nature. There may be and ought to be differences of sentiment among good men on Christianity and the doctrinal interpretation thereof.

Nor does this mean we are to keep silence when error is taught. There is no need for us to surrender points of doctrinal belief in order to compromise on a lesser ground of truth and thus remove doctrinal distinctions. We have been advised in Scripture to prove all things, to hold fast the form of sound words and to contend for the faith. But the spirit of Christ and of this prayer is aimed against sectarian division, prejudices and strife. When a group of men constitute a denomination and make universalistic claims, they become schismatic in that very act. Their spirit is not the spirit of Christ.

II. THE PRESENT POSSIBILITIES OF FULFILLMENT

A. THE ECUMENICAL MOVEMENT

Some equate the ecumenical movement with the fulfillment of Christ's prayer in John 17:21. Unity has almost become a fetish, worshipped by some ecclesiastical leaders. Certainly no believer should have an innate opposition to unity in the Church. The uniting of men for testimony and work is to be desired. But a believer in the inspiration of the Scripture as God's revelation and the ecumenical doctrines of Christianity expressed in the first great councils of the Church cannot feel at liberty to sacrifice these great convictions for the sake of unity with men who often do not believe this content of Christianity. We cannot believe that the Lord Jesus Christ was praying for the organizational unity of the Church.

B. THE EQUATING OF THIS PRAYER WITH THE ROMAN CATHOLIC CHURCH ORGANIZATION

Romanism, of course, makes the claim that it is the only Church, that it has an organizational continuity since the time of Jesus' establishment of His Church. Romanism admits that there are some people who are members of the soul of the Church but not the body of the Church. But Romanism claims that if such persons are enlightened as to the nature of the Church and still remain outside of it, they are in invincible ignorance and there is no salvation outside of the Church. Romanism is guilty of schism.

C. THE ENUNCIATING OF A SPIRITUAL UNITY

We believe that the Lord Jesus Christ prayed for a unity of spirit in born-again believers to cross all divisional groups. He prayed that the believers would have the attitude of not cutting themselves off from other believers by condemning them, but regardless of any organizational limitations, recognize them as brothers. This is as near as we can get to organizational unity. Many of our organizations are unnecessary and can be sloughed off in the interest of true ecumenical Christianity. But where convictions are sacrificed, this should not be done.

III. THE PURPOSE OF THIS UNITY

Jesus prayed, "That the world may believe." As a result of union among believers, the unbelieving world may have an historical faith but not necessarily an evangelical faith. They may intellectually perceive and know the divinity of Christianity, but that does not mean they will submit and yield to its authority; in fact, we have no promise in Scripture that the world will be saved.

A. WHAT WILL THE WORLD BELIEVE?

Christ is the propitiation for the sins of the world, but the world will not accept Him. Some will believe and commit themselves to Him, thus being changed from children of wrath to being elect (Eph. 2:1, 2). Some will be convinced but will make no committal, and hence will be doomed. Some will be as the demons who believe and tremble, but are not saved.

B. Will the world believe so as to be saved?

Christians are not universalists. The Bible describes two groups — the saved and the lost, the children of God and the children of the devil, the kingdom of light and the kingdom of darkness. The world throughout the Scripture is the unsaved world. This world must be convinced and condemned if it does not believe. We must differentiate this world from those who believe on the ground of the disciples' testimony (v. 20).

C. Will leave the world without excuse

The oneness of the Church spiritually, its effective example, its fulfillment of the mission Christ gave to it will convict the world and thus glorify Christ. Those who do not respond affirmatively will be irretrievably lost, but they will be left utterly without excuse.

CONCLUSION

There is a unity which we may know if Christ-formed in us through the new birth, so that we are adopted as the sons of God. As a result, we will love one another and by this love the world will know and believe. Our cry is, "Jesus, continue to pray that we do not fail Thee before the world. Let our testimony be effective."

6

PRAY THAT WE MAY GO TO HEAVEN

FRIDAY — THIRTY-FIRST DAY

TEXT: John 17:24. "Father, I will that they also, whom thou hast given me, be with me where I am; that they may behold my glory, which thou hast given me: for thou lovedst me before the foundation of the world."

SCRIPTURE: Acts 1:1-11

This prayer demonstrates the coincidence of the will of Jesus with the will of God. He said, "I will." Let us remember that we are standing on holy ground, overhearing the intercessions of Jesus who as an equal makes claims upon God which are based upon an eternal relationship and agreement. It is as if a veil were drawn aside and we were permitted to overhear the prayers being made at the golden altar in heaven now. For this, we should have a reverent spirit.

A. A RIGHT CLAIMED FROM THE WILL OF GOD

In the garden Jesus prayed, "Not as I will, but as thou wilt." Here He asserts the fulfillment of His will. The word used is *thelo,* meaning desire or petition (John 7:17; Rom. 12:2) . This expresses the same thought as a prayer, for in one place He says, "I pray," and in another He says, "I will." The Greek softens the expression greatly. It describes the wish of Jesus that His people, namely, those given Him by the Father, those for whom He died, will be with Him in heaven eternally. He prays as the God-man, the mediator, not as absolute God or it would have been settled and decreed. Then the word would have been in the Greek *boulomai.*

B. CONDITIONED UPON THE LOVE OF GOD

Here Christ pleaded the love of God for the Son in pre-earthly ages on the ground of the love covenant which is the strongest motive in the world. In this pleading, He placed His people, those He represented in His life, death and mediatorial ministry on the same ground of love. God the Father not only loved Him but those represented by Him with an everlasting love. Praying like this is the most effective interceding there is. God will not and cannot deny His love. It was this which initiated creation and redemption and it is this which holds us securely.

C. CONCERNED WITH THE PRESENCE OF GOD

Christ was to be with God and He wanted His people to be "with me where I am." Proleptically, He anticipated the ascension to heaven whither He was soon to go. Wherever Jesus is, it is heaven. He is described as being at the right hand of God and there His people will be. Here is comfort for the dying and courage for the bereaved (Phil. 1:23; Luke 23:43; II Cor. 5:1-9). They were not only to be with God but to see God. He prayed "that they may behold my glory." His glory was suggested in the transfiguration (II Pet. 1:16) and in the revelation of the Christ of glory (Rev. 1:10ff) and as Paul saw Him on the Damascus Road (Acts 9:11). Some day the pure in heart shall see God. Moreover they shall be like God. As we are at present constituted, we could not stand the beatific vision, but "we shall be changed" (I Cor. 15:52; I Thess. 4:17; II Cor. 3:18; Phil. 3:21). The goal and objective of the Christian is to be with Him and to be like Him in heaven (I John 3:2, 3). Thus this prayer tells us something about the heaven where Jesus was to go and to which He is to take us.

I. THE PRE-EXISTENCE OF JESUS IN HEAVEN

A. THE LEAVING OF THAT HEAVENLY STATE OF GLORY

In verse 5, Jesus prayed, "Glorify thou me with thine own self with the glory which I had with thee before the world was." He left that state of glory and came into this world to take upon Him human flesh. Of all beings, Christ alone came into this world trailing clouds of glory. All other souls are created, but He was not (Micah 5:2; Heb. 1:5; Isa. 9:6). Hence, when He came, the angels worshipped Him. He abandoned the courts of heaven for this earth, for human nature, for humiliation by lowly birth, poverty, rejection, meekness and death. The beauty, purity and harmony of heaven can never be described.

They are only presented to us by symbol. Yet He left it, and accepted the lowly position of a servant, a minister, a redeemer (Matt. 20:28; Phil. 2:6).

B. THE LIVING WITHOUT GLORY

The song says —

> "Veiled in flesh His Godhead see;
> Hail, incarnate deity!"

On earth, Jesus' glory was veiled. Isaiah describes Him as "no beauty that we should desire him." He was smitten, bruised, rejected and despised (Isa. 53:2-6). In this state, He consecrated Himself to the daily tasks of home, the routine of a family, to the mundane things of this world, and finally to all the sufferings humanity is heir to, including death itself.

C. THE LONGING FOR RESTORATION OF GLORY AND TO SHARE IT

The burden of Jesus' prayer, "glorify thou me with thine own self with the glory which I had with thee before the world was," shows that He was homesick for heaven. This is the meaning of the words describing Him in Gethsemane when it says, "He was very heavy." This literally means "away from one's people." He had a memory of heaven and all that it meant, and He longed for its restoration. Moreover, He included in this restoration the blessing of this glory upon His people. Not only was His incarnate humanity to be exalted to the right hand of the Father and filled with glory (Phil. 2:9-12; Eph. 1:20-22; Acts 2:33), but also He was to elevate His people to the same status so that they might share His glory with Him (Rom. 8:16-23).

II. THE PROMISES OF JESUS ABOUT HEAVEN

We may not know very much about the place called heaven, but Jesus' word concerning it is enough for us. He said that the angels of heaven behold the face of the Father and that they are dispatched in protective care over God's children. He said that the saints in heaven will neither give nor receive in marriage. He spoke of the mansions in heaven and of the place which He had prepared for us. He spoke of the rewards in heaven and of the treasure in heaven, and of the blessings of heaven, and of the kingdom of heaven. We may be sure that

Jesus would never have promised all this had there been no heaven.

III. THE PURCHASE BY JESUS OF AN INHERITANCE IN HEAVEN

No one ever had a right to go to heaven, for this demanded the perfect fulfillment of God's law. But since all have failed and sinned, all are under condemnation (Rom. 3:23) and hence all are excluded from heaven because of sin. Yet we are told that we have an inheritance in heaven. This has been wrought for us through the positive fulfillment of the law by Jesus Christ. He lived without sin. This was the witness of Pilate, of Herod, of the centurion, of the thief and of His contemporaries among the religious leaders. He perfectly fulfilled the covenant of works. He came to do the will of the Father. Hence, Christ earned a right to eternal life because He had no sin (John 8:46; Heb. 4:15), and due to His sinlessness, He conquered death in the resurrection, for death could not hold its prey. In addition to this, He negatively assumed our guilt and sin on the cross to make a satisfaction for our transgression and our failure. The sufferings of Calvary were the price of heaven for us.

"There was no other good enough to pay the price of sin,

He only could unlock the gate of heaven, and let us in."

IV. THE PASSING OF JESUS TO HEAVEN

The Bible leaves no doubt that Jesus arose from the dead. He came forth from the tomb in the same body in which He died. All evidences given to His followers convinced them of this. To Thomas, He said, "Be not faithless, but believing." Through His appearances, they came to touch Him, to see Him, to hear Him, to eat with Him, and they were convinced that He was risen. By examining the open tomb, they knew that the body was gone. Thus the incarnate God-man demonstrated to His people that He had risen from the dead. After forty days, He left them. His appearances ceased as He went to heaven. As He taught them, and as He prayed in this prayer, He went to some place for His body was not ubiquitous but was in one place at one time. Wherever He remains until He comes again is the place called heaven. There He was coronated, exalted to His throne, given the Holy Spirit to bestow upon His Church and there He exercises His mediatorial ministry (Acts 1:11, 2:33; Rev. 3:21).

V. THE POSITION OF JESUS IN HEAVEN

In heaven, Jesus is exalted, glorified, coronated and reigning in a mediatorial kingdom. Thus Stephen saw Him in his vision standing at the right hand of God. He is exercising His priestly function as intercessor, guaranteeing the blessings of salvation and eternal life for the people whom He has purchased. Just as Satan could not possess Peter when he sifted him because of Christ's prayer, so Satan cannot possess any of God's people because Christ is our advocate in heaven, withstanding the accuser. As such, He endues His people with the Holy Spirit who enables them to live acceptably to God (John 20:22; Acts 2:33).

VI. THE POSSESSION BY JESUS OF A PEOPLE IN HEAVEN

This gives us assurance concerning our departed loved ones. They are "with Christ." It gives us an anticipation of a meeting which is to be. We too will stand with all "whom thou hast given me," according to Christ's prayer. Here is the picture of a great multitude — the saved of all ages — that go beyond our fondest hopes who shall be gathered in His presence. Christ did not labor and did not suffer in vain. All this should lead us to accept a place in the kingdom of heaven by acknowledging Christ's right to rule our lives.

VII. THE PRESERVATION FOR HEAVEN

On the ground of Christ's offering up of Himself upon the cross as a victim, and now on the ground of His intercession as high priest, we know that we are secure until He takes us to be with Him in heaven. In this assurance, we know that we have an inheritance incorruptible and undefiled that fadeth not away, reserved in heaven for us who are kept by the power of God unto salvation ready to be revealed at the last time (I Pet. 1:6).

7

JESUS' TEACHING ON PRAYER

SATURDAY — THIRTY-SECOND DAY

TEXT: Luke 11:1. "Lord, teach us to pray, as John also taught his disciples."
SCRIPTURE: Luke 11:1-13

Our text is a plea from those who know not how to pray, and the chapter constitutes the largest section on prayer in the Bible. There are other sections such as II Chronicles 6, John 17 and Daniel 9, but this is the most prolific source of knowledge of prayer we have in the Bible.

A. THE CRY IN A CRITICAL TIME OF NEED

This text is an expression of the age-old feeling of dependence and of the need to know how to pray. It expresses the aspiration for know-how in this all-important practice. It is a desire for a sense of accomplishment, for a victorious prayer life, for getting through to God. It expresses a desire to get answers when we pray, to enjoy fellowship with God, to be faithful in prayer, to have a burden of prayer and to be able to express oneself in prayer. Attention to this need was given by Jesus and attention to it ought to be given by those who teach in the church.

B. THE CONTRASTS OF JESUS' PRAYING WITH OUR PRAYING

Most Christians pray in a lifeless, weak, easy, lethargic and moribund way. Against this, the Bible contrasts Jesus as praying with strong crying and tears (Heb. 5:7, 8). If Jesus is too high for us in example, let us consider Elijah at Carmel, Jacob at Peniel, Hannah at Shiloh, Abraham at Mamre, the disciples at Pentecost. Our conclusion must be that something is wrong with our praying.

C. THE CONVICTION THAT WE OUGHT TO BE TAUGHT BY JESUS IN THIS MATTER

We are as one with the disciples who cried, "Lord, teach us to pray." Do you really mean it? Do you want to pray? Then listen to the principles, precepts and promises of this most concentrated teaching on prayer in the Bible. It all comes from the Master Himself, in fact, the whole subject arose because of His own prayer life which was an example. Let us not forget that Christ is not only Saviour but is an example for us (I Pet. 2:21).

I. THE PRACTICE OF PRAYER

We read, "As he was praying in a certain place, when he ceased. . . ." This describes the place of prayer, the practice of prayer and the personal need of prayer.

A. THE PLACE OF PRAYER

The place of prayer is a necessity and without it, it is difficult to pray. Since Jesus had no home, He made His places of prayer in a garden, on a mountain or at the side of a lake. Hence, He had to pray in the early morning, or late at night, or as high up on a mountain as it was accessible, sometimes with His disciples on guard to guarantee privacy. The disciples apparently always knew where to find Him when He was in prayer. Even Judas at the time of the betrayal led the soldiers and priests to Gethsemane, the place of prayer. Do people ever think of a particular place when they want you, knowing that you are at prayer? Jesus had no shame, no fear that someone might overhear, and no hiding of His prayer life. It is true that if we pray in secret, we shall be rewarded openly. But we are not to pray so secretly that no one ever knows that we pray. Our prayer practice may have a mighty influence upon our family and even upon others.

B. THE PRACTICE OF PRAYER

Jesus left us an example of the faithful practice of prayer. He arose a great while before day and went out into a solitary place and prayed (Mark 1:35). He withdrew Himself into the wilderness and prayed (Luke 5:16). He went into a mountain to pray (Matt. 14:23; Mark 6:46). He prayed all night (Luke 6:12). He was alone praying when Peter made his confession of

His deity (Luke 9:18; Matt. 16:13). He was praying when His countenance was changed in the transfiguration (Luke 9:29; Matt. 17:2). He prayed for His disciples on Solomon's Porch (John 17). He prayed in Gethsemane (Matt. 26:36, 39). He prayed on Calvary (Heb. 5:7). Such an example should stimulate us as Christians to the practice of prayer.

C. THE PERSONAL NEED OF PRAYER

All this praying on the part of Jesus was consistent to His being filled with the Holy Spirit (John 3:34) and with His being the second Person of the Trinity in His humiliation. The true human nature of Jesus necessitated prayer. How much more then should we need such hours of prayer.

Prayer sustained the Lord Jesus Christ who was tempted in all points like as we are. It refreshed Him after He gave of His strength to the multitudes. It enabled Him to walk on the sea and still the waves. It calmed Him in the face of the scribes' opposition. It transformed Him personally as He prayed. It gave Him wisdom to meet difficult situations, and it instilled peace in Him when He faced death after His Gethsemane struggle.

This was the reason for the disciples' request when they said, "Teach us to pray." They saw that the great moments in His life were connected with prayer. They realized that He prayed regularly with nothing interfering. They knew that this was contrary to their nature and that they must be taught or disciplined if they would pray.

II. THE PATTERN

In response to their request, the Lord Jesus gave unto them the perfect pattern of prayer, which is commonly known as the Lord's Prayer. According to historical criticism, both the record of the prayer given in Luke and in Matthew end without the doxology. The doxology appears, however, in many of the ancient versions and is in complete accord with the spirit of prayer, so we need have no hesitancy in using it.

A. THE PERFECT PRAYER

This prayer was delivered to Jesus' disciples to pray. It was not to be prayed as a vain repetition but as a model, or form, or pattern of prayer. No one can form a more perfect prayer than this. Hence, it merits profound study if one would be expert in prayer. It may be divided into three sections: the invocation or address, the petitions, and the ascription or doxology. The earliest manuscripts make the ascription a gloss, but it is quite generally used in the churches. Those who doubt the validity of the petitions of the Lord's Prayer in the era of grace are wrongly dividing the Word of truth. This prayer is not a legal prayer. It is a prayer to be prayed by Christ's disciples.

B. THE PETITIONS

The petitions of the Lord's Prayer may be divided into three and four; three representing the Trinity, four representing the world, and the union of them effectuating the reconciliation of the world. Everything is involved here for which we may pray. The sevenfold request involves the hallowing of the name of deity, the prayer for the rule of Christ and of God now, for the coming of the kingdom in power and glory, for the will of God to be done on earth as it is in heaven through the working of the Holy Ghost and the willing of the will of God, for the granting of material bread as meeting our mundane needs both spiritual and material, for the forgiveness of our debts because we are still sinners and need a sense of sorrow over them, realizing that our justification does not rest on our forgiving spirit, but our filial spirit does, for guidance against our proneness to fall into temptation and our susceptibility to weakness, and finally for deliverance from evil, the escape from which lies in Christ, His cross and His Spirit.

C. THE PEOPLE WHO PRAY THIS PRAYER

The disciples of Christ, the Church, the redeemed, the followers of Christ are to pray this prayer. If you do not know how to pray, begin here and follow this pattern of prayer. If you have prayed all your life, you may end here. Always guard against the danger of vain repetition, of speaking "Pater Nosters," of thinking you will be heard for your much speaking.

III. THE PRESSURES OF PRAYER

Christ then gave the illustration of the importunate friend (Luke 11:5-8).

A. THE PRESSURE OF NEED

Here it was for bread, for material, tangible substance. Our need may be physical, material, spiritual, social, intellectual, but when it comes, it exerts a terrific pressure on us. Some people break under those pressures. Others find a way of rolling them over on Jesus and letting Him carry them. The time that the need came was midnight. It was a most unexpected emergency. One can never know when the pressure of need will come upon him. How wonderful it is to be able to go to Christ in such an hour, to find grace at the throne of prayer. The place of your need may be your home, your life, your business, but when it arises, be sure to know where to go.

B. THE PRESSURE OF FRIENDSHIP

How happy that this individual could go to a friend and say, "Lend me . . . for a friend is come." This friend was in a mediating position. He found himself between one who had not and one who had. He was the only link between the two. His friendship with both obligated him. Thus it is that a Christian is in a mediating position between those whom he serves, such as the congregation, the heathen, the world, and Christ who is the source of every blessing. Many have no access to God, but they come to him, and he has the great privilege of mediating spiritual food, comfort and direction from God to others.

C. THE PRESSURE OF PERSISTENCE

The emphasis here is not that the friend will not give on the ground of his friendship, but that he will much more give because of his urgency and his pressure. Thus the Bible speaks of the necessity of fervency, urgency and intensity in this matter of prayer. Witness Elijah. Such persistence is rewarded (James 5:16).

IV. THE PROGRESSION IN PRAYER

Then Jesus presented the promise of Luke 11:8, 9 in a threefold way. He said, "Ask . . . seek . . . knock."

A. ASK IN ACCORDANCE WITH CONDITIONS

The conditions of asking are faith (Mark 11:24; Matt. 21:22; Matt. 7:8-11), agreement (Matt. 18:19, 20; John 14:15) and submission or abiding in Christ (John 15:7, 16).

B. SEEK THE OBSTACLE TO ANSWERED PRAYER

If prayer answers are suspended, seek the reason (James 4:1-4; I Pet. 3:7). Our prayers may be hindered by many things. Sin will effectively block prayer. Seek it out, confess it and break with it.

C. KNOCK IN PERSEVERANCE

When some people ask and do not receive, they grow cold. Instead, Jesus said be bold, claim the promises, storm the gates of heaven and lay hold of the horns of the altar. Let your knocking be with tears, with pleading, with promises. Be like Jacob at Peniel and the answers will come.

V. THE PARABLE OF PRAYER

Thus Jesus in Luke 11:11-13 gives a comparison between the willingness of a heavenly Father to give good things to His children and the willingness of a loving earthly father to give good things to his children who ask him. Ask for the highest. Ask for the Holy Spirit. And with the Holy Spirit you will get all good things.

AT THE CROSS OF CHRIST

AT THE CROSS OF CHRIST

Introduction

Since the cross of Christ occupies more space than any other single subject in the four Gospels, we inevitably return with a second weekly series to the cross. Lent, Holy Week and Easter should center on the cross and terminate in the resurrection. Calvary and the purpose of Calvary should be the undertones of all Lenten preaching.

The personalities centered around the cross hold permanent interest to us. They form a mirror in which we may see ourselves as those who are spectators, enemies, curious, indifferent, friends, sympathizers, and worshippers at that cross. The attitudes of these persons reveal every possible attitude toward Jesus and toward Calvary.

It may easily be seen that the cross divides just as it unites. Christian people should find themselves united at the foot of Calvary in affirmation of the blessed faith of a Saviour who redeems. Christians also should find themselves separated from those who do not believe, who hate, who repudiate, who attack, who ridicule or who indict Calvary. The preacher, as a psychologist, may find ample subjects to present Christian truths through biographical preaching at its best in the passion narratives. We merely make suggestions, believing that a vast reservoir of material may easily be tapped by the sincere student.

1

THE SIGNIFICANCE OF THE CROSS

Text: John 12:32. "And I, if I be lifted up from the earth, will draw all men unto me."

Scripture: John 12:20-36

At the time of the last Passover of Jesus' life, certain Greeks came to Jerusalem to the feast and said, "We would see Jesus." They were pagans who had become God-fearers and were worshipping at Jerusalem. They were interested in Jesus, they desired to see Him, to evaluate Him and to know Him. They had heard of His teaching, His works, His person, and His triumphal entry. When they came to the disciples, Philip and Andrew brought them to Jesus who told them of His cross, of His death and the termination of His earthly ministry. Apparently, He considered His crucifixion the most significant fact to declare unto them. So it must be to every person who would evaluate Jesus today. If you would see Jesus, if you would understand Him, it must be through the cross.

A. Foretelling His own death

The only ground on which these Greeks could approach Him, could understand Him and could share His work was through Calvary. The Gentiles are still aliens to the commonwealth of God and strangers to His promises. They are made nigh only through the blood of the cross. The ultimate victory of Calvary was suggested by the coming of these Greeks. They represented the masses from the nations of the world who would believe. Only a few of the Jews accepted Him, but countless masses of the Gentiles have believed (Isa. 53:11).

He stated the principle unto them, "Except a corn of wheat fall into the ground and die, it abideth alone: but if it die, it bringeth forth much fruit." The practice of this principle was

"He that loveth his life shall lose it; and he that hateth his life in this world shall keep it unto life eternal." And the pattern was given in His own experience, for He said, "And I, if I be lifted up from the earth, will draw all men unto me." All this was connected with the judgment of this world and the prince of this world.

B. FOREORDAINED OF GOD

The crucifixion was a deed of rebellion of wicked men who with devilish ingenuity expressed their antipathy, hatred and rejection of Christ. Peter said, "Him ye have taken, and by wicked hands have crucified and slain." This displayed the depth of human depravity, iniquity and evil in the crucifying of a man so good, noble, kind, true and humble. He was righteousness incarnate, but men did not want Him. Nevertheless, all this was determined by the divine wisdom and love so as to turn this evil of men into an atonement for those who crucified Him. He returned good for evil, love for hate, forgiveness for insolence. God overruled the worst that man could do for his own good.

C. FOUNDATION FACT OF REDEMPTION

Many facts about Christ are true and necessary, such as His deity, His virgin birth, His sinlessness, His miracles, His resurrection, but none of these can be called the center point of redemption. When we consider the imperative condition of salvation, we are brought face to face with the significance of the cross. It is the heart of all that God has done for us (Gal. 6:14). We may preach about the good life, about the Christian revelation on God, about eternal life, about the forgiveness of sins, but if one does not preach the cross, he is not preaching the gospel (I Cor. 1:23; I Cor. 2:2).

I. THE SIGNIFICANCE OF THE CROSS IN CHRISTIAN REVELATION

A. THE PLACE OF DIVINE REVELATION

1. In the law

We have above stated the principle of the cross involved in the law. The Lord decreed that the shed blood of animals was given by divine appointment to be used as an atonement for sin, to effect expiation and cleansing. The blood was given as a means of atonement for the soul (Lev. 17:11). This blood could not be shed by any except through divine permission (Gen. 9:9; Deut. 19:11-13). When shed, the blood covered sin and made expiation until Christ should come, whose death would take away the guilt of sin (Gen. 3:15; Heb. 9:22; Rom. 3:25). Such a substitute life was laid down in expiation and had the value to cover but not to remove sin. It was symbolic of the great sacrifice in the shedding of the blood of Christ on the cross for man. The great ritual of this atonement occurred on what was called the Day of Atonement (Lev. 16). Yet this ritual was fulfilled and abrogated by the full atonement. Thus the veil of the temple was rent from top to bottom, the way into the Holiest of All was opened, the remedy for sin had been offered in the cross of Christ.

2. In the prophets (I Pet. 1:10)

The prophets had difficulty with this thought of a suffering Messiah, and yet they found ample teaching concerning the necessity of His sufferings. A brief glimpse at Psalms 22 and 69, Isaiah 53, Daniel 9:26, Zechariah 11:11-13 and 13:6, 7 will give ample evidence of the presence of this prophecy of suffering in the prophets. Even the Lord used these to prove His identification with the Messiah to His own disciples (Luke 24:26, 27).

3. In the Gospels

Here we see the importance of the cross by the fact that at least one-fourth of the Gospels is given to the passion of our Lord. The event was interpreted by Him so as to infuse the proper meaning in His own death (Matt. 20:28; John 12:24, 3:12; Matt. 16:22). When this suffering and death was united with His resurrection, it constituted the gospel (I Cor. 15:1-3). Thus He was the innocent lamb (John 1:29) who became sin (II Cor. 5:21; I Pet. 2:24) under the wrath of God (Gal. 3:13) and endured the curse of hell in our place (Eph. 4:12; Heb. 2:14).

B. THE PURPOSE IN REVELATION

The cross exhibits God's righteousness and holiness. God did not spare His own Son (Rom. 8:32). He spared many before Him, both individuals and nations (Rom. 1:18), but not His own Son Christ. God's full judgment on sin fell upon Christ.

All that holiness could do was done to sin in Christ as He became sin for us. God need never again visit His wrath upon men because His holiness is satisfied by this infinite atonement. Simultaneously, it exhibited love and mercy. This act of giving His only begotten Son demonstrated the attribute of divine mercy which initiated our redemption. Love found a way. It went deeper than all our sin. Simultaneously, it displayed wisdom. No man would have invented such a means of salvation. Man always leans to works, but God's wisdom provided One good enough and worthy enough to pay the price of sin.

C. THE POWER OF THIS REVELATION

The preaching of the cross has power. It is a declaration of the riches of God's grace offering forgiveness, regeneration and inheritance in heaven. This is a message sufficient to enkindle the enthusiasm of all. Thus it moves to repentance and faith. It is strange how the thoughts of what our sin did to a God who thus loved, suffered and redeemed moves the hearts of men. The preaching of the cross makes the sinner a new man by the cleansing of the blood of Christ, by the creative work of the Holy Spirit and by his changed status in justification. This preaching also motivates life, inspiring love and devotion in God's service.

II THE SIGNIFICANCE OF THE CROSS IN CHRISTIAN EXPERIENCE

There are three phases of the cross which the Christian must experience. No more and no less. The preaching of the cross must include all three.

A. SALVATION

The primary meaning of Calvary is that our salvation is provided through Jesus' death. An examination of the emphasis which Christ put upon the cross and the background of the Biblical exposition of its necessity and of the interpretation placed upon it by the epistles makes us realize that our faith in the substitutionary death of Christ brings us a declarative righteousness and opens to us the flow of regenerate life. Gratitude should inspire us for salvation provided.

B. SANCTIFICATION

He who is born again through faith in Jesus' crucifixion is

born crucified. He takes a position of identification with Christ on the cross, so that he is crucified to the world without and the world within. This results in the power of deliverance from all evil and the inner impulsion of the Holy Spirit to identify us with the life of Christ. This truth was presented in Romans 6-8.

C. SERVICE

The third principle represented by the cross is that of self-denial, surrender and service (John 12:25). Just as Christ left us this pattern of self-denying service, He expects us to practice it in order to be like Him. We too must take up our cross and follow Him.

III. THE SIGNIFICANCE OF THE CROSS IN HISTORY

A. RECONCILIATION OF GOD AND MAN

When Jesus Christ on the cross cried, "It is finished," it meant that men no longer have their sins imputed to them. God is reconciled, satisfied, and nothing can be added to the work which has been done. There is now a redemptive power in history. The harlot, the thief and the murderer may now be forgiven. Men are not lost because they are sinners, but are lost because they do not believe on Jesus Christ who satisfied divine justice. Mankind, therefore, must abandon its religion of works and merit and be accepted with God through Jesus Christ.

B. REDEMPTION OF THE CHURCH

The cross made possible the Church of Jesus Christ. From Calvary, came the birth, the growth and the witness of the Church. Christ loved the Church and washed it with His own blood; He constituted it His body. The conquest and victory of the Church are due to the presentation of the truth of Calvary.

C. RENEWAL OF THE WORLD

By Calvary, all things are reconciled to God. This includes nature (Rom. 8:23), animals (Isa. 11:6, 7) and the heavens and the earth (II Pet. 3:10).

CONCLUSION

The significance of the cross is that it separates men from sin and the saved from the lost. The cross is God's means of salvation of the lost.

2

GAMBLERS AT THE CROSS

MONDAY — THIRTY-FOURTH DAY

TEXT: Matthew 27:35. "And they crucified him, and parted his garments, casting lots: that it might be fulfilled which was spoken by the prophet, They parted my garments among them, and upon my vesture did they cast lots."

SCRIPTURE: Matthew 27:35-44

Gambling is one of the most universal vices of men. Gambling today supports syndicated crime in America. It bleeds at least fifteen billion dollars a year from the income of the nation. Men gambled at the cross.

A. GAMBLING AS A PRACTICE

Playing games of chance is as old as history. Records of gambling exist in the earliest writings of man. The culpability of gambling lies in its perversion of the holy. In the pre-Christian era, the will of God was known by the lot, and the casting of a lot for the sake of playing games of chance is a perversion of divine sovereignty. It means that one exchanges chance for providence and parodies the precious trust in God. A gambling attitude soon becomes a habit and takes man into bondage.

B. GAMBLING AT A TRAGEDY

These soldiers had just crucified Jesus. The Jewish nation had just sold its birthright and repudiated its Messiah. Then they gambled. Jesus had been brought to Golgotha after being scourged and mocked, which had produced both physical and mental pain. He had fallen in the carrying of His cross due to weakness from scourging. When they reached the place of the skull, the point of execution for criminals, He was well nigh exhausted. There they crucified Him, driving the nails into His hands and feet and transfixing the cross between heaven and earth. Dreadful above all punishments was crucifixion. Yet, in the midst of it, the Lord Jesus prayed for their forgiveness because they were merely fulfilling their duty and they had no intimation of the consequences of their deed. They had already put His title upon the cross written through the malice of Pilate, "Jesus of Nazareth the King of the Jews." They wrote the title in three languages so that they might tell the story to the world. Then there was little for them to appropriate as executioners but His own clothing, so they sat down to gamble over this.

C. Gambling an insult to God

Their irreverence in gambling and the incongruity of their casting dice over His clothing in the very presence of the incarnate God is impressive. Consider the One who is dying on the cross as a man, and then as the incarnate God. Perfect, sinless, majestic, mighty, victorious, yet there He hung as a criminal, and they were totally indifferent to Him. Thus many even today are indifferent toward God in human suffering.

I. THE OBJECT FOR WHICH THEY GAMBLED

They said of Christ's garment, "Let us not rend it, but cast lots for it, whose it shall be." It was a seamless robe, a peasant's outer garment and of little value, but it was all that He left.

A. They stripped Christ of His garments

Like Joseph was stripped of his garments when sold into slavery, so Christ when He would flee this evil world, left His garments in their hands. It is interesting that He left no riches, no houses, no lands and no accumulation, but only His garments. When Adam sinned, God clothed him with the skins of an animal to take away his nakedness. But now men took away the clothing of the second Adam that His shame and nakedness might appear.

B. These garments are types of spiritual clothing He gives us to cover our nakedness

Paul tells us to put on Christ, and Christ Himself says, "Buy of me white raiment." From the hem of that garment, virtue had gone forth to heal wounded lives. The woman with an infirmity of twelve years had wanted to touch Him but was able only to touch the hem of His garment and she was healed. We are not to think that there was any virtue in the garment itself but only as it lifted a person's faith to Christ Himself. It is mentioned by all four evangelists, and apparently it is worthy of careful notice.

Who made this garment? His own mother? or Salome? or Mary Magdalene, or Mary of Bethany? It was homemade or it would have been in two parts, but this was a seamless robe. The garments of Christ were divided among the four soldiers, but each desired His coat. Was it a coat of value like Joseph's coat of many colors? If it had no value, why would they want it? For this seamless robe, they agreed to throw the dice.

C. What the robe for which they gambled represents

The fathers uniformly considered this robe to represent the Church — one unit throughout. They believed that the universal Church was one, that the people of God are united, knit together and an entire whole. When Christ was transfigured on the mountain, this robe glowed. So does the Church when it glorifies Christ. Others have thought that the robe represented the righteousness of Christ. In the Old Testament, the rending of a garment represented the dividing of a kingdom. Abijah took his own new garment and tore it into twelve parts, giving ten parts to Jeroboam to symbolize that the kingdom was rent from the house of David and ten parts were given to Jeroboam. Thus also Saul tore Samuel's garment, and Samuel interpreted it as meaning that the kingdom was rent from Saul. When blasphemy was performed, the High Priest usually rent his garment before judgment was pronounced, but Christ's garment was not rent. When Christ died, the veil of the temple was rent from top to bottom, but not the robe of Christ. The robe had passed into the ownership of these Gentiles.

II. THE ATTITUDE OF GAMBLING INDIFFERENCE

A. Gambling in the face of what occurred on Calvary

Only hardened men, we think, could gamble in the face of the sufferings of the Lord Jesus Christ. But these soldiers had witnessed and endured many hardships, they had seen many people suffer, and they had become impervious to it. Even in the wars of our own generation, men became impervious to the sufferings of the masses. The cheapness of human life inures men to danger, suffering, poverty and need. After all, the birds sang, the flowers bloomed and nature still put forth life while Christ was dying. Too often, it seems, the universe is impervious to our sufferings. Ought we then to accept chance as the ultimate of life or is order, law and providence final? What does reason say about these things?

B. GAMBLING PRACTICES TODAY WITH ETERNITY BUT A STEP AWAY

Thus the gospel is offered now — the one chance to be saved — yet men are willing to miss it. A mighty occurrence was taking place on that cross. The greatest transaction was transpiring in the history of the world, but the soldiers were missing it. That body was being broken for the sins of the world. People in all ages have gambled and played while the world was being crucified. They have frittered away their time on nonessentials while humanity suffers. They have fiddled while Rome burned. Men gamble with eternal life every day. They say, "I'll take my chances." When they should have certainty, they accept chance. Never did a generation of greater gamblers exist than today.

C. GAMBLING IN FULFILLMENT OF SCRIPTURE

God knew what these soldiers would do, and He foretold it in the Scripture but He did not stop it. He also will not stop you. The part of these soldiers was described in Psalm 22, written a thousand years before the event. In this alone we have a great proof of inspiration, and an intimate and detailed description of Calvary. God's prophecies stand. Many of them are fulfilled and many will be fulfilled, yet the world is utterly indifferent to prophecy today and the sovereignty of God which stands back of those prophecies. God has control of the world, and He is preparing it for the fulfillment of prophecy in the coming of the kingdom. Which attitude is yours? Do you trust to good providence or rely upon fortuitous caprice?

III. THE RESULT OF GAMBLING — CALLOUSNESS

The Scripture then tells us, "And sitting down they watched him there."

A. THEY HAD DONE WHAT CAUSED HIS DEATH, AND ALL OF ANY INTEREST WAS OVER

Now they looked on in indifference. They had no emotion over what the Lord Jesus suffered. They were utterly blind to what was really transpiring. They were so hardened by this attitude of life that they were unreached by the best that God could do. They were indifferent to the one event which could have changed their status from condemnation to justification, could give them eternal life, could transform their present existence.

B. THE WONDERS THEY SAW AS THE SCENE WORE ON

After their gambling, came darkness, earthquake, anxiety, fear and dread. Now their interest was aroused. Was it the interest of mere observation of spectators, of onlookers? Even in the presence of such supernatural phenomenon, they were unmoved and indifferent.

C. HOW AT LEAST ONE CAME TO BELIEVE

We have the record that the centurion who had controlled all this crucifixion proceeding finally came to the conclusion, "Truly this was the Son of God." Perhaps he had been the one who won the robe and was to carry it away. At least he had a conviction as to the character and nature of Jesus.

CONCLUSION: RESCUE FROM THE GAMBLING ATTITUDE

A great and good providence has permitted us gamblers to learn that a robe of righteousness is prepared for us to be given to us not by chance, but by sovereign grace through faith. If you see this truth, you can be delivered. Christ was unclothed that we might be clothed. He went from this world, but He left with us righteousness and a Church. That robe is now transformed from an execution mantle to a wedding garment of His people, namely, the righteousness He gives.

3

SPECTATORS AT THE CROSS

TUESDAY — THIRTY-FIFTH DAY

TEXT: Luke 23:35. "And the people stood beholding."
Matthew 27:36. "And sitting down they watched him there."
Matthew 27:39. "And they that passed by."
SCRIPTURE: Matthew 27:32-40

Man possesses a sense of curiosity. This may be seen in a child who asks seemingly embarrassing questions or a scientist who faces nature with prying questions. Curiosity may be a very good characteristic or a morbid characteristic.

A. A DISPOSITION PRYING INTO THE STRANGE

Whenever a tragedy in the form of an accident occurs, or a kidnapping, or a murder, the inquisitive nature of people often prevents efficient treatment of a victim or apprehension of a criminal. In a recent Brooklyn kidnapping, the letters and telephone calls from cranks actually prevented the solution of the crime. Charles Dickens protested the public executions in his day because of the morbid interest of the masses of people in the way people met death. Instead of helping to deter crime, it almost seemed to stimulate crime. Public interest will demand front-page coverage of such cases for months and far more important things are passed by with a mere paragraph. This displays idle curiosity, the attitude of spectators seeing a play or separated from the sorrows of life.

B. A DETESTABLE CHARACTERISTIC OF MANKIND

Luke tells us concerning the Athenians at the time of Paul's evangelization of Athens that they spent their time telling and hearing some new thing. Unfortunately, the Athenians were not the only ones who had such a disposition. The attitude of inquisitiveness into others' business is found among many people. This was one aspect of Calvary. Great crowds of people came out of curiosity to see how this miracle-worker, this man who claimed to be equal with God, this man who proclaimed Himself as a king would die under the authority of Rome.

C. A contrast of perspective

In modern writing, it has been popular to contrast the two perspectives of the balcony, which is that of the spectator, and of the road, which is that of the person of experience. There is a school of thinkers who declare that all truth must be understood in an existential way, that it is impossible to stand off from the experiences of life and to evaluate them. Others tell us that it is possible to either enter into the experiences of life or to stand off and view them as spectators. One may have one of these two views pertaining to life and it was possible in Jesus' day to take one of these views pertaining to the cross. The great masses of people round about Calvary were viewing it as one would view a parade from a balcony. They were examining the events with a detached curiosity which ultimately had no meaning to them personally.

I. COMMENDABLE CURIOSITY A BENEFICIAL THING

A. That which leads to discovery and knowledge

We read in the Scripture that "man sought out many inventions." Curiosity and the powers of observation constitute two of the basic characteristics necessary for a scientist. Man must dedicate himself to the pursuit of universal truth and this is carried on by the satisfaction of curiosity. Most commendable was Madam Curie's investigation of pitch blend which constituted the first step in the recovery of radium and the long process toward the mastery of the structure of the universe in atomic energy. Had Madam Curie had no curiosity concerning the radioactive element in pitch blend, radium probably would never have been discovered in our day. There are those who believe that knowledge itself comes from a trial and error method. It is curiosity plus the powers of combining, comparing and contrasting that gives us the grist for our mill of knowledge.

B. THAT WHICH LEARNS THE TRUTH AND ACTS UPON IT

To merely view all the world with life, struggle and truth as
a spectacle is vanity. It is one thing to dwell in a house by the
side of a road, but it is another thing when dwelling in that
house to be a friend to man, not merely to observe his struggles
along the road. One of the devastating aspects of the destructive
Nazi view of education was its "emancipation from objectivity"
so that science and investigation were instrumental to ulterior
ends. Truth is one and God is truth, although all truth is not
necessarily God. It is a commendable attribute to be willing to
act in accordance with the truth. The knowledge of truth must
be forged in the experiences of life.

C. THAT WHICH LOOKS TO CHRIST WITH INQUIRY AND WILLING-
NESS TO RECEIVE

An open mind is not one which allows truth and facts to
merely flow through it, but it is one which, in receiving facts,
retains them and which accepts the truth which it discovers.
Hence, there is a great difference between looking at Calvary
as a spectacle or as the greatest manifestation of truth of the
ages. The differences in our relationship to that truth make
pain, light and life to us. Thus those who stood at Calvary had
a condemnatory rather than a commendable curiosity.

II. CURIOSITY AT THE CROSS

A. THE CURIOUS ON GOLGOTHA

Calvary was something unusual, extravagant, odd, rare and
novel. Crucifixions occurred rather regularly under Roman dominion, but there was something unusual in this crucifixion due
to its connection with what these people already knew about
the Nazarene. He was no thief, or murderer, but a man who
went about doing good and who had been attested with the
credentials of the supernatural. This mysterious aspect caught
the imagination of the multitude, and they came to see how He
would die under suffering. Yet Calvary has always held the
curiosity of men throughout history, and those who have studied
it have often been conquered by the events of it.

B. THE CURIOUS ONES

The Scripture tells us of the crowds which followed the events
pertaining to Jesus' passion from the triumphal entry to

Golgotha. They were there when He cleansed the temple, when He upbraided the Pharisees, when He wept over Jerusalem, when He answered the questions of the Herodians, the Sadducees and the Pharisees, when He carried His cross along the Via Dolorosa. They had stood at the Gabbatha and heard Pilate say, *"Ecce homo,"* and now they were gathered at the cross to see His crucifixion. They wanted to see what would happen.

Then also there were the passersby who had merely heard about Him and now stopped, gaped, asked questions, read the inscription, wagged their heads and passed on. Perhaps there were some newcomers, some foreigners, some strangers who knew not of the things that had taken place at Jerusalem.

Then also there were the soldiers who sat down to watch after they had gambled over His clothing. To them, there was little difference externally between the crucifixion of Jesus and the crucifixion of other criminals. Yet they also sensed something mysterious here. If we should contrast this unconcern or this indifferent curiosity of men with the concern of angels at this spectacle, we would be appalled, for the angels knew that this was the Son of God, this was the Creator of the world, this was the Judge of mankind who was now being crucified at the hands of men, and they did not understand. Kierkegaard describes this difference in the figure of a professor who indifferently studies Calvary with curiosity and an apostle such as Paul to whom the cross was everything. It is the antithesis between a sympathetic understanding of Christ's sufferings and a detached curiosity in an historical event.

C. Detached curiosity as to the world's suffering today

Many people today may read of the massacres, the wars, the famines, the earthquakes with a similar disinterestedness which is almost brutal. They are curious but only idly so, mere spectators. An age is known by what it tolerates, by the things it gets used to — even horrible things. If we can gaze on suffering in a dog without doing something for him, we do not know Christ. Thus Emily Dickinson wrote,

> "If I can ease one heart the aching,
>   Or cool one pain,
>   Or help one fainting robin to his nest again,
> I shall not live in vain."

III. THE OBJECT OF CURIOSITY

A. WHAT WAS IT ON WHICH THEY GAZED?

Crucifixion was the most terrible kind of physical suffering possible. Any encyclopedia of religion and ethics will describe crucifixion, but here something more than physical suffering occurred. The picture of the suffering of Jesus on Calvary may be gleaned from His struggle in Gethsemane when the cross was placed before Him mentally. There with strong crying and tears He asked to be saved from it because of the contents of the cup of spiritual suffering which were to be drained by Him there. At first, we only see the pain accompanying Calvary, but then we see something of the meaning of Calvary. If pain were the only phase of it, we should honor the Penitentes of New Mexico and Colorado who so similarly scourge themselves and some of whom are crucified. The trouble with these spectators was that they saw nothing of the spiritual meaning of the external suffering.

B. WHAT THIS CRUCIFIXION MEANT

Some go beyond curiosity and see a demonstration of justice at the heart of the universe being exhibited in Calvary, but if that is all, then the universe is not on the side of justice. Some see in it an example of love in sacrifice, showing what must be done to meet sin. Some see moral persuasion in it in order to lead men to turn from sin. But Paul and the apostles saw in Calvary the Son of God bearing our sins, dying in our place, making an atonement for us (II Cor. 5:21; Rom. 5:8; Heb. 12:13).

C. WHAT THEY COULD HAVE LEARNED HAD CURIOSITY LED THEM AS FAR AS THE THIEF

Had they seen, as the thief finally saw, that Jesus was dying for their sins, Calvary could have meant their redemption. It would have led them to the act of repentance. They could have experienced forgiveness. They might have known the assurance of possessing eternal life, but this they did not see in their idle curiosity.

CONCLUSION: THE RESULT OF CURIOSITY AT THE CROSS

Such curiosity either brings salvation from sin or sin against the Holy Ghost (Heb. 6:4). There are curious ones today who may turn to Christian believers. They will act upon the new knowledge that they receive. The gospel asks you to look at Calvary, but it asks you to look in order that you may believe and live.

4

ENEMIES AT THE CROSS

WEDNESDAY — THIRTY-SIXTH DAY

TEXT: Matthew 27:41, 42. "Likewise also the chief priests mocking him, with the scribes and elders, said, He saved others; himself he cannot save."

SCRIPTURE: Matthew 27:39-44

Calvary bristled with a sense of antipathy and hostility. Always someone exists to travesty truth, caricature character and parody purity. It is impossible but that mockery should have been present at earth's most sacred hour. The record tells us that men mocked, laughed, derided, scoffed and railed on Jesus at Calvary.

A. THIS VERY ANTIPATHY AND OPPOSITION WAS PROPHETIC

By this opposition, Psalm 22 was fulfilled. Little did these people know that their banter and bestiality was ordained by God to His own glory. Out of the dreadful, brutal deeds of man, God's great architectural scheme of redemption was being reared. All this should be to His praise and glory. Through it, men should see the beauty of the divine plan which would include even the worst man could do for a high and holy purpose. Peter said, "Him, being delivered by the determinate counsel and foreknowledge of God, ye have taken, and by wicked hands have crucified and slain." The evil, guilt and responsibility were there, but God embraced them in a greater good.

B. THE OPPOSITION WAS AN EVIDENCE OF THE CRUCIAL CONFLICT BETWEEN LIGHT AND DARKNESS, GOOD AND EVIL, WHICH CONSTITUTES THE DRAMA OF THE AGES

We must ask, Is the struggle eternal, as the Zorastrians say, or did Jesus Christ win a victory here? Satan certainly inspired man to vent his hatred upon Christ. He was back of the leering,

211

laughing faces of prejudice, hatred and malice. Back of those characters was a greater force and power, as Jesus said to Pilate, "Thou couldest have no power at all against me, except it were given thee from above."

C. SOME PART OF THIS OPPOSITION WAS IGNORANCE

Men often do things in a heat out of ignorance, for which they are later sorry. At least some of this crowd must have been in the Palm Sunday crowd which had sung "Hosanna," unto Him. Surely, when Jesus said, "Father, forgive them; for they know not what they do," Jesus prayed for the soldiers and possibly for others who did their deeds in ignorance. Peter later ascribed their crucifixion of the Lord of glory to ignorance (Acts 3:17). Ignorance does an appalling work of brutality and wickedness in the world.

I. RECOGNIZING HIS ENEMIES

Were we to take inventory of the enemies of Jesus, we would find a considerable catalogue. Christ knew what was in man, and so He knew what was being displayed by each one of these.

A. THE CHIEF PRIESTS OR THE ECCLESIASTICAL AUTHORITY OF THE LAND

These were the opponents of Jesus from the very beginning (Matt. 9:3). Throughout His whole ministry, they were spying and protesting against Him. They were making tests of His attitude. One of the notable aspects of their opposition was over the Sabbath, which they had perverted (Matt. 12:2; John 9:16). Constantly they asked Him entangling questions seeking to entrap Him, and finally they themselves originated the intention to kill Him (John 11:56). These priests had all the evidence necessary concerning the nature of His person and work, but they resisted the truth. Hence, His terrible denunciation of them in Matthew 23. The constant tendency for ecclesiastical authority, tradition and routine is to oppose Christ at work today. This raises an interesting question. Is it ever possible to reform a church from within? The story of history has usually been to oppose this. New wine needs new bottles, and a new spiritual outburst of life needs a new organizational form.

B. THE RABBLE OR MULTITUDE

It is very hard to believe that those over whom He was so moved with compassion, whom He healed, whom He fed and whom He blessed should thus deride and mock Him on Calvary. Yet it is apparent through the narrative that they did. This raises the question, Can we trust the crowd? Can we believe in the common people? Woodrow Wilson's thesis was that we could believe in the people, and the people foresook him and he was broken by it. Does this mean that we should take skepticism as a way of life? Some think so. People follow whatever leaders they have. In Germany they followed Hitler, in Italy they followed Mussolini, in Spain they followed Franco, in Japan they followed Tojo. It is very easy to make the people the enemies of the right. The reason for this is ignorance as well as corruption.

C. THE SOLDIERS REPRESENTING THE AUTHORITY OF THE STATE

The state in itself is a good thing. It is the power established by God to restrain evil and violence in the earth. But in the hands of corrupt men like Pilate and Herod and later Nero, the state becomes a great enemy of right, and even of the Church. It is very easy for the state to violate conscience, to compel conformity, and to kill and hurt the person. A notable example of this is Martin Niemoller in Nazi Germany. Wherever statism is established, the individual is crushed.

D. THE BRIGANDS

These thieves personified wickedness. They were guilty of murder, robbery, adultery and other crimes. Such wickedness is always antithetic to the holiness of Christianity. The thieves on the cross felt this difference between Him and them. They said, "We indeed (suffer) justly; for we receive the due reward of our deeds: but this man hath done nothing amiss." Wherever corruption and organized evil appears, it is the deadly enemy of Christ.

E. SATAN

At the cross was the prince of darkness, the prince of this world, "the prince of evil," as Jesus called him. Satan had dogged the footsteps of Christ while He was in this world from His birth to His death. From Herod the Great's attempt to kill

Him when He was a baby, through the temptation in the wilderness, through Peter's suggestion that He abandon the cross, through Gethsemane, and now on Calvary, He faced Satan in conflict. Calvary, according to Jesus, was the judgment of Satan. It was His victory over Satan, and it was the rescue of the saved from Satan. Hence, we may be sure that this great enemy of Christ and of the redeemed was present at Calvary.

II. LISTENING TO HIS ENEMIES

A. THEIR MOCKERY

These enemies of Christ reproached Him with His mighty deeds of compassion, such as raising the dead. They said, "He saved others; himself he cannot save." They reviled His trust in God by saying, "He trusted in God; let him deliver him now, if he will have him: for he said, I am the Son of God." They ridiculed the saving act in which He was engaged. They said, "Let him save himself, if he be Christ, the chosen of God." They rejected Him as king, saying, "Let Christ the King of Israel descend now from the cross, that we may see and believe."

B. THE MEANING OF WHAT THEY SAID

There was truth in all their statements of ridicule. Even in their derision, they confessed to what He claimed and what He did. He was Saviour, He was Son of God, He was Christ, He was King and He was Messiah. There could be no better witness than this to what Jesus both claimed to be and was. Yet they made a false statement, for they said they would believe on Him if He demonstrated His power. He had done more than what they asked and He later even rose from the dead, but they would not believe. When men will not believe in the face of the best evidence, there is nothing more which we can do for them. Men must repent from this attitude as the thief did if they will be saved.

C. THE MODERN COUNTERPART OF THIS

The enemies of Christ are doing and saying the same things today. They ask, Where is God? Why doesn't God do something to save the just and the innocent? This is exactly the same problem which they faced in Jesus' day, and the cross is the clue to the answer. The mockers, scoffers and skeptics will look at present-day suffering and say, It proves there is no God. Because the world is turned from time to time into an inferno of hate and brutality by war does not prove that there is no God.

III. OVERCOMING HIS ENEMIES

A. HE SUBMITTED TO THEM

He then, as we now, could have met His enemies with fire, sword and hate, but He chose the bowed head. On the cross, He gave a complete example of His teaching concerning non-resistance of evil. To me this is the hardest aspect of the teaching of Christ. I can accept it among believers, but to meet the world in its force with a bowed head is most difficult. If there is an example to us as Christians in this, it would surely mean that we have to refuse to participate in vindicating ourselves at any point.

B. HE PRAYED FOR THEM

While these classes were doing their worst to Him by scourging, beating, spitting, reviling and crucifying, He prayed for them and asked for their forgiveness. He did more than pray for them. He died for them, at least for those in the group who later were to believe, like the priests (Acts 6:7). Many legions of angels could have been summoned by Him for deliverance, but then He would not have been the Saviour.

C. HE OVERCAME THEM

By Calvary, Christ overcame His greatest enemy and defeated him (John 12:31, 14:30). The cross was Satan's greatest attack upon Christ. The darkness was caused by his presence as he tried to black out the soul of Jesus. It was the culmination of conflict, curse and condemnation, and yet it became the means of Satan's defeat. By enduring and overcoming, Christ gave Satan the death blow (Rom. 16:20). He is forever defeated and is overcome. The sentence has been passed on him, and it will soon be executed. By this, even the lesser enemies were delivered from the great enemy.

CONCLUSION: MANY STILL TAKE POSITIONS WITH HIS ENEMIES' MOCKING

Some think that Rome, Jerusalem and the priestcraft are all gone, but the same attitudes persist. People still sit in the scorner's seat, but there are some who kiss the Son, who recognize that He gave a ransom for them, and that He delivered them from their greatest foe. Thus in humility, they bow and worship Him. The cross will reveal whether you are an enemy or a friend of Christ.

5

THIEVES AT THE CROSS

THURSDAY — THIRTY-SEVENTH DAY

TEXT: Luke 23:33. "There they crucified him, and the male-factors, one on the right hand, and the other on the left."
SCRIPTURE: Luke 23:33-43; Matthew 27:11-31

These thieves on the cross were representatives of mankind. They represent us in our corruptions, they represent us in our possible reactions to God's offer of salvation, and they represent the difference between the saved and the lost.

A. THE IMPENITENT THIEF

Tradition going back to the Gospel of Nicodemus calls the impenitent thief "Gestas." Both thieves were guilty of revolt against society and no doubt had been companions of Barabbas in robbery, murder, insurrection and plunder. Periodically, these wild groups would gather on the periphery of Judah's borders and would engage in their misdemeanors. Probably they were part of a larger wild group which was a constant problem unto the Romans.

There was justice in their awful punishment. They were to be executed because they had shed men's blood. Execution came as a result of a just trial and a condemnation under the authority of the government of the day. Scripture tells us that such government is to restrain evil and is representative of the authority of God. These thieves were to carry their crosses, they were to experience the same physical pain that Jesus experienced, and they were to die.

In the early hours of their crucifixion and suffering, both of them ridiculed Christ in the same terms as the Pharisees and others ridiculed Him. They said, "He saved others; let him save himself," and "If he be the King of Israel, let him now come

217

down from the cross, and we will believe him. He trusted in God; let him deliver him now." And Matthew says, "The thieves also, which were crucified with him, cast the same in his teeth." No doubt these thieves knew something of His teachings, of His claims and His actions during the three years of His ministry. They were hardened criminals and were suffering the just effects of their deeds.

B. The penitent thief

A similar tradition calls the penitent thief "Dumas." As the time passed while they were hanging upon the cross, a change came over Dumas. He stopped his jeering; he did some serious thinking; and finally, when his companion railed on Christ saying, "If thou be Christ, save thyself and us," he rebuked his companion and said, "Dost not thou fear God, seeing thou art in the same condemnation? And we indeed justly; for we receive the due reward for our deeds: but this man hath done nothing amiss." His was a powerful testimony to the sinlessness of the Lord Jesus Christ.

Suddenly he cried out from his cross to Jesus hanging on the center cross, "Lord, remember me when thou comest into thy kingdom." One wonders what caused the change in the life of this penitent thief. Was it pain? Pain sometimes works marvels in the lives of people, and yet it hardens some and softens others. Many are embittered by pain. This is what pain did to the first thief, but to the second thief it brought mellowing.

Was it the prayer that Jesus prayed for those who crucified Him? We have evidence that Stephen's prayer, that the Lord would not lay to the charge of those who stoned him their sin, lodged in Paul's mind and became a prick in his conscience. Why could this same process not have worked more quickly here?

Was it Jesus' reference to His mother? Did this bring back all that was tender and good in the man's youth to his memory? Was he convicted because of this reference? Had he been brought up in a godly home?

Was it a look from Christ? Remember how the look of Christ made Matthew leave his receipt of customs, how it transformed Zaccheus and how it brought Peter to repentance. It was a look from Christ that even threw the mob backwards in the garden.

Just a look from Jesus may have done something to this thief which changed his life.

Or was it the gathering darkness that was an intimation of the coming judgment when men must stand before the throne of God and answer for their deeds? The imminence of death with its great darkness has a tremendous power to turn men to Christ.

Whatever the reason, this thief turned his attention to Jesus in repentance, contrition and faith. He confessed that he was suffering justly, that he was a sinner, that Jesus was Lord, that He was King of a spiritual kingdom, that He had the power to save him. Here is an instance of a man "justified by faith" without the works of the law. He is certainly the first trophy of the cross and the apocryphal gospels picture him as being the first to enter the gates of heaven leading Adam, Noah, Abraham, Moses, Elijah and the long roster of the saints.

C. THE THIRD THIEF

One wonders what had happened to Barabbas who also had been appointed to crucifixion but who, at the last minute, had received his reprieve from Pilate because of the custom to release a prisoner to the Jews at the Passover. He was a far more famous criminal than the two who were crucified, but by a strange twist of fate, the people had demanded his release instead of the release of Jesus when Pilate had presented them their opportunity.

Barabbas' name means "son of a rabbi." He was an insurrectionist, a murderer and a robber, and he was worthy of death on at least two points. It had been Pilate's hope that when this man was contrasted with Jesus, the Jews would have asked for the release of Jesus, but instead they chose Barabbas. One wonders if Barabbas was in the crowd, obscured and swallowed up, but intently watching One suffer in his place along with his erstwhile companions in evil. If so, there is no better illustration of the substitutionary work of Christ for us than is given in the deliverance of Barabbas and the death of Jesus. It may be that he saw and listened to Christ with a faith like the penitent thief, or he may have gone back to his old companions of sin, but it is hard to think so. He must have taken one of these two ways, for there is no middle ground.

I. THE AUTHORITY OF CHRIST TO REDEEM

To this repentant thief, the Lord Jesus answered, "Verily I say unto thee, Today shalt thou be with me in paradise." This is the divine answer to a repentant sinner. God manifests mercy. Never did Jesus turn one away. This was a cup of solace which Christ did not reject on the cross as He did the cup of narcotic, but it was a balm to His soul. The words of the thief revealing his change deadened the static of the multitude. It made clear to Him the music of heaven. From this incident we may step to the division of the whole of humanity into two classes by their attitude toward Christ.

Well might we ask as the Pharisees did, "Who is this that forgiveth sins?" The answer is Jesus Christ, the Lord, who won this right to forgive sins through His work on Calvary.

A. THE RIGHT TO FORGIVE A SINNER SUCH AS THE THIEF RESTS IN THE WORK ACCOMPLISHED BY THE LORD ON THE CROSS

Now He has the power to open the gates of life to human wrecks who otherwise could never enter. This thief did not steal heaven, or pick the gate of heaven as one has said. He had the gate opened by One who had the right to open it, who possessed the keys. The meaning of Calvary is that the divine Son became our substitute. His blood was shed for us. He came to save us from the guilt of our sin.

B. WHAT HE WILL REDEEM

There is no sin too low, too hideous or too great for Christ to forgive. He can redeem us from dishonesty and greed as He did Zaccheus, from impurity as He did the harlot in the Pharisee's home, from disloyalty as He did Matthew, from instability as He did Peter, and from all manner of sin.

C. HOW HE REDEEMED MEN

This redemption was wrought by finishing the work God gave Him to do. That work was yielding a perfect obedience to the will of God in fulfillment of the law and taking the penalty of sin, or of the broken law. He made a satisfaction as our substitute, and His sufferings were sufficient to reconcile us to God. His sufferings were sufficient for the redemption of the world.

II. THE CONDITION OF REDEMPTION

A. TRUE REPENTANCE TOWARD GOD

The one condition manifested by this thief was repentance or a change of mind. It is interesting to note that repentance is not remorse or a tendency to despair. It involves a fear of God, for the thief said, "Dost not thou fear God?"; a sense of condemnation for sin, for he said, "Thou art in the same condemnation"; a willingness to confess, "and we justly"; and a recognition that he was suffering the consequences of his own evil, "we receive the due reward of our deeds." Here was a man who had violated God's law and he knew it, but he turned in repentance and contrition.

B. FAITH TOWARD GOD

This penitent thief recognized the validity of Christ's claims. He said, "This man hath done nothing amiss." He believed Him to be the Messiah or the King, for he adds, "Lord, remember me when thou comest into thy kingdom." This took a tremendous courage on the part of the thief, for in addition to his physical pain, he would then necessarily become the butt of the ridicule and the attack of his fellow in sin and also of the masses that were round about the cross. His, however, was a plea of mercy, for he knew that he needed divine help.

III. THE ESSENCE OF REDEMPTION

A. THE PROMISE TO THE THIEF OF LIFE AFTER DEATH

In response, the Lord Jesus promised the thief that that day he would be in paradise or heaven. Nothing that Jesus would do for him in this world could make any difference to him. The only thing now which counted was heaven. So it is with countless other people in the world. The possession of an inheritance in heaven is the greatest gift that we can receive.

B. HEAVEN OR PARADISE

Christ promised that the thief would be "with me." Wherever Jesus is is heaven. When Paul expressed his desire to go to heaven, it was "to depart and be with Christ." The song says, "Where Jesus is 'tis heaven to me." Today, wherever Christ is, that thief is. Heaven can be on earth if Christ is with you, but heaven is also a place to which Jesus took the repentant thief.

C. WHEN WE GO TO HEAVEN

Jesus said, "Today." He did not refer to a long future time at the resurrection of the body, but now. The time of redemption is now. We may be saved now, and if we depart this world, we will go to be with Christ in heaven now. There are those who would tell us that the soul sleeps until the day of the resurrection. This cannot be justified from the Bible either from this text, or from Philippians 1:21-23, or II Corinthians 5:1-9. The Bible leaves no doubt that to be with Christ is to be in heaven.

CONCLUSION

The thieves stand as two classes — one on the right and one on the left of Christ, as the sheep and the goats. Thus Christ will divide all sinners in this world into the saved and the lost. Those who are saved will be saved because they have believed in Christ and have accepted His mercy. Those who are lost will be lost because they have rejected Jesus Christ. We may be saved as the penitent thief was saved.

6

GOD AT THE CROSS

FRIDAY — THIRTY-EIGHTH DAY

TEXT: Matthew 27:54. "Truly this was the Son of God."
SCRIPTURE: Matthew 27:45-54

Our text is the conclusion of the centurion when the crucifixion was over. The curiosity of this soldier resulted in his conviction. The man who died on the center cross was God's Son.

A. THREE PERSONS OF THE TRINITY WERE AT CALVARY

James A. Francis says, "All there is of God is in the Father; all that was ever seen of God is in the Son; all that was ever felt of God was in the Spirit." Jesus addressed the Father as "Thou," and He commended His spirit into the Father's hands. It is the Trinity which puts meaning into Calvary. Otherwise Calvary would only be a martyr's death of a hero. God suffered on the cross, but in a more direct and real way than He suffers in our suffering. God the Son was in Jesus on Calvary.

B. THE PERSONALITY OF GOD HAS BEEN QUESTIONED AND DENIED

Einstein echoed the view of Renan, Darwin and Huxley when he said, "In this struggle for the ethical good, teachers of religion must have the stature to give up the doctrine of a personal God — that is, give up the source of fear and hope." G. Studdart Kennedy, the King's bishop following World War II, raised this question of the existence of God in the presence of such universal suffering as was seen in the war. Ernest Fremont Title summarized an impersonal god as "objectified desires and thoughts in a blind universe." This he ridiculed by raising the question of how we could quote the Twenty-third Psalm and the Lord's Prayer without a personal God. There can be no peace from such a conception.

C. THE KIND OF GOD WE BEHOLD IN LOOKING AT THE CROSS

Calvary reveals a concept of God thoroughly consistent with the entire Biblical revelation of God. It is fully harmonious with what our moral sense tells us God must be, both just and merciful. In the death of Jesus Christ, He demonstrated and exhibited His justice. In the atonement made by Christ, He demonstrated and exhibited His mercy. This revelation of God is sufficient to meet the need of our sin-burdened hearts.

I. A SUFFERING GOD

A. IF GOD EVER WAS ANYWHERE, HE WAS IN JESUS

As Jesus said, "He that hath seen me hath seen the Father." In Jesus, men saw God and walked with God. They saw the wonders which He did, His omnipotence in the realm of nature as He controlled humanity, demons, elements and death. They saw His compassion in His deeds of mercy to publicans, harlots, sick, strangers and all who came. They listened to teaching which was beyond anything that had ever been given by man. They concluded, "Never man spake like this man." They listened to the Sermon on the Mount, chapter 14 of John, the message on Olivet contained in Matthew 24, and they knew they were in touch with ultimate truth.

B. IF EVER GOD WAS SEEN IN JESUS, IT WAS ON CALVARY

Here we see one suffering innocently when He could have avoided it or could have defended Himself. But He said, "I lay down my life." Here we see one forgiving in the midst of the most flagrant wrongs and insults and pain. He said, "Father, forgive them for they know not what they do." He knew that they did it ignorantly. Here we see one giving gratuitously, as when He said, "This day shalt thou be with me in paradise." Here we see one loving, taking care of an earthly mother from whom He was now snatching Himself away. Here we see one dying in submission and in fellowship with the Father. Perhaps even His last prayer was a reflection of one taught to Him as a little child by His mother when He said, "Father, into thy hands I commend my spirit."

C. IN THAT VOLUNTARY SUFFERING, WE BEHOLD A MIGHTY, EVER-
   LASTING, SACRIFICIAL LOVE

This suffering was endured voluntarily, it had been pursued
as a life course, and it had been chosen deliberately because it
manifested the determination to do the will of the Father.

II. A JUDGING GOD

A. THE REVELATION OF THE MAJESTY AND UNAPPROACHABLENESS
   OF GOD

God is not only merciful, kind and loving but also holy and
just. God is unapproachable. No man has ever seen Him. He
dwells in a light that no man can approach unto. He is a God
afar off, transcendent, glorious, separate from man. He is a God
of eyes too pure to behold iniquity. No sin exists in His
presence. A gulf which separates sinful man and God has to be
bridged. This bridge was built by God Himself in coming to us
in the person of Jesus Christ. Without this mediatorship of
Christ, man would have perished alone. Such justice man
deserved.

B. THE MYSTERY OF THE WORDS, "WHY HAST THOU FORSAKEN
   ME?"

On the cross Jesus cried, "Why?" The "why's" of life are
like daggers. Why should we have war? Why should good men
die while bad men live? Why is right on the scaffold and wrong
on the throne? Why do the innocent suffer? Why all the horror
and brutality in the world? Thus men cry, "Why, Why, Why?"
In the terrible darkness on Calvary, a great "Why" was raised
by Jesus Christ. God's face was veiled. Heaven was shrouded.
The harmony between the Father and Son was ruptured. Deity
apparently was divided. The depth of this hour can never fully
be fathomed. There are those who try to interpret it away by
saying, "My God, my God, for this have I been kept." Or, as
one said, "The Twenty-second Psalm had begun to be quoted
and He was interrupted." But these are too shallow interpretations of Jesus' suffering. Rather, the Scripture tells us that He was
the true substitute, that He became one with guilt and sin, that
He had imputed to Him our judgment, that in that moment the
harmony of the Trinity was disrupted and a terrible mystery

was enacted in which Jesus could say, "Why hast thou forsaken me?"

C. WHATEVER IT MEANS, JESUS WAS DOING GOD'S WILL AND IN HIM GOD WAS WELL PLEASED

God was never His adversary, but He was the adversary of sin. And when Jesus became sin on Calvary, it did something to the nature of the Trinity. Sin was judged and that judgment was borne by the Son of God. God took sin into Himself that He might forgive it in man.

III. A FORGIVING GOD

A. THE PROBLEM INVOLVED IN FORGIVENESS OF SIN

Sin violates God's sanctities, profanes His being and, having come in history, it must continue forever. It cannot be lost from the divine consciousness. If it is to be forgiven, it must be dealt with so as to satisfy God's holiness and justice. God must so relate it to the harmony of the whole that it will reveal the divine holiness. The question is, Can sin be so related? The cross of Christ and the subsequent resurrection of Christ declare, "Yes." Sin may be forgiven and God may still be God — holy, just and good.

B. THE CROSS SHOWS GOD'S FORGIVENESS

On the cross, Christ, who knew no sin, became sin for us. He took the judgment of God on sin. Thus God took into His own life our death, the penalty of our sins and our estrangement from Him. Christ died and was buried. He brought deity into all of our experiences and He brought our experiences into deity. This satisfaction ever stands over against man's sin and man's necessary death. By faith in this great act, we may have the forgiveness of sins. God does not pass sin by. He forgives it because of a sufficient satisfaction.

C. THE HIGHEST REVELATION OF GOD IS THE CROSS

On Calvary we see the acme of redemptive love. Holiness was not only satisfied but love was manifested. Love could not stand apart in our need. God's love made Him become one with a sinful race. "Herein is love, not that we loved God, but that he loved us, and sent his Son to be the propitiation for our sins." God joined Himself to a lost race, a fallen people, a cursed mankind to be one with them to lift them into fellow-ship. It is this love of God which melts our hearts, shows the futility of our sins and wins us to Him. As we see God broken on the cross for our sins, we also are broken at the cross. Thus this cross of Christ has been transformed from a symbol of criminality and disgrace into the highest place the universe knows.

CONCLUSION

Let us relate Jesus on the cross to Jesus the teacher, the sinless man, the miracle-worker, the prophet, and then we will say, "Truly this was the Son of God." With Nathaniel, with Thomas and with Peter, we will fall down in worship saying, "Rabbi, thou are the Son of God," and "Thou are the Saviour of the world."

7

BEARING THE CROSS

Saturday — Thirty-ninth Day

Text: Mark 15:21. "And they compel one Simon a Cyrenian, who passed by, coming out of the country, the father of Alexander and Rufus, to bear his cross."
Scripture: Luke 23:26-31

In life, great things often come from queer quirks. The lowliest experiences often bring the greatest blessings. Clarence Edward Macartney tells us about Stanton's relation to Lincoln. In the 1850's a famous trial in Cincinnati occurred in which the McCormack Reaper Company was suing the Manning Company for infringement of patent, and because it was thought the case would be heard by a Western judge, the eminent lawyers for the Manning Company, Harding, Stanton and others, secured the services of Abraham Lincoln, but when Lincoln appeared at Cincinnati with his umbrella with a blue cotton ball on the handle, they gave him the cold shoulder and froze him out of the case. Stanton said in the hotel so that Lincoln heard it, "I won't associate with such a damned long-armed, gawky ape as that. If I can't have a gentleman with whom to associate in this case, I'll have nothing to do with him." That was Stanton's first verdict concerning Lincoln. His last — twenty-two minutes after seven, April 14th, 1865, with his left hand supporting his head and his right hand on his left elbow, and holding his high hat, Stanton stands by the bed in the house on Tenth Street, tears flowing down his cheeks. And when Lincoln ceases to breathe, he puts his hat for a moment on his head, then removes it, turns and touches Dr. Greeley of the New York Avenue Presbyterian Church on the shoulder and says, "Doctor, lead us in prayer." When the prayer was ended, Surgeon General Burns turned and pulled down the blinds to shut out the April sunlight and then Stanton gave his final verdict, the greatest

228

biography of Lincoln ever written, "Now he belongs to the ages."

A. THE STRANGE ASCENT TO IMMORTALITY OF MEMORY

Mary of Bethany made this ascent to immortality by the breaking of an alabaster box and the pouring of the ointment over the head and feet of Jesus Christ as He sat at meat. Of her Jesus said, "Wheresoever this gospel shall be preached in the whole world, there shall also this, that this woman hath done, be told for a memorial of her." Others have come to immortality in other ways — Zacchaeus by climbing a sycamore tree, Bartimaeus by being willing to cry out to Jesus in spite of the rebukes of the multitude, Nicodemus by hazarding his position as a ruler of the Jews in order to come and follow Jesus. But Simon of Cyrene was catapulted into immortality of fame by being compelled to do what must have seemed an onerous task at that time, namely, to carry the cross of Jesus Christ.

B. THE STRANGE PROVIDENCE WHICH SEIZED UPON SIMON

Simon had come in out of the country at this particular moment. Whether he was a farmer from Judea or a traveler from a far country we do not know. We know this was the season of the Passover and that Jews came from far places. I, myself, have seen during the feasts at Jerusalem huge black men from Africa with their tribal markings upon their faces walking the streets of Jerusalem. Simon had no expectation that anything unusual was about to come to pass. And yet, as he was present on the Via Dolorosa when Jesus was carrying His cross, he was impressed into a service which was destined to change his entire life. Thus sometimes the little things of life will change the whole course of life.

C. THE STRANGE MEANS OF IDENTIFICATION WITH JESUS

This must have been an unwilling service into which Simon was pressed, for no one would want to identify himself with a criminal about to die. Thus men in the English cities, especially the ports a century and a half ago, were pressed into service in the Merchant Marine and the Navy of Britain, sometimes leaving whole families in desperate need when press gangs seized upon them and compelled them to undertake their service.

One wonders whether Simon's attention to Jesus as he carried His cross was not an unwilling one. Perhaps his first impressions were to flee as soon as his job was done and to get as far away from this situation as possible. But as he went along the way following Jesus, he had opportunity to observe Him, to hear what the women said to Him and what He said to them, to see the nobility of His carriage and finally, when he arrived at Calvary, something held him irresistibly to see what occurred to this Jesus.

There he heard His seven sayings. He found that Jesus exercised some unexpressible power over him. And, when the crucifixion was over, he followed the band of believers who were apparently intimate with Christ. Undoubtedly on the Day of Pentecost when Peter preached, Simon believed for he became an early evangelist, if we are to identify him with the mention made in Acts 11:19 and 13:1. Paul later tells us that he was the father of preachers (Rom. 16:13). There is no good reason why we should not identify Simon with this later leader of the New Testament church.

I. THE PROMINENCE OF THE CROSS IN JESUS' EXPERIENCE

A. The teaching of Jesus

Again and again, Jesus repeated to His disciples that it was necessary for Him to go to Jerusalem, to suffer many things of the scribes and the priests, to be turned over to the Gentiles to be scourged and to be crucified (Matt. 16:21, 17:9, 20:18, 19). The Lord Jesus plainly fused the meaning into His own death by declaring that it would be the giving of a ransom for the sins of the world and would be in substitution for sinners (John 3:14, 12:32; Matt. 20:28). He used the expression as synonymous with the cross, "the cup" (Matt. 20:22) and "the cup that the Father hath given me" (Matt. 26:39).

B. His purpose for coming into the world

The cross was the deliberate choice of the Lord Jesus. Mark tells us that He set His face toward Jerusalem and they were amazed and afraid (Mark 10:32). And when He went up to Jerusalem to heal Lazarus or to raise him from the dead, Thomas said, "Let us also go, that we may die with him" (John

11:16). The final review of the end of His life and the purpose
He had for coming into the world was given to Jesus in the
Garden of Gethsemane. There in a last struggle, He faced this
purpose of His life and dedicated Himself to it (Heb. 5:7). In
His high priestly prayer, He said, "I have finished the work
which thou gavest me to do" (John 17:4). Thus when Peter
preached at Pentecost, he could say, "Him, being delivered by
the determinate counsel and foreknowledge of God, ye have
taken, and by wicked hands have crucified and slain" (Acts
2:23). The divine purpose of God had embraced the necessity
of Christ's death on the cross.

C. THE LARGE SECTION OF THE GOSPELS DEVOTED TO THE DEATH
   OF CHRIST REVEALS ITS IMPORTANCE

Other biographies pass over a man's death in a page or a
paragraph, but the Bible devotes about forty per cent of the
Gospels to the last events of His life. A memorial was established in the Lord's Supper to remember His death. The
apostolic and the Pauline interpretations coincide in the emphasis upon the death of Christ as the fundamental and primary
aspect of His coming into the world.

II. THE PLACE GIVEN BY JESUS TO CROSS BEARING

The Gospels emphasize that Jesus laid a great importance
upon His disciples and followers taking up the cross and coming
after Him (Matt. 10:38, 16:24, 20:28; John 12:24).

A. THE ESSENCE OF CROSS BEARING

We cannot take up the physical cross of Christ as Simon did
and carry it. The obvious principle enunciated by Jesus is that
of self-sacrifice, self-denial, self-renunciation for the sake of Him
and His kingdom. Though such taking up the cross does not
make us Christians, it shows that we are Christians and that we
are followers of Him. Without adopting this attitude, we are
no disciples. There is too much easy Christianity preached in
our day which allows people to merely accept salvation and
justification without taking up the cross. This is why so few men
are available for the mission field. We see little separation,
sacrifice and self-denial.

B. TWO SENSES OF THE CROSS

We have seen that the cross reconciles us to God (Ps. 85:10; II Cor. 5:19; I Pet. 2:24; Eph. 2:14). This is the great truth of forgiveness by the remission of blood of the Lamb of God. It is the only gospel which saves. Yet there is the second sense of the cross in that we must re-enact Jesus' sacrificial life. There must be a recapitulation of His humility, His service, His self-denial and His death to self. In fact, in the early Church there was a theory of the atonement called "recapitulation." A balance must be maintained between the objective and the subjective phases of the cross. Dead orthodoxy emphasizes the first but produces no redemptive Christianity, no great sacrifices, no great missionary movement and no great evangelism. Modernism emphasizes the latter and has no power to save from sin. A vital Christianity means both. Christian sacrifice cannot redeem, but Christians must live redemptive lives. The magnificent story of men like David Brainerd, Adoniram Judson, Hudson Taylor and others exemplifies such a balance between Christian doctrine and Christian deeds.

C. THE ASSUMING OF THE WAY OF THE CROSS AS A REALITY

Christians must voluntarily accept the cross and consecrate themselves to it. Sometimes the cross is forced upon us in an involuntary way but is accepted with joy and results in the same testimony. However it comes, it is necessary that the cross must be there. There is a great truth in the hymn which says —

> "I must needs go home by the way of the cross,
> There's no other way but this;
> I shall ne'er get sight of the Gates of Light,
> If the way of the cross I miss."

III. THE POWER OF THE CROSS IN CHRISTIAN EXPERIENCE

A. THE MEANS OF CRUCIFIXION OF SELF

The means of our voluntary identification with the cross is given to us in Romans 6. Here we learn of the sanctification of the spirit of the believer. It is not when we are near the cross in meditation and life that we are tempted to sin. Calvary has not only a forensic reality but an experiential reality. The position we assume when we are baptized with Christ into His death must be maintained by reckoning ourselves to be dead to sin, by realizing our unity with Him in resurrection life and by a presentation of our members as instruments of righteousness. Thus the crucified and resurrected Christ releases the Holy Spirit in the life of a crucified believer. Where self is on the throne, the Spirit cannot be. Where identification to Christ is realized, the believer voluntarily is motivated to service (II Cor. 5:14).

B. MAKING UP THAT WHICH IS LACKING IN THE SUFFERINGS OF CHRIST

This was the personal experience of Paul (Col. 1:24; II Cor. 11:23-28). How is it that we as Christians expect to get away so easily in our Christian experience in a world under the dominion of Satan where we must resist sin unto blood? Why should we complain when we suffer or are persecuted? We should expect it (John 15:19).

C. MIRRORING THE LIFE OF GOD IN MAN

Paul said, "Be ye imitators of me as I am of Christ." We are definitely to follow the example of Christ. Our purpose is not to look for the stigmata by meditation or by some fanatical repetition of flagellation and asceticism, but we have the need of following Christ in self-denying service in the world. We will never save the world by being little Jesuses. Jesus alone is the Saviour. But we may worship Him, and obey Him, and make Him known by our life and service.

> "Must Jesus bear the cross alone,
> And all the world go free?
> No; there's a cross for ev'ry one,
> And there's a cross for me."

CHARACTER CONFLICTS AT CALVARY

CHARACTER CONFLICTS AT CALVARY

Introduction

On entering Holy Week or the last week of the life of our Lord, an almost unlimited range of subjects presents itself to us for consideration. In fact, most of the subjects treated so far could be used during Holy Week with appropriate results. All that Christ taught and did points toward this consummation of His life. Even His incarnation was for the purpose of dying upon the cross. Other subjects which may be suggested would be a treatment day by day of the events of the last week, or a treatment of the high hours of Holy Week such as The Happiest Hour or His Triumphal Entry, The Most Blessed Hour or The Last Supper, The Most Trying Hour or His Period Before Pilate, The Darkest Hour or The Experience on Calvary, and The Brightest Hour or The Resurrection Morning.

Another series might be —

Sunday . . . . . Behold, A King Cometh
Monday . . . . . A Door Opens to the Court of Suffering
Tuesday . . . . . A Power Opposes an Easy Victory
Wednesday . . . A Hand Thrusts Him Into the Conflict
Thursday . . . . A Glimpse Into the Glory Awaiting
Friday . . . . . . The Meeting Place of Light and Darkness
Saturday . . . . . Friends Who Impeded God's Plan

One could even take the Beatitudes and adapt them for Holy Week. Happily, there seems to be no limit to the subjects available to the preacher for use at this time of year. Thus the minister who launches into regular services and does his own preaching during Holy Week or even during Lent, may be sure that he has an inexhaustible treasury from which to draw, and, in conjunction with it, he is constantly presenting the Gospel which is the power of God unto salvation.

1

THE TRIUMPHAL ENTRY

SIXTH SUNDAY — FORTIETH DAY

TEXT: Matthew 21:9. "And the multitudes that went before, and that followed, cried, saying, Hosanna to the son of David: Blessed is he that cometh in the name of the Lord; Hosanna in the highest."

SCRIPTURE: Matthew 21:1-17; Luke 19:44ff

The triumphal entry initiates Holy Week. Christ's public and private ministry were over; now He was to enter His passion. There still remained three days of solid teaching by parable and a response to interrogation. There also remained such events as the cleansing of the temple and the upbraiding of the Pharisees. There was the precious time of fellowship with His disciples in the upper room. There was teaching given to them, such as chapter 14 of John and the high priestly prayer of John 17 and there were those last precious hours that led from the fellowship of Solomon's Porch through Gethsemane, unto Caiaphas' Hall, the Gabbatha of Pilate, the Via Dolorosa, and then Calvary. This moment of adulation and praise on the Bethany road was both a happy and a sad hour.

A. HAPPINESS OF THIS HOUR

After Christ's circumlocution of the seizure of an ass upon which to ride and the attendant excitement, He mounted Himself upon the animal, and surrounded by His disciples, began His ride to Jerusalem. The ass was covered with their garments and the colt tagged along. As they left Bethpage, skirted the top of Olivet toward Jerusalem, the crowd which had been resting on Olivet, near Bethany, in the gardens on the sides of Olivet, soon gathered. Most of them were Galileans and readily joined the procession as soon as they heard who its center was. Children also came and joined the multitude.

As they rounded the top of Olivet and began to descend the Roman road, the people took upon their lips Psalm 45 and Psalm 118 and began to proclaim Christ as King. From the palm trees they ripped branches and cast them in His way. The steep and uneven road finally comes out to a place where a marvelous view of Jerusalem is afforded. Most of these people were not the people who gathered at Pilate's hall and cried for Him to be crucified. These were Galileans. The others were the natives of Jerusalem under the control of the priests. If ever Jesus' kingly nature and regal beauty shone forth it was on this ride. He was majestic, radiant and loving as He received and returned the greetings of His followers. It was one moment of joy and was a harbinger of His coming kingdom.

B. THE ADULTERATION OF THIS HOUR WITH SADNESS

It would be expected that Judas was also singing along with the others. This would moderate Jesus' joy as He knew what Judas was about to do. Moreover, when the procession came into the full view of Jerusalem and He remembered all that this city had received spiritually and what this city would do to Him and what would happen unto the city, He broke into weeping. There He saw Herod's magnificent temple, He saw the acres of the temple area, He saw the tower of Antonia and the white buildings of the city. He envisaged the day when not a stone would be left upon another and these people, after dreadful suffering, would be led forth into desolation and dispersion. The crowd observing Him was hushed with awe, then heard His voice cry out as He stretched forth His hands over the city saying, "If thou hadst known, even thou, at least in this thy day, the things which belong to thy peace! But now they are hid from thine eyes. . . . Thou knewest not the time of thy visitation" (Luke 19:41-44).

I. THE SCENE WAS APPROPRIATE TO CHRIST'S BEING

A. REMEMBER WHO THIS WAS

Some requested Christ to rebuke His disciples but He said, "I tell you if these should hold their peace the stones would immediately cry out." He was supremely conscious that He was pre-existent deity. He had said to these people, "Before Abraham was I am." He had been with God and was God and by Him all things had been created and now He was conscious of that nature. As the only begotten Son of God He was the revelation of God in the flesh and in Him the fulness of the Godhead dwelt bodily. The glory had been veiled, the essence of His being was there. Thus it was, as King of Kings, only Potentate, Judge of all the creation before whom every knee shall bow in heaven and earth, that He rode into Jerusalem. But He rode in humility.

B. REMEMBER WHAT HE WAS DOING

Jesus was going to His death. By this act He was revealing His love for the human race (I John 4:7ff). It was the self-giving of the Son of God on Calvary that revealed the heart of God. He was going to bear the sin of mankind, to become sin for us, though He knew no sin. He was to set aside the demands of justice which His only holiness required in order that we might be forgiven. He was to make an atonement which would reconcile a condemned and lost race to a holy God through His own suffering love.

C. REMEMBER WHY HE WAS HERE

All this took place according to the fore-ordained plan of God (Acts 2:23). He was the lamb slain from the foundation of the world (I Pet. 1:19, 20). The covenant of works established by God had to be fulfilled or no man could be saved. Thus Jesus lived a perfect life of obedience and the covenant of grace which opens to man the reservoir of divine love and forgiveness is made possible by His taking the guilt and penalty of our sin into His own body. Surely, if men had held their peace, the very stones would have cried out at the presence of such a Person.

II. THE CROWD WAS AN EARNEST OF THE MULTITUDE WHICH WOULD WORSHIP HIM IN AGES TO COME

A. THAT WORSHIPPING CROWD

Among those who sang Hosanna were His own immediate disciples. These had left all and had committed their lives to Him and deeply loved Him. Then there were the Galileans. These had seen His miracles and had heard His teaching in the north. They loved Him and wanted to make Him King even if they did not wholly understand Him. They were sincerely happy. Then there were the children whose purity and innocence made them love Him from the very beginning. Children always responded to Jesus when He came in contact with them. Thus, He had received them unto Himself and said, "Of such is the kingdom of God," and He told men that except they became as little children they should not enter the kingdom of God. Yes, there were many sincerely adoring people in this crowd on Palm Sunday.

B. THE WORSHIP HE WOULD RECEIVE ON EARTH WAS TYPIFIED

We are often sentimental about this crowd and its songs and are condemnatory of the chief priests, but in what crowd are we today? There are those who worship Christ. There are many people who are willing to sing Hosanna to Jesus on Palm Sunday but who will neglect Him throughout the entire year. They take no part in keeping His testimony in the Church or in spreading His testimony throughout the mission fields by prayer, service and giving. Then, of course, there are those who do not worship Him. They either neglect or reject just as many did in those days. But this early crowd was a harbinger or a foretaste of the great multitude that would worship Him across the years.

C. THE WORSHIP IN HEAVEN

Revelation declares unto us that a vast assembly of people from every tribe and kindred, tongue and nation shall be gathered before the throne and shall worship Him saying, "Worthy is the lamb that was slain." There will be songs to His glory, His power, His honor, by an innumerable multitude in heaven whom no man can number who have been saved by His redeeming work. It is utterly incongruous for us to expect to enjoy that there if we do not enjoy the singing of hymns, the uttering of prayers, the service of God and the worship of Christ on earth.

III. THE HOUR OF THIS TRIUMPH WAS PROPHETIC OF HIS ULTIMATE TRIUMPH

A. IT WAS A TRIUMPHAL RIDE

Christ had triumphed over temptation in His own life. He had triumphed over His humanity in all His sufferings, over weariness in Gethsemane, and now, even in His deepest and greatest humiliation, He was the victor over the sufferings that were to come to Him. He had triumphed over sin. The prince of this world had found nothing in Him and thus was cast out. Calvary was soon to break the power of Satan and Christ was to take captivity captive. Believers would forever overcome "by the word of their testimony by the blood of the Lamb." He also triumphed over death. He was now subjecting Himself to the powers of death in order that He might defeat them and forever deliver His people from the fear of death. With the same body that suffered death He was now to come forth from the tomb to be the first-fruits of the resurrection.

B. It suggested His triumph in many hearts

Christ is the Lord of those who follow Him in His way of humiliation. He told us that one must humble himself to be exalted, he must confess himself to be a sinner to be saved. He is a Saviour of those who believe in what He did. By faith they become justified and are made new creatures. Thus He is established as king over those who live resurrected lives. This was a suggestion of the triumphal domain of Christ in the hearts of millions of believers today.

C. It pointed to the last great triumph of which the Bible speaks

One day the Lord will come, not on an ass, but on a white magnificent horse followed by ten thousands of His saints and shall judge the ungodly of their ungodly deeds. This will be the coming in His kingdom. Then every eye shall behold Him and all people shall see His glory and worship Him. Then the knowledge of the Lord shall cover the earth as the waters cover the sea. Then all enemies shall have been put under His feet and He shall have put down all rule and all authority and have all power.

CONCLUSION

Happy should we be to be privileged to join in these hosannas on Palm Sunday and thus to add to the cup of His happiness. Let us do it with sincerity and faithfulness and due appreciation for that which He has done for us. Truly He is King of Kings and Lord of Lords.

2

THE UPPER ROOM

Text: Mark 14:15. "And he will show you a large upper room furnished and prepared: there make ready for us."
Scripture: Mark 14:12-26

The upper room has an indispensable place in the last week of our Lord's life. It symbolizes to us the intimacy of spiritual fellowship.

A. The upper room is a synonym for devotion

We even have a devotional magazine by the title "The Upper Room" urging daily devotions for families and individuals. The practice of the upper room directs our hearts in the love of God and consideration of spiritual fellowship. Spiritual life depends upon some such practice of maintaining an upper room. It perhaps may be figurative but it must be real. It may be the same room in which we live, eat and sleep but it will be transformed at times by devotions into an upper room. There can be no enjoyment of fellowship with God without a continuous upper room experience. David Brainerd made the forest an upper room. Adoniram Judson made his Ava prison an upper room. Others have made their kitchens an upper room.

B. The upper room receives a great emphasis in Scripture

The first emphasis of the upper room is in connection with this Passover at which our Lord died. No doubt it was prepared by the owner as the meeting place of his family for the Passover celebration but was gladly surrendered for the use of Jesus and His disciples. It must have been a large, airy, well-appointed room. The second mention of it is preceding Pentecost when the disciples and apostles gathered for a ten-day prayer meeting. There never was a deeper devotional meeting than this protracted prayer meeting. If ever the Church is to experience the power of Pentecost, it must be by the observance of such upper room experiences. The third mention of the upper room is at the prayer meeting which delivered Peter from the prison of Herod (Acts 12). Here was a wonderful demonstration of power which produced a special providence of God that delivered Peter from the prison.

C. THE UPPER ROOM IS CONNECTED WITH JOHN MARK AND WITH YOU AND ME

This upper room in so constant a use in the early church is believed to be the home of Mark from the references to the mother of Mark in Acts 12:12 and by the reference of Mark to the young man who followed Jesus (Mark 14:51, 52). From that upper room emanated an influence upon all who came under the sway of such prayer power. Mark's own life was transformed from failure into victory through the power of that prayer meeting. Every church ought to have prayer rooms and prayer seasons for the empowering and extension of its work.

I. MAKING READY FOR FELLOWSHIP — PREPARATION

A. COMMANDED BY JESUS

The subject of the Passover was first broached by our Lord (Luke 22:8). When He was questioned by His disciples as to where it should be celebrated He directed them to go into the city where they should see a man carrying a pitcher and to follow him to his home. This was most unusual for the water-carrying was done by the women and it would be very easy to single out a man who was carrying a pitcher of water. Even this displays the omniscience of Christ and the knowledge He has of every step we take. By this device the Lord maintained the secrecy of the place of His meeting the disciples so that even Judas who had already agreed to betray Him (Luke 22:6) would not know where they were going to celebrate the last supper. Jesus did not want that event to be interrupted. Hence it was that Judas had to leave the upper room and go to the priests in order to take them to Him. He probably returned to that upper room after Jesus and the disciples had gone to Solomon's Porch and then to Gethsemane. The Lord Jesus needed strengthening and companionship that night for the ordeal which was before Him. It is a great Scriptural truth that we are strengthened by the mutual faith one of another (Rom. 1:12). He needed the fellowship of His disciples.

B. CONDITIONED BY OBEDIENCE

Peter and John went to do as the Lord commanded them although they felt it was a very mysterious way to do it. They did not understand the implications pertaining to Judas. They found things just as He had said and, after all, there must be obedience in this matter of preparation for fellowship if we are to enjoy intimacy with our Lord. Jesus said, "To obey is better than to sacrifice." People who let their fellowship with God slip by omitting the upper room experience, think that they can compensate for it by some sacrificial deed, are mistaken. Special providences will meet us as we obey God in this matter of preparation for the upper room. Ancillary to it we may experience conversions, wonderful answers to prayer and events which we personally could not control.

C. THE COST OF SUCH PREPARATION

Preparing for the Passover consumed an entire day for these disciples. Time for most people seems to be the most scarce element of life. Time must be set aside if we are to have an upper room. It is the basic element of Scripture to experience. We must have a regular set time for communion with God. This was the value of the established hour of prayer held by the early Methodists. Let us take time for personal devotions, for united prayer meetings, for spiritual undertakings, knowing that it is essential. Preparation involves effort. People who will devote effort to every other objective but who give no energy or attention to this matter of spiritual fellowship with God are again in error. We must not assume that it will take care of itself. There is no end of inconvenience involved in having an upper room experience. We must rise early, we must devote our hours to it, we must meet with others, we must follow the example of men of prayer. God's promise of fellowship is to those who seek him (Jer. 29:13). Such preparation may even cost considerable money. We may have to let some things which are financially prosperous go in order to have spiritual prosperity and it is certain that we will have to observe the Biblical teaching concerning tithing, giving offerings to missions, evangelism and

Christian education in order to reach the unsaved. It was the unwillingness to meet this that partially caused Judas' betrayal.

II. THE MAR ON THE FELLOWSHIP

A. THE INTIMACY OF THAT HOUR

At eventide of the Passover the Lord Jesus met together with the twelve saying, "With desire have I desired to eat this Passover with you." He had an overpowering desire for their fellowship before He suffered. This was His last opportunity for teaching them. Only a slender thread held his Church on earth together. He was to give them His farewell. He said, "I will not drink of the fruit of the vine, until the kingdom of God shall come." This dinner that they had together was an expression of His love (John 13:1). "Having loved His own, He loved them to the end." This expressed both intensity and extensity of love.

Together they remembered what God had done for the Israelites at the exodus, their identity of faith with those people of God, and their sharing in the redemptive purposes of God. When they came to the eating of the lamb, it had a special meaning, for Jesus is the Lamb of God. No doubt their conversation centered on these great redemptive acts of God.

B. THE INTRUSION OF EVIL

When the supper was ended, the devil put into the heart of Judas to betray Him (John 13:2; Luke 22:3). The prince of evil now had access to the apostolic band and to Jesus through one life. Thought processes of betrayal were Judas' but the plan of betrayal was Satan's. Let us remember that Satan can have no access to us without our will. Then it was that Jesus made the startling announcement, "One of you which eateth with me shall betray me." Here again supernatural knowledge was revealed and shown. Apparently Jesus was still reaching for the conscience and soul of Judas, giving him a last chance to change. God never seems to tire of seeking us for Himself. Evidently the son of perdition was not yet lost. The result of this was that the disciples searched their hearts, saying, "Is it I?" It is better to realize the depth of soul and the evil of which we are capable than to affirm, "I will never deny thee." Do not think too highly of yourself (I Cor. 10:13; II Kings 8:13).

C. THE INSTITUTION OF A NEW SYMBOL OF FELLOWSHIP

When Judas was gone and only the faithful disciples were present, the Lord instituted the new memorial of redemption (I Cor. 11:26ff). Only those have a right to sit at the Lord's table who are His faithful followers. In the institution of the Lord's Supper the Old Testament Passover was forever abolished. That to which it looked forward was fulfilled in the sacrifice of the Lamb of God for the sins of the world. Christ, our Passover, is now sacrificed for us. This fact forbids any other interpretation of the death of Christ than that of a substitutionary sacrifice for sin. The Holy Communion commemorating that is a means of fellowship with Him and with each other. We recognize Him as the head and all believers as equal members of His body. If we cannot meet in unity at His table, we have no unity whatsoever.

III. THE MANIFESTATION OF FELLOWSHIP

A. A COMMON LOYALTY TO CHRIST

Our fellowship with Him is a fellowship of love. He said, "Do you love me?" (John 21:16), and "If ye love me, keep my commandments" (John 14:15). Our fellowship is one of faith. He said, "Believe me . . . the word . . . the work . . . the record." Our faith is in Him. Our fellowship is one of obedience. We are to call Him Master and Lord and to do the things which He says.

B. A COMMON EXPERIENCE

Our fellowship is a fellowship of life. We are cleansed by His Word just as He declared when He washed His disciples' feet at that supper. They were called to discipleship through many exigencies: from the lake, from the customs, out of the fig tree, from the remnant, and yet together they were bound into a Church or a body by the baptism of the Spirit. They were one in life.

C. A COMMON TASK

Ours is a fellowship of service. At a later supper He quoted, "As the Father hath sent me so send I you" (John 20:20-22). This was again given in the same upper room. To these disciples He gave the commission to carry the gospel to the world (Matt.

28:18-20). He declared to them in that upper room that "forgiveness must be preached to the nations beginning at Jerusalem" (Luke 24:49). This, then, is the great commission to the Church of Jesus Christ and its greatest fellowship rests in fulfilling it.

CONCLUSION: THE INVITATION TO THIS FELLOWSHIP (I John 1:3-9)

The basis of this fellowship is what the disciples had seen, heard and handled of the Word of Life, that is, of the events from the baptism to the ascension of Christ. Through this knowledge they declared the gospel that by partaking of that gospel others might have fellowship with them. When we accept the gospel we enter this great fellowship of the Church. Such continued fellowship may be enjoyed by walking in the light as He is in the light and knowing that the blood of Jesus Christ cleanseth us from all sin. The greatest privilege given to man is to meet God and his fellows at the Throne of Grace in fellowship.

3

GETHSEMANE

TUESDAY — FORTY-SECOND DAY

TEXT: Matthew 26:39. "And he went a little farther, and fell on his face, and prayed, saying, O my Father, if it be possible, let this cup pass from me: nevertheless not as I will, but as thou wilt."

SCRIPTURE: Matthew 26:36-46

Hoffman's picture of Christ shows Him kneeling by a rock with hands clasped, face uplifted, darkness lowering about Him but light breaking through the clouds, suggesting an ultimate victory. The dark shadows reveal in the distance the dim lights of the group coming with Judas to apprehend Him.

A. JESUS CAME TO THE GARDEN OF GETHSEMANE ON THE NIGHT BEFORE HIS CRUCIFIXION TO PRAY

It was His habit to pray before great events such as choosing His disciples, such as rejecting the offer of the kingship, such as stilling the tempest, such as facing His decease on the Mount of Transfiguration. Now He needed prayer more than at any other time in His life for He was facing the greatest crisis of His life. Here His humanity was being tested and the certain knowledge of what He was to suffer on Calvary (Heb. 2:14).

B. JESUS BROUGHT HIS DISCIPLES WITH HIM

This is a suggestion of the circles of His communion. He left eight of the disciples at the entrance to the garden and took three with Him to watch and pray with Him and the twelfth one, Judas, was off betraying Him. Each of us is on one of these three circles in relationship to Christ. Then He said to them to watch and pray while I go yonder. Jesus needed to be alone and yet He needed fellowship. He needed sympathy from His friends and strengthening from God, for His flesh trembled before the

248

sufferings of Calvary and His spirit quailed before the judgments of God's wrath upon sin. It was soon revealed that the
disciples could not go through this experience with Him. They,
His closest friends, failed Him that night by sleeping. They reported what they saw but what they did not see has never been
revealed. We are appointed to be His faithful intercessors and
prayer partners today. Are we failing Him or are we in prayer
with Him, releasing spiritual power by which He is able to rule
in the hearts and lives of men?

C. JESUS WENT A LITTLE FARTHER

This describes Jesus going into His greatest temptation and
battle. He had said, "The prince of this world cometh and
findeth nothing in me." Satan could get no foothold in Christ.
He had tried Him in the wilderness, he had tried Him through
Peter's suggestion to abandon the cross, and now he tried Him
in Gethsemane but he could get no response. Thus Jesus declared, "Now is the prince of this world cast out." He was
totally defeated on Calvary (Col. 2:14, 15). In this struggle
Jesus went farther than anyone else. He demonstrated the
religion of the greater price so that He had a right to ask
others, "What do ye more than others?" He did more than all.
He fell on His face under the burden, being unable to stand
or to kneel. He went as low as He could get in utter prostration.
We do not mention this to arouse pity for Him but to show
what He has done for us. In this awful agony and struggle God
placed before Him the chalice which He was to drink. He had
foretold His disciples that He would drink it. Now he tasted it
and knew He would have to drain it to the dregs on the morrow.

I. THE CUP THAT WAS OFFERED

A. THE TEMPTATION TO ABANDON CALVARY

Some think that Jesus was offered the cup by Satan in the
form of temptation to die and thus to escape Calvary but this
is an unsubstantiated theory. The cup that was offered was
death through crucifixion in becoming sin for us. He was not
crying for deliverance from premature death, but He was crying
for deliverance from the death in which He would become sin
for us, in which all the wrath of God that had been dammed
up from the first sin of mankind would break forth upon the

Son of God as our substitute. Christ had been tempted to abandon Calvary in the wilderness when Satan suggested He use His power for selfish purposes but He had resisted that temptation. He had resisted it when Peter said, "Far be this from thee" and now He was resisting it again although His prayer was that if it were possible, salvation might be wrought in some other way.

B. THE PRAYER HE PRAYED

His prayer was one of communion. He said, "O my Father." God, the Father, was there with Him. The cross had to be suffered, salvation had to be accomplished but He needed the presence of God. Thus we, too, in our suffering, in our testing, in our homesickness cry out for God's presence. He said, "If it be possible." It was the man who was speaking here as representative of humanity. He was asking if there couldn't be some other way but the answer was that this was the only way. Why then should we speculate on what would have happened if Jesus had not been crucified, if the Jews had accepted Him? This had to be. The law had to be met. Thus, that law was the law of the nature of Christ and of God and it could not be avoided. If forgiveness were to be wrought, the justice of God had to be satisfied and the cross was the only way. It is at this point that Islam shows its weakness because it throws law and justice to the four winds and declares that forgiveness may be arbitrary. He said, "Let this cup pass from me." He had lifted it to His lips and tasted it and He knew what He must suffer on the morrow. It was the vicarious death of Calvary. It was the hour when the Father's face should be turned away. It was the time of forsakenness. All the bitterness of agony should be His.

C. THE TWO CROSSES OF JESUS

Actually the Lord Jesus suffered the agony of Calvary in Gethsemane. There His will was crucified although His body was crucified on the cross. It was in Gethsemane He resigned Himself to death. It was on Calvary He experienced death. The cross may be set up in one's mind just as much as in one's experience.

II. THE CONTENTS OF THE CUP

A. LONELINESS

The word translated *heavy* comes from a Greek word meaning "away from one's people," that is, not at home, and implies homesickness. In the garden Christ was homesick for heaven, for glory, for the Father and the angels. He had emptied Himself of that glory, He had left heaven, He had laid aside His authority, now He was homesick, lonely and desirous of returning to the presence of the Father. How unutterably alone He was can only be seen as He left this garden and went to Calvary. He had invited His disciples to watch with Him and they had failed. He longed for sympathy as He went through the trial, the carrying of the cross, and the death on the cross, but all He tasted was the depths of loneliness for us that we might not be alone. No one need ever be alone as He was for now He stands with us, comforting and strengthening us. Thus a great English churchman once said, "Never so little lonely as when alone," because Christ is with us.

B. SORROW FOR THE WORLD

We read, "He began to be sorrowful." There are two kinds of sorrow that are related to sin. One is remorse. It is the sorrow of the wicked sinner who hates God and who is sorry because of the effects of his own deeds but not because he has sinned against God. Judas had this kind of sorrow and he went out and killed himself. Sorrow according to the world does not save.

But there is a Godly sorrow which one may have after he has done wrong and which reveals a truly converted and contrite heart. Thus Peter went out after his denial and wept bitterly. His heart was full of grief and it turned him to the Lord. True sorrow is called a sorrow according to God and when it says that Jesus began to be sorrowful we believe that He offered a true sorrow to God for sin and its consequences. He gave in the garden a complete repentance for the sins with which He was identified. No one else ever could do this. It was this sorrow for the sin of others that broke His heart. Our sins added to that grief when He was "sorrowful to death." But even that sorrow was not enough for atonement as some declare. His soul had to be poured out unto death for He made our atonement in His death on the cross.

C. SUFFERING OF ALL KINDS

In that cup came all manner of suffering. Physical pain was there. He was to taste it fully on the morrow in the smitings of Caiaphas' servants, in the scourging, in the crowning with thorns, in the nails, in the thirst, finally with the spear. Rejected love was there. He was love incarnate and yet His love had been rejected and unrequited. Loneliness was there. There is no greater suffering than loneliness. To be alone in the crowd is unbearable and yet it says concerning Jesus' disciples, "They all forsook him and fled." Poverty was there. For our sakes He became poor and at this point He reached the depth of such poverty. Social ostracism was there for He was called "a friend of sinners." Class consciousness was there for He was designated "a carpenter's son." Race prejudice was there for He was described as "the King of the Jews." Spiritual struggle was there as though all the powers of hell were arrayed against Him.

D. IDENTITY WITH SIN

We read that "He was made sin for us, who knew no sin." Atonement was to be made by Christ in bearing our sins in His body on the tree. He was to take the punishment due to us, to bear the curse, endure the wrath and suffer the pains of hell. The depth of that spiritual suffering on the cross we will never know. Light was plunged into darkness, life was poured out by death, the sinless one became sin, all that we might be forgiven.

III. THE CONSECRATION TO THE CUP

A. THE HUMAN NATURE OF JESUS CAME INTO A PERFECT ACCORD WITH THE DIVINE

He declared, "Not as I will, but as thou wilt." The wish, the desire, the prayer of Christ became identified with the will of God.

B. THE LAST TEMPTATION TO FLEE THE CROSS WAS CONQUERED

After this Jesus never wavered. He was in complete control of Himself. He had absolutely and completely surrendered Himself to the will of God. He was to make a voluntary sacrifice in laying down His life for us (John 10:17; Heb. 9:14).

C. THE PROCESS WAS GRADUAL

Three times Jesus went to His disciples and three times returned to pray. He found them asleep and sadly awakened them and reproached them and then went off to continue His vigil alone. How sadly He looks at us in our prayerlessness and our indifference in the great spiritual struggles going on in the world today. Finally he said, "If it be thy will, that I drink it, I will." It is obvious He had not drunk it yet, that He was looking forward to the morrow on Calvary. He fought His battle through alone and then the angels came and strengthened Him (Luke 22:43). The disciples could sleep on now and take their rest for the struggle was over. The hour had come.

CONCLUSION: THE BETRAYAL

Almost immediately Judas came with a multitude of priests and soldiers and rabble. He greeted Christ with a kiss and received his rebuke. The Lord demonstrated His own power by overcoming them with a word and then voluntarily yielded Himself up to their control. Thus He gave Himself to die for us on the cross.

4

JUDAS' BETRAYAL

Wednesday — Forty-third Day

Text: Matthew 26:24. "The Son of man goeth as it is written of him: but woe unto that man by whom the Son of man is betrayed!"

Scripture: Matthew 26:14-25, 47-50; 27:1-10; Acts 1:15-25

There are two theories concerning the character and purpose of Judas in his betrayal of Christ.

A. The theory which excuses Judas or at least explains his motive in betraying Jesus

This is held by Marie Corelli in the novel "Barabbas," by Parker in The Peoples Bible, by Leslie Weatherhead and others. The thesis is that Judas was a splendid youth, faithful and zealous of the cause of Christ, devoted to the kingdom of God but that he resorted to ideas of statesmanship and means of diplomacy rather than loyalty to Jesus and consistency with a spiritual kingdom. These persons excuse Judas for betraying Christ on the ground that he was desirous of having Jesus Christ reveal His authority as the Son of God, His glory as King and Messiah and His kingdom as inevitable.

The thought is that Judas attempted to force the hand of Christ to compel Him to exercise the authority and power which rightfully belonged to Him. This authority was demonstrated in the Garden of Gethsemane when with a word He compelled the soldiers and priests to fall backward to the ground. Had that same authority been exercised toward the Romans and those who would apprehend Him, Jesus would have been unveiled as the Messiah. The thesis is that Judas knew that Jesus was the Christ, that he believed in Him but that he thought He was making a mistake and he wanted to create the situation which would compel Christ to reveal Himself as Messiah.

It is obvious that he missed the spiritual meaning of Christ's mission and the meaning of the teaching of Christ as He had given it for three years. When Judas finally apprehended what he had done he took his own life by suicide but even this was because of repentance and sorrow and therefore he was saved.

B. THE COMMON VIEW

Historically the Church has believed that Judas was a false disciple who had been chosen because of his potentialities but had let the baser elements of his character triumph and so became a rascal, a demon, a son of perdition, a thief and a traitor. The sin of Judas in betraying Jesus was inexcusable, made him the instrument of Satan and condemned him to his own place which is hell. Thus the name Judas has become synonymous with traitor. The preponderant weight of Scripture seems to designate Judas as one who had an opportunity but perverted it.

C. THE CONFLICTING TEXTS ABOUT JUDAS

After preaching on Judas, I received a letter from a theological student who said, "In your sermon on Judas' fatal decision, you did not have time to touch on certain texts treating of Judas and his fatal act. This is one of the incidents in Scripture that I confess has bothered me considerably. Was it foreordained that Judas was the man? If I understood correctly, you stated that Jesus chose Judas as a promising young man. Are we to understand in this interpretation that when Jesus chose him He did not know that he, Judas, was the man? It was prophesied in Psalm 41:9 and fulfilled as stated by Jesus in John 13:18 how the Lord should be betrayed, 'He that eateth bread with me hath lifted up his heel against me.' How then must we construe such recorded statements as John 6:64, 70, 71 and John 13:10, 11, 18 and 27?"

Jesus said of Judas, "Have not I chosen you twelve, and one of you is a devil (demon)?" (John 6:70). Also, "For Jesus knew from the beginning who they were that believed not, and who should betray Him" (John 6:64). Jesus said, "The Son of man goeth as it is written of Him: but woe unto that man by whom the Son of man is betrayed! it had been good for that man if he had not been born" (Matt. 26:24; Mark 14:21; Luke 22:22) and in the garden Jesus said unto Judas, "Friend, wherefore art

thou come? . . . Betrayest thou the Son of man with a kiss?"
(Matt. 26:50; Luke 22:48).

I. JUDAS WITH THE PRIESTS

A. THE OCCASION WHICH CRYSTALLIZED JUDAS' DECISION TO BETRAY CHRIST

The chief priests, elders and scribes had been seeking a way
in which they could take Jesus by subtilty in quiet and put Him
to death (Matt. 26:3-5; John 11:49-51). Then it was that the
event occurred which determined Judas' course. In the house of
Simon the leper in Bethany, on the Sabbath before the Passover,
a feast had been given to Jesus and His disciples. During the
feast Mary of Bethany brought a very expensive alabaster box
of ointment, broke the box and poured the contents on Jesus'
head and on His feet. It was Judas who expressed the indignation of the disciples and asked what purpose this waste since
this could have been sold for three hundred pence and have
been given to the poor. John tells us that "this he said, not that
he cared for the poor; but because he was a thief, and had the
bag, and bare what was put therein" (John 12:6). Matthew
and Mark tell us that immediately after this Judas went unto
the high priest and covenanted to betray Jesus and deliver Him
unto them for thirty pieces of silver.

This action reveals Judas' indignation at the course which
was being pursued by Christ in deliberately going to His death
(Matt. 26:2). It reveals an utter lack of comprehension of the
last days of Jesus and of the meaning of His mission in the
world. Judas had been with Jesus for three years and yet he had
a complete blind spot as to the nature and purpose of Christ's
work. Paul later said that the things of God are spiritually
discerned and the natural man cannot understand them. This
is the only explanation we can give concerning Judas.

B. THE ACTUAL BARGAINING WITH THE PRIESTS

It is here that the theory of forcing Christ would come in. If
Judas had thought that Christ was making a mistake and that
placing Him in conflict with the authorities would compel Him
to reveal His authority and power, he still would have lacked
comprehension of the purpose and mission of Christ. Yet the
emphasis by Matthew and Mark is upon "how much will you

give me, and I will deliver Him unto you?" He met with an acceptance of his proposition for they were anxious for such an opportunity to apprehend Christ but he met with opposition concerning the amount that they would give so that he accepted the price of a slave, or thirty pieces of silver. However we may look at this, there was no excuse for Judas accepting money in order to reveal the meeting place of Jesus. He sold his Lord and Master for a paltry sum.

C. The expression of evil in Judas

It was foreordained that the Lord Jesus Christ would be betrayed. The Scripture had foretold this and such foreordination must be connected with the foreknowledge of God concerning the details of the event. The question then arises, was Judas so predestined to reprobation that he could not have been a faithful disciple of Christ? The same question arises concerning all those who will be elect or reprobate. One system of interpretation declares that all is dependent upon the good pleasure of God and that only the elect will believe. However, according to Ephesians 1:4, it is possible to believe that God has elected all who are in Christ and that He does not predetermine who shall be in Christ but that they are predetermined on the condition of their repenting and believing. Just so, the individual choices of Judas brought him into the position where he fulfilled the Scripture in reference to Christ. No violence was done to the will of the creature. When the Lord Jesus chose him, after a night of prayer, along with the other eleven, he apparently had all the possibilities of being a Peter, or a John, or a James. He was given a magnificent opportunity. Yet, as the days went on and the reactions of the disciples were watched by the Lord Jesus, He was able to say as early as John 6:70 that one of the twelve was a demon. Without going into detail as to the analysis of the character of Judas, we can only conclude that he had an opportunity but he did not respond affirmatively and early in his relationship to Christ he revealed his corrupt motives and tendencies. Thus, when he came to the end, he was a thief and was stealing from the common treasury. This would confirm the fact that he was not betraying Christ to force His hand but in order to profit by it.

II. JUDAS WITH JESUS

A. THE DEVIL ENTERED INTO JUDAS

There is no more beautiful and solemn occasion in the New Testament than the upper room fellowship of Jesus with His disciples at the Passover when He instituted the Lord's Supper. Yet, we are told that Judas was so irritated with it all that the devil entered into him (John 13:2). One wonders what his thoughts must have been as he let Jesus wash his feet. Perhaps even that self-emptying of Christ confirmed him in his decision to betray Him.

B. THE DEPARTURE TO DO HIS DEED

During that supper the Lord announced that one would betray Him and He both covered up for Judas and yet designated him as the one who would dip the sop with Him in the dish. It seems that the Lord was still reaching for Judas' conscience and still giving him an opportunity to change and repent. But finally He informed him, "What thou doest do quickly," and Judas went out for the purpose of betraying Him. The Scripture says it was night. It is always night for a soul when that soul turns his back upon the light or upon Jesus and right. The condition of Judas must have been desperate as he turned his feet away from that fellowship with the disciples and made his way to the high priest, led them and the soldiers back to the upper room in the home of the father of John Mark, and discovered that the disciples were gone so that he had to lead them to Jesus' trysting place in Gethsemane in order to turn Him over to the priests.

C. THE DELIVERY IN THE GARDEN

Jesus had had time enough for His three periods of prayer when He faced the cup, struggled against it and then surrendered. His own personal needs had been met and He was serenely composed through all that was to follow in His trial and crucifixion. Then it was that He interrupted His fellowship with the Father, knowing that Judas was at hand to betray Him, along with the soldiers and priests. He awakened His disciples so that they were with Him when the end came. Judas approaching, in the light of the flares of those who sought out Jesus, greeted Him with a kiss, a sign of intimacy, and heard the words from Jesus, "Friend, betrayest thou the Son of man with a kiss?" Once again it seems that Jesus was still reaching for Judas' conscience as He called him friend. But the deed was done, the disciples were allowed to disperse and they apprehended Jesus and led Him to Caiaphas' hall.

III. JUDAS WITH HIMSELF

A. His CONVICTION

Scripture says, "When he saw that he was condemned." It was when Judas saw the consequences of his deed that he was convicted, full of remorse, and tried to change his action. How strange it is that when the sinner sees the consequences of his deeds that his remorse comes. When the landlord sees a penniless and sick family turned out, when the prodigal sees the effect of his sin upon his aged and Godly parents, when the sinful wife sees the pain in her husband's eyes, then understanding is given. Strange that temptation blinds but sin opens the eyes. But such opening of the eyes is too late. When Judas saw what he had done it was too late for him to rectify his deed.

B. His REMORSE

Perhaps there is no hard and fast rule concerning repentance and remorse. Peter is always used as an illustration of one who repented, going out and weeping bitterly. Judas is given as an illustration of one who had remorse. Repentance is sorrow according to God for one's sin; remorse is sorrow according to the world for one's sin. Repentance is sorrow because of the deed which we have done; remorse is sorrow because of the consequences of the deed. When Judas saw the consequences of what he had done, he took his coins to the high priest and threw them before him, declaring, "I have betrayed innocent blood." Was this real restitution or was it a mere attempt to get rid of the consequences of one's deeds?

C. His SUICIDE

The end of Judas was terrible. He hanged himself, the rope apparently broke and as he plunged down the precipice his stomach was ripped open and his bowels came out. He was buried in a potter's field which then was named the field of blood. Had Judas truly repented, he would not have taken his own life. He would have known that he could have gone to Jesus and found forgiveness as did Peter. His sorrow, his tears, would have led him to a transformed life.

CONCLUSION

Judas went to his own place (Acts 1:25). Was that place with the devil and his angels or was it, as some affirm, heaven and the saved? Christ, in His high-priestly prayer, declared, "Those that thou gavest me I have kept, and none of them is lost, but the son of perdition; that the scripture might be fulfilled" (John 17:12). Was Judas saved and then lost? This is a perversion of the teaching of the text. Christ said that He had lost none. Judas was the son of perdition. He went to his own place. The implication is that he was lost. Lost by his own choice of evil in the presence of the magnificent opportunity for salvation and service.

5

PETER'S DENIAL

Thursday — Forty-fourth Day

Text: Luke 22:31, 32. "And the Lord said, Simon, Simon, behold, Satan hath desired to have you, that he may sift you as wheat: But I have prayed for thee, that thy faith fail not: and when thou are converted, strengthen thy brethren."

Scripture: Luke 22:31-34

These words of Jesus were spoken at the Last Supper after the departure of Judas. Almost immediately afterwards Jesus took His disciples to Solomon's porch where He gave them the teaching contained in John 15, 16 and 17. From there they crossed the Kidron and went part way up the Mount of Olives into the Garden of Gethsemane where the sifting of Peter by Satan should begin. It is here that we begin the drama of Peter's temptation.

A. So often they had been in Gethsemane

It was in Gethsemane where Jesus and His disciples had gone to sleep during Holy Week, that is, when they did not go all the way to Bethany. Like other pilgrims, they simply slept out in the open. It was on the Mount of Olives, just above this very place where Jesus had given them His great teaching contained in Matthew 24 and 25 concerning the final events of the age. It was on the Mount of Olives, not far from Gethsemane, where the Lord had stopped on His triumphal entry to weep over Jerusalem and to proclaim its future destruction. This Gethsemane was a very familiar place to them.

B. So different a place today

Except for the mountain itself, for the valley of the Kidron, for the old Roman road and for some gnarled olive trees which may go back close to the time of Christ, Gethsemane is greatly changed today. Now there is a chapel, a church, some priests who tenderly tend the old olive trees and the garden round about them. At least one of these trees is between three and four feet in diameter. If these or the rocks could speak, they would tell us the secrets that they heard in Jesus' prayers when He conversed of love, of sorrow, of heartache, of remorse, of faith, of hope, of loyalty with His Father. But if they could have talked, man would long ago have removed them. Their testimony rests in their silence. It is here in the topography of such a place where one feels nearest to the Lord when visiting Palestine.

C. So WONDERFUL AN APPEAL THAT NIGHT

Here Jesus came to pray, to prepare Himself for the tensions, the struggles and the sorrows of the day of His crucifixion. Here He wanted fellowship with His disciples in prayer. Here He sought the face of His Father. It was in this precious garden outside the Holy City in the quietness of the night that Jesus prayed. To this experience Peter was invited.

I. PETER'S EXPERIENCE IN THE GARDEN

A. ONCE MORE IN THE INTIMATE CIRCLE

Peter had several times been designated for the place of honor with James and John in the inner circle of the disciples. Thus they had gone to the Mount of Transfiguration and thus they were now asked to watch with Jesus and pray with Him as He went forward to struggle and to enter into agony alone. Perhaps intimacy breeds contempt for these three knew what had been revealed on the Mount of Transfiguration and they had seen the demonstration of Jesus' person when He had raised the daughter of Jairus from the dead with all others excluded. Now they were to see something that appalled the angels. Jesus asked them to share with Him His spiritual suffering. There are many derogatory theories about Peter which present him as a base, harsh individual who condemned others and forgave himself, who was forever wavering and dissembling. But it is only right in defense of Peter to say that though he was weak, yet he was also strong. As his name was Simon, bespeaking weakness, his name became Peter, bespeaking firmness. It was a name given by Jesus because only grace could bring that characteristic of him out. He had shared with Jesus in His temptation and now he saw Jesus go forward, bow to pray, and then fall upon His face. He, along with James and John, heard Him pray, "If it be possible, let this cup pass from me." Perhaps Peter, James and John prayed with Jesus for a while, then the exertion of the day, the food they had eaten, the lateness of the hour combined to overwhelm them with sleep so that they ceased praying and heard the voice as if at a great distance and then heard Jesus no more.

B. Now the special object of Satan's attack

Jesus said that Satan had desired Peter and now was to make him a special object of attack. It must have been something like the attack of Satan upon Job when he accused him before God and when God permitted him to be tested by Satan. Probably because of Peter's future destiny in the Church Satan now desired him and began to tempt him. The sleep that overcame the three in the garden may have been from Satan himself. The Lord had warned Peter that Satan desired him and now, in the garden, he admonished, "Watch and pray, that ye enter not into temptation." The sifting process began through sleep, "the spirit is willing but the flesh is weak." The natural demands of the body became a source of temptation. These disciples needed sleep and they deserved it but in this case it should have been foregone for Jesus' sake. The spiritual power that Peter needed for the next few hours was lost while he slept. Prayer will prepare the Christian for anything. John Wesley arose every morning at five o'clock and devoted one hour in prayer. Luther spent at least an hour in prayer in the morning. Thus Jesus prayed. Thus Daniel prepared himself to face the hostile king and princes. Had Peter prayed, his mind would have been illumined concerning the sayings and doings of Christ and he would not have denied Him.

C. Still determined to die for his Lord

Peter meant the vow he made in the upper room when he said, "I will die for Thee." Here in the garden he drew his sword and faced the multitude, ready to fight. His demonstration of resistance was vain, as Jesus showed him. Peter's effectiveness in fighting was very small. All he did was cut off the ear of the servant of the high priest. But supposing Peter had cut down these enemies as a Samson would have done, what good would have come of it? The Lord showed him that He had authority to call upon the Father and at least seventy-two thousand angels would come to His relief and one alone would be sufficient. He also showed him that His kingdom was not established by the sword. But if Peter was too sleepy, or too confused, or too amazed, we do not know. He apparently did not understand the action of this voluntary surrender. Perhaps he was even wounded in spirit at the rebuke. Secretly Peter may have hoped that when this time arrived Jesus would have declared Himself and utilized His own power to set up His kingdom.

II. PETER'S FOLLOWING AFAR OFF

A. THE SCENE OF THE MOB TAKING JESUS TO CAIAPHAS' HALL

At the request of Christ, the disciples were permitted to disperse. They left Him to the soldiers and the priests. Being bound, He then was led down the old Roman road, across the valley of the Kidron, through the sheep-gate into Jerusalem, across the parade ground and the street of David to the hall of Caiaphas. The rabble, the soldiers, the priests must have created some disturbance going through Jerusalem even during the night. No bonds could hold Christ, not even the bonds of the grave, and yet He submissively followed His captors.

B. THE VIEW OF PETER AT A DISTANCE

Let it be said to Peter's credit that he followed Christ although he followed afar off. He did not want to get mixed up with this but he was involuntarily drawn after Christ and followed. He may have begun to think that he had made a mistake. All his doubts may now have been telescoped into a few moments and he may thus have been spiritually prepared for his renunciation of Christ. At least, the devil was at work on him. We see him a picture of a baffled, bewildered, perplexed, amazed individual; loyal but fearful; hoping, and yet despairing; totally unable to devise the ways and means of Jesus. How many, like Peter, have been baffled by events God has let come into their lives and hence they have followed Him afar off? They love this Christ but they do not know what to do about Him. So many people would not turn against Christ or abandon Him, but they cannot seem to throw their all in with Him.

C. THE END OF THE JOURNEY

Thus they came to Caiaphas' hall. Thus Jesus was immediately led in with the priests and the soldiers while the servants entered the portico, passed through the gate, and milled about in the courtyard. Jesus was taken to the place where the Sanhedrin was illegally meeting in the night while Peter gained entrance to the courtyard and mingled with the servants and the inquisitive strangers. He came to see the end. His important words reveal his attitude of mind for he thought it was all over.

III. PETER'S PRESENCE IN THE HALL OF CAIAPHAS

A. THE INTERROGATION OF JESUS BY HIS ENEMIES

Peter, from his refuge at the fire of the servants, heard of the progress of the trial which was reported outside from time to time. He heard of their seeking the false witnesses and finding none from the servants who were coming and going, of their finally getting two who themselves could not agree on that of which they accused Christ. He heard how that they accused Him of intending to destroy the temple and to rebuild it. Above all, he heard that Jesus had stood holding His peace, being "led as a lamb to the slaughter, as a sheep before her shearers is dumb, so he opened not his mouth"; that He was eloquent in silence. He heard of the oath Caiaphas had asked of Christ concerning His Person, saying, "Art thou the Christ, the Son of God?" He understood that He had said yes and that He would come in power and in glory, in clouds and with angels. He was reaffirming the same thing He had taught them as disciples. He heard the accusation of blasphemy and the demand for His death. Then, news seeped through of His mistreatment and His being mocked.

B. THE IDENTIFICATION OF PETER BY THE ENEMIES

Now, three times in a few brief moments, the finger of scorn was levelled at Peter. Back of it, of course, was Satan who was sifting Peter. First the damsel who saw Peter by the fire in the courtyard where Peter warmed himself said, "Thou wast with Jesus of Galilee," and before all about the fire Peter denied it, saying, "I know not what thou sayest." He pleaded ignorance and in confusion he left their presence, attempting to go from the courtyard. As he went to the porch over which he must pass to get out the gate, another damsel met him and said to some, "This fellow was with Jesus of Nazareth." The word *fellow* and the word *Nazareth* revealed the scorn with which she held him. In fear that he would be discovered, Peter denied with an oath, saying, "I do not know the man." Then, rather than go out, to reinforce his bravado, he returned to the fire and evidently was talking, for someone standing there said, "Surely thou art one of them, for thy speech betrayeth thee." Peter could not hide it. Then it was, with cursing and swearing, he renounced his knowledge of Christ and he said, "I know not the man."

C. The indictment of Peter by his conscience

Several things occurred at that moment. First, the cock crew. Second, they were leading Jesus from Caiaphas' hall by a balcony which overlooked the courtyard, a way to take Him to Pilate (Mark 14:72; Luke 22:61). Then Peter recalled to mind the words Jesus had said unto him (Mark 14:72). He remembered the tender scene at the Last Supper when Jesus washed his feet. He remembered his professions of loyalty. He remembered that Jesus said he would betray Him and he thought a dog would have been more faithful than that. Just at that moment "the Lord turned and looked upon Peter" (Luke 22:61). That was the look which caused the soldiers to fall back in Gethsemane. That was the look which caused Zacchaeus to give half his goods to feed the poor. That was the look which caused Matthew to leave the seat of customs. This was the look that sinners could not stand. As Peter looked into those searching, knowing, loving eyes a flame was kindled within him and he knew that Jesus understood all. Then Peter went out and wept bitterly. The probabilities are that he stumbled out from that group, he retraced his steps back to the garden of Gethsemane where he had first begun to fall. Peter was convinced even here that Christ was the Son of God. He knew that he had failed Him and his strength and his courage were gone. It is possible that Peter missed the rest of the tragedy: the trial, and the Gabbatha, the sufferings of Christ along the Via Dolorosa, and finally His death on Golgotha. But certainly he experienced the earthquake, and the darkness. It may be that he even sought death. But Jesus had prayed for him, that his faith would not fail.

CONCLUSION

"The Lord appeared unto Peter."

We cannot leave the story here. Peter went out and wept bitterly. He revealed his contrition. He made his repentance and on the resurrection morning the Lord appeared unto Peter. Some would like to have this left as an historical story only and not apply it to themselves but this cannot be done. "All scripture is given for reproof, for correction, for instruction in righteousness." Some of us are willing in spirit but weak in the flesh. We are following afar off. We are warming ourselves at the fire of the enemy. We are, in fact, renouncing Christ. This may have put us in darkness. Let us take an example from Peter and manifest due contrition and repentance that there may be a spiritual resurrection. Jesus is praying for us though the sifting is heavy and hard. If we are converted we may strengthen others.

6

THE SEVEN LAST WORDS

Good Friday — Forty-fifth Day

SCRIPTURE: Luke 23:13-46; John 19:16-30; Matthew 27:39-49

The seven last words of Christ embrace the most solemn, sacred and saving period in the history of the world. It is the center point of time and eternity. We do well to commemorate it. Whatever hope man has for forgiveness of sin and for eternal life rests on what happened on Calvary.

A. THE INDIVIDUAL SENTENCES

Statements of Christ on the cross number seven in the following order:

"Father, forgive them for they know not what they do" (Luke 23:34).

"Woman, behold thy son! . . . Behold thy mother!" (John 19:26, 27).

"This day thou shalt be with me in paradise" (Luke 23:43).

"My God, my God, why hast thou forsaken me" (Matt. 27:46).

"I thirst" (John 19-28).

"It is finished" (John 19:30).

"Into thy hands I commend my spirit" (Luke 23:46).

B. THE INDIVIDUAL REALMS REPRESENTED BY THESE SAYINGS

So much is covered by these statements of Christ on the cross that they constitute an opportunity to evaluate each major field of Christ's life. Under them we may recapitulate the different realms or chapters of His biography: His first prayer would well suggest to us the study of His prayer life; His reference to His mother, a study of His family life; His promise to the thief, a study of His redemptive life; His question concerning forsakenness, a study of His deity and the mystery of His unity with the Father; His reference to thirst, a study of His human life; His statement that it is finished, a reference to His life work; and, His commitment of His spirit unto the Father, a study of His eternal life. These sayings open to us a rich mine of spiritual truth by which we may apprehend the revelation given in the life of Christ.

C. THE INDIVIDUAL STATEMENTS VIEWED AS A UNIT

Taken together, the exposition of these seven sayings might well tell the complete story of the facts of the Christian religion centering in the work of redemption. It is strange that there are just seven statements. This is not arbitrary for no one evangelist records them all. It is only a composite statement of all four evangelists that we get the seven statements. In Scripture, three is the number of the Trinity, four is the number of the world, and seven represents the world and God in reconciliation. Thus it is used in the seven parables of Matthew 13, the seven petitions of the Lord's Prayer and in the seven promises of Christ's epistles to the churches in Revelation. A careful study of these statements on the cross reveals four dealing with man and three dealing with God. And here, the redemption, planned in eternity, wrought in time, was finished by the work of Christ on the cross. We shall summarize the meaning of these and hope that they will suggest a far more full treatment.

I. THE FIRST THREE WORDS

A. THE MEANING OF JESUS' PRAYER

Here, on the cross, the Lord Jesus prayed, "Father, forgive them, for they know not what they do." These were His enemies. They were treating Him despitefully. They were mocking Him. They were reviling Him. They were inflicting pain upon Him and yet He prayed for them. He had taught His disciples to pray for their enemies saying, "Pray for those who despitefully use you." Here He personified His own teaching in action under duress. In the prayer He embraced those who sinned ignorantly. There is evidence that many of the priests later believed on Him, that many of the masses were converted at Pentecost and afterwards. It is possible that even the centurion and soldiers were led to believe on the Lord Jesus Christ. If prayer means anything, divine mercy was extended to many of those who afflicted Him on Calvary. It represents the intercessions of Christ for those who sin out of ignorance and it shows God's love for men who are in revolt and in the practice of wickedness. In it we have an example to pray for those who sin without knowing the truth.

B. The meaning of Jesus' request from John

As the time passed on Calvary, Jesus "said to his mother, Woman, Behold thy son! Then saith he to the disciple, Behold thy mother!" Apparently Mary, who had watched the crucifixion, at this point was led away by John and thereinafter protected and kept by him. The Lord recognized human responsibility to His parents. It calls to mind the fact that He had been subject to these who had brought Him up as a baby and a child. Although the Lord later withdrew Himself from the authority of His family and universalized the family relationship by saying that he is My brother who doeth the will of My Father in heaven, He nevertheless discharged His responsibility in this hour. Here is a revelation of self-forgetfulness in suffering and of concern for those in one's family which opens a whole realm in instruction and example for the believer. The Lord chose John who had been most intimate with Him in love and fellowship to extend this care and relationship for His earthly and physical mother. These human relationships have been established by God and it is in them that we may display our achievements of Christian character.

C. The meaning of His promise to the thief

To the penitent thief the Lord said, "This day thou shalt be with me in paradise." The immediacy of His response to penitence on the part of so low and so corrupt an individual reveals that the Lord can save from the uttermost to the uttermost. No time is too late and no condition too evil. He is willing to accept all who come to Him in contrition and in commitment of faith. Here is a reply which declares on the authority of Jesus Himself that heaven and eternal life begin at physical death. This is a permanent disproof of the doctrine of the sleep of the soul and it demonstrates that our Lord has the power to redeem sinners.

II. THE FIFTH WORD

In the midst of His sufferings and as His agony intensified, the fever of His body increased and with it the awful attendant circumstances of thirst. This was in fulfillment of Scripture and it even suggests that He may have had Psalm 22 in His mind while He was hanging on the cross. At least, by it the Scripture was fulfilled, when He cried out, "I thirst."

A. His longing for water

Here was a picture of terrible human anguish, of longing for that which would assuage the need of His body. What a paradox it was that He who is the living water and who offered to men water so that they would never thirst, had to cry out, "I thirst." What a paradox of His nature that He was divine yet could essentially be human and suffer under human needs. What a paradox, also, that He could succor all others but could not satisfy Himself. Others had failed under thirst, such as Hagar, Samson and the Israelites in the wilderness, but the thirst of crucifixion surpasses all this. The passion of Christ is bound up in the fact that He was subject to suffering and death. All this was revealed in the words, "I thirst."

B. His thirst for the grace of God

The object of the thirst of Christ was primarily water. This was obvious. In answer to this, they set a vessel full of vinegar, filled a sponge and put it to His mouth. But far more than water was symbolized in this. Chronologically, this cry came after His cry, "My God, my God, why hast thou forsaken me?" It was in the midst of His early anguish, as darkness began to descend. It was then that He was shut off from that stream of life of deity. The Holy Spirit is symbolized in the New Testament by water. Christ now thirsted for the streams of grace without which any life becomes a spiritual desert or waste place. It was such that Jesus felt Himself becoming for us upon the cross.

C. His thirst for faith of humanity

The Lord Jesus longed for the belief of others in Him. His nation had rejected Him, had plotted to put Him to death. One of His disciples had betrayed Him, one had denied Him, and all had deserted Him. He was utterly alone. He longed for the love, the belief, the trust which would be as cool water to a thirsty soul. In the light of this we can see what the confession of the thief meant to Him while He was on the cross. Isaiah said, "He shall see of the travail of his soul and be satisfied." In the thief's repentance there was given to Him the satisfying portion for which He longed. But the Lord is still thirsting for the faith of men.

III. THE OTHER THREE WORDS

A. THE MEANING OF THE WORD, "MY GOD, MY GOD, WHY HAST THOU FORSAKEN ME?"

This was a quotation from Psalm 22 and it describes an experience, the depth of which can never be fathomed by us. In this moment He was enduring the pains of hell for us, He was tasting spiritual death and in some way a division or rupture entered into deity, a momentary separation between the Father and the Son. Thus, sin separates man and wife, or two friends, or man and God. Thus deity took into Himself the experience of forsakenness and separation. Here is real evidence that the Father was not suffering in the human Jesus but that the apparatus of the God-man was used and that the judgments for sin were poured out upon the Mediator, Christ Jesus.

B. THE MEANING OF THE WORD, "IT IS FINISHED"

This can refer to no other thing but our redemption. It is salvation wrought by Jesus for those whom He represented. He finished the work He came to do. It was a cry of triumph, of victory, of completion of the covenant of redemption. His sufferings were now about over and all that was required was done except to physically die. He had drained the cup of its last drop. He had purchased a people from the authority of Satan. He had made atonement for all who would believe. He had undone the work of the evil one. How wonderful to know that it is all finished and there is nothing we can add by way of merit or works to obtain our salvation.

C. THE MEANING OF "INTO THY HANDS I COMMEND MY SPIRIT"

This was the last act of Christ. He was now to die. Then this experience of death was even proof of the existence of the Trinity. Now death was to be taken into the nature of deity.

Now the sting of death was to be pulled. Now God's people were to be delivered from the bondage of the fear of death. Into God's hands was God's keeping of the security of heaven. Jesus passed through death. It has become nothing but a shadow for all who are His people.

CONCLUSION

The seal upon the atonement of Christ was His resurrection from the dead. By coming forth from the grave Jesus vindicated completed redemption. The Father accepted the offering and salvation was complete. Here we can do no other than bow in worship and adoration and thanksgiving.

7

DEATH, BURIAL AND HELL

Saturday — Forty-sixth Day

Text: I Corinthians 15:1, 3, 4. "I declare unto you the gospel which I preached unto you . . . how that Christ died for our sins according to the scriptures; and that he was buried, and that he rose again the third day."

Scripture: John 19:38-42

When Paul preached his gospel he declared the faith with no hesitancy, equivocation, apology or fear, but with confidence, joy and delight. The gospel which he preached included Christ's death for our sins, His burial and His resurrection.

A. The gospel

The gospel constitutes the good news of salvation, a message of what God has done for the believer. It includes three salient facts, all of which are essential: First, that Christ died for our sins; second, that He was buried; and third, that He rose again.

B. Tradition

Paul refers to this gospel as being handed down in the Church. He speaks of the gospel "which also ye have received and wherein ye stand." Paul himself had received his gospel "by revelation" (Gal. 1:12) but the people who comprised the Church had received theirs by tradition. This was an oral tradition, passed on by preaching and only later to be inscripturated. When the epistles of Paul were written and the Gospels recorded, the gospel had been delivered to the Corinthians, they had received it, believed it and they were saved unless they had believed in vain. Thus, also, all who have received this gospel through the millenniums since have been saved.

C. AUTHORITY

Paul declares that this is "according to the Scriptures." Thus, there was ample authority for the substitutionary death of Christ given in the Scriptures and also ample authority in the Scriptures for His resurrection from the dead and the gospel which was preached by oral tradition in the days of Paul was confirmed by the authority of the Old Testament Scriptures.

I. CHRIST DIED FOR OUR SINS

This is the primary truth of the gospel, without which there would be no gospel.

A. THE FACT — "CHRIST DIED"

The death of Christ is an historical event which cannot be gainsaid. It can be demonstrated. No historian of reputation would attempt to deny it for He died a painful, ignominious, cursed death outside of Jerusalem in 29 A. D.

B. THE INTERPRETATION — "FOR OUR SINS"

This phrase interprets the fact of His death in a doctrine. It defines what we are to believe about the fact. It connects that fact with our sins. Not His own, but our sins, sent Him to the cross. It proclaims substitution and expiation. Out of this statement is born theology and a particular doctrine called the substitutionary vicarious atonement of Christ, namely that in His body on the cross He carried our guilt and made a sufficient satisfaction and expiation for the sins of men. The blood of Calvary was redemptive and by it reconciliation between a just God and a guilty world was made.

C. THE ACCEPTANCE

Paul said, "By which ye are saved if ye keep in memory what I have preached unto you." It is the acceptance of this interpretation of the death of Christ which brings salvation. This is the affirmative reception of the gospel. It is possible to have an unworthy or an untrue basis of faith, hence not to continue in the faith and thus to believe in vain. But when this faith concerning Christ is substantiated by the resurrection, it establishes the individual.

II. CHRIST WAS BURIED

A. THE BURIAL IN A TOMB

The synoptics describe the burial of Christ by Joseph of Arimathea and Nicodemus. The reality of Christ's death was attested by His burial. Death, burial and tomb were real. The centurion delivered the certificate of death. The blow from the spear settled the question that He was already dead. It was no swoon that claimed Jesus but a true death. The women saw them close the tomb of Joseph, leaving Jesus' body within. The seal of death under the Roman authority was placed upon the tomb in order to guard it from a fraud. We may be thankful for that emphasis of the New Testament upon the tomb of Christ.

B. THE INTERVAL OF DEATH

Death but not corruption claimed the Son of God. He tasted death for every man that He might destroy him who had the power of death (Heb. 2:14). He laid down His life in order that He might take it up again, thus conquering death (John 10:17). This enabled Him to give the assurance of the ultimate end of death's power. Thus death only refers to the body of men. To declare that the soul also sleeps as the body appears to do, is unscriptural. The spirit of Jesus, disembodied as all men are disembodied at death, went to Paradise. This intermediary state of the human personality reveals that man is a spirit with a body, not a body with a spirit. He is like God. Death's power will end at the resurrection when the bodies of believers will be raised. Yet the interval for Jesus was the time of His leading forth the waiting spirits of the just from Sheol into Paradise. We are not to think that Jesus went to preach to spirits imprisoned at this time, thus giving them a second chance, as some affirm. Their chance had been given by the Holy Spirit who preached through Noah unto them in the days before the flood. But the Lord led captivity captive and brought all those who had been redeemed by faith before His death on the cross into heaven.

C. THE MEANING CLARIFIED

Death did not mean that Jesus suffered in hell. Hell was suffered by Him on the cross, not after death. He descended into the grave and from the grave He ascended into heaven. How much more the clauses "He descended into the lower parts of the earth" in Ephesians 4:6 means, we do not profess to know, but wherever Jesus went, He called it Paradise. The language will not permit "this day" to refer to a future age but compels it to refer to the day of crucifixion. If the thief was to be with Jesus in Paradise, then Jesus had to go to Paradise on that day. Thus it is also that the New Testament tells us that to be absent from the body is to be at home with God and to depart this world is to be with Christ for the believer (Phil. 1:21; II Cor. 5:1, 7, 8). Jesus was not in hell for three days nor did He go to preach to the spirits in prison. He went into the Father's presence.

III. CHRIST AROSE AGAIN THE THIRD DAY

If we were to leave Christ in the grave, all would be darkness and despair. There would have been no Church. There would have been no hope of salvation. There would have been no seal upon the atonement. There would have been no evidence of the acceptance by the Father of the work of the Son. The outlook would have been as the outlook of the disciples was before they knew that Christ rose from the dead. Hence, the gospel must include not only the death of Christ for our sins, and His burial, but also His resurrection from the dead. Happy are we as believers who are not left in that darkness but have the evidence of the completed resurrection.

A. THE EVIDENCE OF IT

The strongest possible attestation of the resurrection is given in the appearances of our Lord Jesus Christ. In I Corinthians 15, five appearances are related: To Peter, to the twelve, to five hundred brethren, to James and to all the apostles. In all the Gospels and epistles some eleven appearances of the resurrected Christ are recorded.

Did the disciples just imagine that they saw Jesus or just persuade themselves that He still lived? Was it a result of their imagination or wishful thinking, or a hallucination, or a tendency to deify a hero? We find that the entire tendency of all the disciples from Mary Magdalene to Thomas was to disbelieve the resurrection and to seek proofs of it. The fact remains that they saw Jesus living after His death and burial.

The independence of the testimony of various witnesses is revealed by their differentiation and their narrative of what they saw but they all agree that they saw Him living. The psychological change in the disciples could be accomplished in no other way. The final appearance of Jesus was to Paul which he describes as before his time. As a result, he was changed from persecuting the Christians to propagating the Christian faith. This change in St. Paul must be explained in some manner. Paul attributed it to grace by revelation of God by the appearance of Jesus Christ. On the ground of it he based his apostleship.

There is also the evidence of the open tomb. This confirmed the appearances of Christ for if the tomb had still been occupied, Christian preaching would have been a lie. The only denial to the resurrection was the story put into the mouths of the soldiers by the priests and even this serves to prove that the tomb was empty. If the enemies of Christ took the body, then they could have produced it to disprove the preaching of the apostles that Jesus was risen. If the apostles themselves had stolen the body, they would have been prosecuted by the Roman law, and moreover, their zeal would have been dissipated for psychologically they could not have preached that Jesus was risen if they themselves did not believe it. All critics, hostile and friendly to supernatural Christianity, admit the early Church believed that Jesus rose from the dead and that it was on the basis of this belief that the Church accomplished what it did and suffered what it did.

B. THE ALTERNATIVE THAT HE DID NOT RISE

Paul, in I Corinthians, considers this alternative and explores the possibility that Jesus did not rise. Then he says, his preaching is in vain, that is, it is false, untrue, a fable and a delusion, and there is no message of salvation. Then their faith is in vain, or has no foundation, and they are yet in their sins. Then the apostles are false witnesses, or liars, and this involves the integrity of Scripture. Then, those fallen asleep in Christ are perished. Then Christians are of all people most miserable.

C. THE IMPLICATIONS OF THE RESURRECTION

But if Christ rose from the dead, then Christianity is true, for God placed a seal upon Christ's death for our sins. Then we are saved, we have the confidence and knowledge of our redemption. Then we also shall share the resurrection of our Lord Jesus Christ; whereas He is the first-fruits, we shall be the full-fruits.

CONCLUSION

This, then, is the gospel, that Christ died for our sins, that He was buried, and that He rose again. Those who believe this gospel and receive it are saved. This is our Holy Week and Easter message.

8

RESURRECTION FAITH
Easter Sunday

Text: Romans 10:9, 10. "That if thou shalt confess with thy mouth the Lord Jesus, and shalt believe in thine heart that God hath raised him from the dead, thou shalt be saved. For with the heart man believeth unto righteousness; and with the mouth confession is made unto salvation."
Scripture: Romans 10:1-18

Salvation is the greatest word in the Christian's vocabulary. It includes love, power, holiness, immortality, resurrection, the forgiveness of sin and life. Easter is the day to proclaim salvation through the resurrection of our Lord Jesus Christ.

A. The meaning of salvation

Salvation is all that is synonymous with the question, "What shall I do to be saved?" or "What shall I do to inherit eternal life?" or "What shall I do to become a child of God?" or "What shall I do to have the kingdom of God within me?" The things of salvation are made very plain in the Scripture which deals with ultimate salvation from the penalty, power and presence of sin, with the mysteries of salvation, with the assurance of salvation and with the plan of salvation. Salvation is deliverance from sin and its consequences. It embraces the plan of God, the work of the redeemer and the application of that work by the Holy Spirit, the actual salvation of the people of God. Salvation is accompanied by satisfying inner peace with God and a rest after striving after the truth.

B. Salvation and Easter

Without the Easter fact, there could be no salvation. One has put it, "Easter is the birthday of hope" (I Pet. 1:3). Without the resurrection our hopes for salvation must be reduced to the despair of the heathen. Thus, salvation is the one message which should be re-emphasized at Easter. It is wonderful that this is the spring of the year when the birds return, the flowers appear and life resurges in nature. But these are temporary things. Were we to mention them only and to pass over the eternal matter represented by Easter, we would be faithless indeed. The contact point in this divinely proffered salvation is faith in the resurrection of Jesus Christ.

C. EASTER EMPHASIS

Easter morning emphasizes the difference between a Christian and a Unitarian, whether he is a Moslem, a Jew or a Modernist. For all but a Christian Jesus is still in the tomb. Hence, there can be no joy of salvation for these unbelievers. Paul felt this for his brethren, the Jews, and it was his heart's desire that they should be saved. They were believers in God but they rejected Christ and hence, Paul declared that they were under condemnation. Paul believed that the key to the conversion of Israel lay in the fact of the resurrection. This alone would lead them to faith in Christ and to salvation. This faith would not raise the sceptical demand of proving that Christ is Saviour by bringing Him down from heaven, or bringing Him up from the dead, for a knowledge of Christ would be present in their experiences in their hearts. Thus this Easter faith is proclaimed in connection with faith in the resurrection, through confession of this faith and through preaching this faith.

I. POSSESSION OF FAITH IN THE RESURRECTION

Paul said, "Believe in thine heart that God hath raised him from the dead, and thou shalt be saved. For with the heart man believeth unto righteousness."

A. THE OBJECT OF FAITH

What is it that we are asked to believe in order to be saved? The resurrection may mean different things to different people. Just what is it that the Gospels narrate in reference to the resurrection of Jesus? It is that the man Jesus who lived in the family relationships of Nazareth, who was human enough to suffer all physical needs, who depended upon prayer for fellowship with the Father, yet who performed miracles through supernatural power and who died upon the cross and was buried, that this same Jesus rose from the dead. The resurrection means that Jesus, without external help, burst the bonds of death, conquered death, and lives today. Now, in a transformed body, He has gone to heaven to rule His spiritual kingdom. The fact of the resurrection thus gives meaning to the cross. Faith in the resurrection makes possible faith in the cross. It is at this truth of the resurrection of the Lord Jesus from the dead that the unbelievers stumble.

B. HELPS TO FAITH IN THE RESURRECTION

We may argue for the resurrection from apriori principles, that is, from known and accepted principles, truths and consequences deducted from them and consistent with them.

1. From the fact of God's love

Can you think of an infinite, omnipotent God creating a universe and peopling it with human beings and then permitting sin to enter and allowing these human beings to continue with the results of sin in suffering and justice and death? A God who would make us and place us in such circumstances is no God at all. The Bible expressly and emphatically declares that it was the love of God which sent Jesus Christ into the world to be our Saviour; to live, to die and to rise again for our justification. Calvary and the resurrection are the greatest demonstrations of God's love that exists.

2. From the kind of life Jesus lived

When one studies the life of Jesus in its manifestation of resurrection power, even before the resurrection, he would never expect death to have power over Him. The experience of His death was what so shattered the faith of His disciples. They expected a different quality of life. If I start from the life of Christ at Easter it is easy to believe, but if I start from the life of Christ at Calvary and terminate the story there, it is impossible to believe. What power could death hold over One who raised other people from the dead, who rebuked the elements and they obeyed Him, who exorcised the demons from the possessed, who conquered every manner of sickness, who opened the eyes of the blind, who healed the lepers and who raised the lame? What power could death have over One who said, "Come unto me all ye that labor and are heavy laden and I will give you rest"? Or who said "He that hath seen me hath seen the Father"? The resurrection was natural to such a Person.

3. From the message of the gospel and the churches

Take the resurrection out of Christian doctrine and the keystone goes from Christian truth. Then we must return to modified Judaism with its merely new ceremonies and new ritual. But with the resurrection the Christian message has power, dynamic, force and compulsion. It is the resurrection message which draws such multitudes to churches on Sunday.

4. From the influence of Jesus in history

Look back by way of the calendar through the medieval church, the Crusades, the Reformation, the establishment of Protestantism, the world missionary movement and you find that there is something that must be explained in Christianity. Universal education, hospitalization for the sick, humanitarianism in every form largely came from the influence of Jesus. All these things help us to believe in Christ.

C. EVIDENCES FOR FAITH IN THE RESURRECTION

In addition to the argument from principles, there are arguments from evidence which we call aposteriori evidence. This may be drawn from the disciples who never could have done what they did unless they believed that Jesus was risen. It was the dynamic that transformed their experience. This may be from the garden tomb which was open and could be examined by friends and enemies. This may be from those early narratives which have been proved to be historical and which record the resurrection appearances of the Lord Jesus Christ. This may be proved from the experience of the resurrection by St. Paul and countless multitudes who have been born again through having known it.

II. CONFESSION OF FAITH UNTO SALVATION

Paul said, "If thou shalt confess with thy mouth the Lord Jesus . . . thou shalt be saved."

A. THE CONFESSION WHICH IS MADE

To confess Jesus of Nazareth as Lord is to identify an historical person with the eternal God and this constitutes a creed. It was the worship of Jesus as Lord that caused Paul to persecute the Jews who thus were guilty of blasphemy. It was because Jesus made this claim that His contemporary Jews demanded

His death. Yet this was the message which Paul carried throughout the Roman world, namely that Jesus of Nazareth was the Messiah, the Son of God. To confess Jesus as Lord is to confess that He is the Lord of history. This confession must go further than mere doctrine, however, and must include the statement, "Jesus is my Lord, my Sovereign." A man must commit himself to Christ in order to be saved. It is not intellectual assent but it is personal commitment which leads a person to a saving faith.

B. THE CONFESSION OF WILLING LIPS

There is a common opinion that the gospel need not be preached or declared by word of mouth but can be lived. This is an error. We can never live and win anybody to Christ by merely a good life. Jesus had the best life that was ever lived and yet they repudiated and killed Him. Those who tell us that we can teach the heathen how to live by example and that will bring them to Jesus are in error. The gospel is a message, a message of the fact that God came into the world, died for our sins on the cross, was buried and rose again from the dead. It is a message of release from sin, of the gift of life and of the possession of immortality. This must be preached. One may believe but unless he confesses Christ as Saviour and Lord, his salvation is not complete. Jesus said "Ye are my witnesses." We must tell what God did for us on Calvary and in us through His Spirit.

C. THE CONFESSION OF A CHANGED LIFE

It must be said on the other hand that it is just as great an error to hold the idea that if one believes these things he will set the world on fire. This is not necessarily true. "The demons believe and tremble." One can lend intellectual assent to truth and yet not have it change his life. The will must be exercised in salvation. It must be "into righteousness." Belief ought to compel action but there is something in human make-up which prevents belief from producing this result. Therefore, a good confession must conclude a character which is a carry-over of the faith which we declare.

III. PREACHING OF SAVING FAITH

A. THE OFFER OF SALVATION

Paul declared, "Whosoever shall call upon the name of the Lord shall be saved." The offer of salvation is universally suitable and adaptable. Men in every nation need it, persons in every class need it, people in every state of education need it. God makes no difference between men. All are sinners, all have come short of His glory and all may find the riches of grace. God does not mock men with His offer. If they respond, they shall be saved. The key is in the human will. This is the promise of God. No man will call unless he believes, therefore, whosoever believes will not be ashamed. God will give him power and strength to be saved.

B. THE ORDER OF SALVATION

The offer of salvation is to be accepted. It must be carried unto men so that they hear it and know it. Thus the gospel must be preached. This is the resurrection commandment of Jesus (Matt. 28:18-20). This was the burden of the resurrection commandments of the Lord. Paul here outlines this mission of the Church in the inverse order as to its causality, speaking of those who are "sent . . . preach . . . hear . . . believe . . . call . . . saved." If the chain of causes is broken the results are not obtained. We are both sent to preach and we must send others to preach. This missionary and evangelistic endeavor is an integral part of our own salvation.

C. THE OBEDIENCE TO SALVATION

Paul said, "But they have not all obeyed the gospel." All have not and all will not obey. The Bible nowhere promises universal application of salvation. Our experience is that some accept and some reject. There are some that will be saved and some that will be lost. A division is always created by preaching, just as there was a division created by the cross. Evangelical obedience is the acceptance of the gospel and the yielding of life and a commitment to Jesus Christ.

CONCLUSION

God has His arms stretched forth to receive you: arms of mercy and justice, of peace and truth, of immortality and life, but God will not compel you. He will only invite, exhort and persuade. "Whosoever will call upon the name of the Lord shall be saved."